FUNNY BUSINESS

FUNNY

THE LEGENDARY LIFE AND POLITICAL SATIRE OF

‹ ‹ ‹ ‹ ‹

BUSINESS

* * * * * * * *

ART BUCHWALD

> > > > > > MICHAEL HILL

FOREWORD BY CHRISTOPHER BUCKLEY

RANDOM HOUSE NEW YORK

Published in the United States by Random House,
an imprint and division of Penguin Random House LLC, New York.

RANDOM HOUSE and the HOUSE colophon are registered trademarks
of Penguin Random House LLC.

Permissions credits are located on pages 289–91.

Library of Congress Cataloging-in-Publication Data
Names: Hill, Mike, author.
Title: Funny business: the legendary life and political satire of Art Buchwald / Michael Hill.
Description: First edition. | New York: Random House, [2022] | Includes bibliographical references and index.
Identifiers: LCCN 2021039045 (print) | LCCN 2021039046 (ebook) | ISBN 9780593229514 (hardcover) | ISBN 9780593229521 (ebook)
Subjects: LCSH: Buchwald, Art. | Humorists, American—20th century—Biography. | Political satire, American—History and criticism.
Classification: LCC PS3503.U1828 Z69 2022 (print) | LCC PS3503.U1828 (ebook) | DDC 814/.54 [B]—dc23/eng/20220318
LC record available at https://lccn.loc.gov/2021039045
LC ebook record available at https://lccn.loc.gov/2021039046

Printed in the United States of America on acid-free paper

randomhousebooks.com

9 8 7 6 5 4 3 2 1

First Edition

Book design by Jo Anne Metsch
FRONTISPIECE IMAGE:
Paul Slade/Paris Match Archive via Getty Images

For Joel and Tamara Buchwald—

who were there for that last glorious bit of laughter

There is only one Art Buchwald, and if you think I am going to say "That's plenty," you are wrong, witty though it would be. I could do with a dozen.

—P. G. WODEHOUSE, British humorist and
creator of the Jeeves and Wooster stories

"Did you read Art Buchwald today?" has become as commonplace as the inevitable answer, "I certainly did."

—JAMES THURBER, American humorist,
cartoonist, and writer for *The New Yorker*

That Buchwald not only sees the world as mad, but that it is mad gives him—as the British say—a leg up.

—DEAN ACHESON,
former U.S. secretary of state

FOREWORD

BY CHRISTOPHER BUCKLEY › › › › › ›

I missed Art Buchwald's memorial service at the Kennedy Center in March 2007, but I had a good excuse. My mother was dying. An apt excuse, too, for she thought Art Buchwald was "the funniest human being on the planet." I first heard her say this when I was about ten years old. She continued to say it after I became a Washington-based political satirist, by which point I began to find it irksome. I finally asked her to stop saying it, at least in my presence. Being a good mother, she did. But then I'd run into someone who'd just been with her and they'd say, "Your mother spent the whole time talking about Art Buchwald's latest column. She thinks he's the funniest man on earth!" I find it interesting, mystically speaking, that both Mum and Art shuffled off this mortal coil at about the same time. This could be a case of taking "Get a room, you two" to the next level. Meanwhile, I'm haunted by the certainty that she's up there, going from cloud to cloud, telling everyone "Art Buchwald is not only the funniest person in heaven but also an absolute angel!" Shoot me.

Being asked to contribute this foreword to Michael Hill's totally marvelous book—Mum would doubtless call it "the best book *ever* written"—is an honor. But I hear Art's distinctive growl muttering, "Damn straight it is!" I gobbled it up in two sittings. It made me wish Art were still around to make us laugh. There's so much going on these days that only Art Buchwald could turn into humor.

Being a diligent person—diligence is one of my many virtues, along with complete absence of envy—I read all the tributes to Art that were published after he died. They'd fill a volume just by themselves. My final act of due diligence was to rewatch C-SPAN's tape of the memorial service that I missed. You should check it out for yourself, but only after you've read Michael's book and bought a copy for every person you know. It's celluloid (pixel? Whatever C-SPAN stores stuff on) evidence that Art Buchwald was not only the funniest human being on earth, but also just maybe the most beloved human being on earth.

I lived in Washington for thirty years. There are two maxims about my dear old former hometown. The first is "If you want a friend in Washington, get a dog." The second is "A friend in Washington is someone who stabs you in the chest."

I loved D.C. and I made good and lasting friendships there, but those maxims are, generally speaking, valid. (Otherwise they wouldn't be maxims, right?) Art's memorial service stands as a maxim-busting testament that Washington can be a place capable of abounding warmth and fuzziness. At least for friends and fans of Art Buchwald.

The last lyric of the last song the Beatles recorded goes, "In the end, the love you take is equal to the love you make." Art Buchwald made more love than Elizabeth Taylor had husbands. He'd have a funnier metaphor, but you get the drift.

How did he manage to turn a city of wolves, baboons, and sharks— yes, Ted Cruz, Matt Gaetz, Marjorie Taylor Greene, I'm talking about *you*—into a petting zoo?

Two ways: 1) he was a mensch, and 2) he made people laugh. Everyone. As you've seen from the epigraph to this book, he made P. G. Wodehouse and James Thurber laugh. And Dean Acheson. I'd bet my fee for writing this brilliant foreword that it was harder to make Dean Acheson laugh than it was Wodehouse and Thurber.*

Columnist Dave Barry, who knows a thing or two about humor, concluded his tribute, "He talked funny, he wrote funny, he lived funny, and damned if he didn't find a way to *die* funny." As the saying goes, "Dying is easy. Stand-up is hard." Art did stand-up for half a century, mostly while sitting down.

His daughter Jennifer told the crowd at the Kennedy Center that she once asked him who he wanted to win the presidential election—the Republican or the Democrat? "He wanted the one who would make his life easiest," she reported. "So that he could do his column and be on the tennis court by ten-thirty." Bet you double or nothing this was the 1968 election. Richard Nixon was proof that God loves political satirists.

In the "Dying Funny" category, Art famously spent five months in a hospice, *not* dying. His son, Joel, said, "Dad was probably the only one in history to gain weight in hospice." A *Washington Post* headline from his year of dying livingly: "Washington's Hottest Salon Is a Deathbed." Daughter Jennifer said the most important lesson he imparted to his children was "Eat ice cream every day." This was, after all, a man who talked his way into a job on the *Herald Tribune* by convincing an editor that his job in the military was "the food taster for the United States Marine Corps." What better qualification for being a restaurant reviewer in Paris?

What fun it must have been to be one of Art's kids. He sent Jennifer a postcard from China in the early 1990s: "All the women here are barefooted and collect rice for 15 hours a day, seven days a week. I think you'd love it here."†

After moving to D.C. from Paris in 1962, Art became an adjunct

---

* $0. Generosity and humility are also among my myriad virtues. Tom Brokaw, one of the eulogists at the memorial service, began his by saying that he could imagine Art saying to him as he reached the podium, "Ya gettin' paid for this one?"

† One of Art's comic talents was the "paraprosdokian." I could explain, but you'll have more fun googling it yourself.

member of the Kennedy family. Ethel Kennedy asked him to be god-father to one of her children. Her eulogy brought down the proverbial house.

The Catholic church, she explained, was not keen on Jewish—and other non-Catholic—godparents. Fortunately, the new parish priest, freshly arrived from Portugal, had a shaky grasp of the English language, so the baptism went forward. However . . . "Artie's familiarity with the rite of baptism turned out to be equally sketchy, as we discovered half-way through the ceremony, when the priest asked him, 'Do you renounce Satan and all his pomps?'

"Artie lost it. He turned pale, fled to the back of the church, and collapsed on a folding chair. Asked what was the matter, highly agitated, he spluttered, 'I'm not *ready* to renounce Satan and all his pomps!'" I cherish this story. It's up there with Voltaire being asked on his deathbed to renounce Satan, and telling the priest, "Is this any time to be making enemies?"

As he was not dying, Art told Tom Brokaw, another eulogist, that the thing he was most looking forward to in the afterlife was "meeting Judas." He planned to ask Judas, "I wanna know—did you betray him, or not? I've been living with this *my whole life*. So, tell me." (What would Mrs. Kennedy's Portuguese padre have made of this? He'd probably have caught the next plane back to Portugal.) Brokaw also asked Art what he was going to miss. Answer: "Global warming."

By this point in the C-SPAN tape, you're wondering if this is a memorial service or celebrity roast. And whether Art was, in fact, deceased. I wouldn't have been surprised if they'd wheeled in a cake and he popped out, cigar in mouth, grinning. You can hear sniffling and hankies dabbing, but the laughter-to-blubber ratio is 20 to 1.

Last to speak was Ben Bradlee, legendary former editor of *The Washington Post* and a buddy of Art's from France in the 1950s. Together they covered the wedding of Princess Grace and Prince Rainier, an event that led to arguably Art's most shimmering satirical moment. He wrote a column explaining that he hadn't been invited to the nups because of a long-standing family feud: "The Buchwalds and the Grimaldis have not spoken since Jan. 9, 1297." The next day, Art received a handwritten invitation to the wedding.

Bradlee told a story that became funnier and funnier as it went along. Art showed up one day at Bradlee and Sally Quinn's new Georgetown manse and affixed to their doorway a mezuzah, the plaque identifying a home as Jewish. If you asked a computer to identify the most goyish couple in the United States, it might very well nominate Benjamin Crowninshield Bradlee and Sally Sterling Quinn. But Art informed them that Georgetown was such a dangerous place that their house needed nothing less than Jehovah-level protection.

Years later, the mezuzah got painted over during a renovation.

"Within three weeks, we'd been broken into three times," Bradlee said. "We called Art and within half an hour he was there with an emergency mezuzah, which still hangs there."

Bradlee concluded by telling about one of Sally's visits to Art at the hospice. Art told her that he'd decided not to die.

"What changed your mind?" Sally asked.

"Well," he said, "I picked up the paper this morning and read where Vice President Cheney shot his best friend in a hunting accident." (Wait for it.) "And I said to myself, 'Life is good. I'm gonna stay.'"

It took a while for the laughter to die down, just as it took Artie a while to die. Bradlee looked up at the ceiling and said, "Okay, Artie. Life *is* good. And *was* good, but it'll never be the same without you."

Amen, as we Jews say.

You've got a treat ahead of you. Please proceed—in an orderly fashion—to chapter 1, and commence laughing, and wondering at the miracle of it all.

CONTENTS

PART IV: TEARS OF THE CLOWN

INTRODUCTION

Before Stephen Colbert, Jon Stewart, Trevor Noah, and even before *Doonesbury*, with its colorful cast of characters, there was Art Buchwald. For more than fifty years his Pulitzer Prize–winning column of political satire and biting wit made him one of the most widely read American humorists of his age. At the height of his career, his column—published three times a week—was syndicated in 550 newspapers in one hundred countries. The power of his wit was legendary, some describing him as "Will Rogers with chutzpah." Dean Acheson, venerable Washington "Wise Man" and former U.S. secretary of state, called Buchwald the "greatest satirist in the English language since Pope and Swift." Columnist Arthur Krock of *The New York Times* compared him to Anthony Trollope, and novelist James Michener said Buchwald had "one of the sharpest wits" he had ever known.

Even political satirists, humorists, and commentators of a later generation acknowledged the singular genius of his work. Maureen Dowd of *The New York Times* called Buchwald the "gold standard" of American columnists, and Garry Trudeau, of *Doonesbury* fame, praised him as the true "Gruppenfuhrer" (group leader) of political satire.

The great British humorist P. G. Wodehouse read Buchwald each morning, then clipped his column from the paper. Even one of America's most celebrated caped crusaders, Batman (Adam West), began each day with a touch of Buchwald in the morning. Fellow columnist Ann Landers (Eppie Lederer) once told Buchwald that on a flight from Paris to London a man sitting next to her "almost fell out of his seat laughing" while reading one of his columns. "In fact," she told him, "the stewardess came by and suggested that he strap himself in— at least until he finished your column."

Creative genius Lincoln Kirstein of the New York City Ballet was an admirer, as were poet Robert Frost and Supreme Court justice William O. Douglas, who quoted a Buchwald column in one of his U.S. Supreme Court opinions. Silent film star Clara Bow ("The It Girl") was a fan, as were filmmakers Alfred Hitchcock, Frank Capra, Mike Todd, and John Huston. His barbs could get a chuckle out of Arthur Schlesinger, Jr., as easily as they could out of President Dwight Eisenhower and William F. Buckley, Jr. Conservative Republican senator Barry Goldwater once told him, "You are one of those people who have the ability to make us think, make us laugh, to make us cry, and love our fellow man. For that, I thank you."

Like Mark Twain, James Thurber, H. L. Mencken, and Dorothy Parker, Art Buchwald was an American original. For more than five decades, millions of readers began their day by reading his column, which playfully satirized political scoundrels, lampooned the powerful and the pompous, and, as he was fond of saying, "worshipped the quicksand" that ten different presidents of the United States walked on.

Over the course of his long career it seemed as if Buchwald had a tongue-in-cheek solution to nearly every problem that America faced. In the spring of 1976 he took on the gun lobby when he wrote a column, "Art's Gun Control Plan," which facetiously demanded a federal mandate to cut off "everybody's trigger finger at birth" in an effort to curb gun violence in America. "The Constitution gives everyone the right to bear arms," Buchwald quipped. "But there is nothing that says an American has to have ten fingers." To entertain his readers Buchwald often created imaginary "skits" in his column with satirical dialogue from a colorful and delightful cast of fictitious characters such as Professor Max Kilaton ("a hawkish nuclear scientist"); Hillary Hazeltine (president of the Pseudo-Intellectual Antidefamation League); Dr. Alfred Thumbsucker (an expert on adolescent behavior); Hiram Bullhorn (head of the Intercollegiate Hecklers Conference, which favored a healthy "exchange of ideas on heckling, jeering and hooting" in order to "find ways of shedding more heat and less light on the basic issues of the day"); and one of Buchwald's all-time favorites, the legendary Dr. Heinrich Applebaum (holder of the "Casey Jones Chair of Railroad Philosophy at Pullman University").

And like Washington, D.C., itself, Buchwald had a mythical lobby group, political action committee, or trade association for any public issue or cause he felt worthy of ridicule, such as the National Pothole Association; the Our Country Right or Wrong Oil Institute; the High Thermostat Manufacturers Association; the Crank Case Oil Workers Union; and an organization called "Students for Utterly Free Speech," whose avowed "purpose [was] to keep speakers who come to college campuses from speaking."

He always found the bewildering complexities of the federal bureaucracy fertile ground for his satirical imagination. During the 1976 Christmas season he couldn't resist having a little holiday fun with the Occupational Safety and Health Administration (OSHA) with a stern yet amusing "Letter to Santa" from "E. Scrooge," one of the agency's toughest bureaucrats, charging St. Nick with a violation of federal regulations regarding the treatment of his reindeer ("Our inspector measured 1.4 inches of hay in Donner's stall and 1.3 inches in Blitzen's stall in contravention of Reindeer Regulation 4s"), and giving a strict warning about the manner in which Santa intended to make his Yuletide deliveries. "You may descend a chimney providing . . . the inside . . .

has steps one foot apart with a safety railing along the side," and once inside the house "the packages must be neatly piled with 1.9 feet between them."

Much to the delight of his readers, every few years Buchwald published a collection of his favorite columns, each book with a catchy title such as *Getting High in Government Circles, The Buchwald Stops Here, You Can Fool All of the People All the Time, While Reagan Slept,* and *Beating Around the Bush.* Each book's dust jacket had a distinctive flair, including an ever-changing array of biographical tidbits—all written by Buchwald himself. On one cover Art described himself as "shy, introspective, and terribly aloof," a man who "rarely leaves his small airless room atop the Washington Monument except to buy *Time* magazine to see if they've put him on the cover." His favorite sport, he quipped to readers, was "social climbing," and he always loved fabricating a whimsical story or two about life inside the White House, claiming that during the Kennedy years he had been the first family's chef until departing in a "huff" after having "a violent disagreement with Jackie [Kennedy] on how long to cook a three minute egg." On the cover of *And Then I Told the President,* Buchwald claimed that his columns about Lyndon Johnson had been so biting and "so outspoken that the last time [he] attended a White House function, Lyndon didn't ask him to dance." And during the Nixon administration he declared that he had been the "chief recording engineer" for all of Richard Nixon's Oval Office conversations, soon earning him the nickname "Little Throat" during the Watergate scandal.

Although Buchwald's satire could be sharp and biting, he was never afraid to poke fun at himself. Once, when his wife, Ann, was laid up with an illness, Art took the helm at the Buchwald household, an experience that produced a witty column about lessons learned on the home front. "A laundry hamper only holds clothes. It does not wash them," he told his readers after returning to work. "Frozen meals taste like frozen meals," he observed, and "taking a headache remedy does not necessarily mean there will be less dust in the living room."

As with any great satirist, his barbs—known in his day as Buchwald's "Buchshots"—could often sting and ruffle a political feather or two. But that was the point. Although he wanted to make people laugh, he also wanted to provoke thought and reflection on many of the political issues of the day. Of the U.S. Supreme Court's 1973 landmark ruling on abortion in *Roe v. Wade*, Buchwald said, "The Supreme Court ruling on abortion did not have the calming effect on people that the justices for the majority opinion had hoped for. More Americans want to kill each other in the name of 'the right to life' and 'freedom of choice' than ever before."

And in May 1985 he wrote a column, "Rewriting History," in which he ridiculed those—both in and out of government—who promoted "historical revisionism." Quoting one of his fictional comic straight men, Dr. Heinrich Applebaum, Buchwald conveyed with biting satire the nature of the dilemma. "You can't learn from history, unless you rewrite it," he quoted his imaginary scholar as saying. "The job of the revisionist is to make people forget the past. The neo-historian looks at what has been printed so far and then asks himself, 'Will this hurt or help our present alliances?' If it hurts, then he must reconcile the facts with what is in the nation's best interests."

At times he could be maddening to those at whom he poked fun. Bobby Kennedy, who was occasionally mocked in Buchwald's columns, once asked him, "How many people take you seriously?" When Buchwald replied, "Oh, about fifty percent," Kennedy grumbled, "Then why don't you knock it off."

And many people *did* take him seriously. When he wrote a column in 1964 titled "J. Edgar Hoover Just Doesn't Exist," in which he claimed that the FBI director was a "mythical person thought up by *Reader's Digest*," he sparked a debate across the country about whether his column was really true. Neither Hoover nor the FBI was amused. Art Buchwald could not have been happier.

At the height of the Vietnam War in the 1960s, Buchwald's numerous columns mocking President Lyndon Johnson's handling of the conflict landed him in hot water with government officials, who grew so frustrated by his ridicule of the president that at one point the

National Security Agency was ordered to conduct a secret high-level surveillance of Buchwald.

By using his gift to make people laugh—and laugh at themselves—Buchwald felt he was doing something to benefit mankind. As he told an interviewer in the late 1960s, "My function—if I have one, is sort of taking the steam out of everything. This is a very uptight country now and if you can take some of the pressure off—maybe you are doing a bigger service than changing things."

And as his friend and fellow columnist Rowland Evans said, "What people don't understand about Buchwald is that he isn't just a funny man. He cares deeply about many things."

He was a fierce defender of freedom of the press, freedom of speech, and the freedom of satire. When editors or close friends urged him to temper his wit or sarcasm about a political figure or issue, he refused to be muzzled. In the 1950s, at the height of Senator Joseph McCarthy's anti-Communist crusade, Buchwald mocked McCarthy in a column he wrote for the *New York Herald Tribune*, claiming the Wisconsin senator was "causing a lot of people grief" in America because he hailed from a "bad strain" of the McCarthy clan in Ireland. When Buchwald submitted the article to his editors, who were "deathly afraid" of McCarthy, they killed it. Undeterred, and perhaps spurred on by the rejection, Art looked elsewhere and sold it to *The New Republic*.

While his humor could be caustic, it was never mean or vicious. He understood that with his style of satire and humor came a measure of influence, a power he recognized and respected. "My style is different than a lot of comedians," he said. "I don't try to be off-color. . . . I don't go for the jugular and if I do I try to sugar-coat it." Cartoonist Garry Trudeau said it best when he told Buchwald that "the gentleness of your satire is one reason you are so beloved."

And his satire wasn't limited to his columns. He had a larger-than-life persona, and during the 1960s and '70s, at the height of his career, he was a much-sought-after lecturer, toastmaster, emcee, and commencement speaker. He had his own radio program and a weekly commentary spot on the CBS newsmagazine program *60 Minutes*. He loved being a journalistic celebrity and he loved being onstage, taking great joy in presiding over the famed Kennedy family pet show each year as "ringmaster," fully attired in a red hunting jacket, high leather boots, and a black top hat. And he loved hosting an Easter party at his home each year, showing up, to the great delight of family and friends, in an Easter Bunny suit.

But despite his public image as a humorist and funny man, there was a darker, more troubling, and more melancholy side to Art Buchwald. For more than forty years he fought bravely against periodic episodes of severe and at times crippling depression, stemming from the trauma and "scars" he suffered during his sad early life as a foster child. And like many creative people who suffer from depression, time and again Buchwald overcame the debilitating effects of his illness by drawing on what he called his "inner strengths and hidden talents" to help him carry on with his life and work. In the 1990s he finally went public about his long-held "dark secret" in a series of television, radio, and newspaper interviews disclosing the details of his lifelong struggle with depression. He even went on the road with William Styron and Mike Wallace, two of his closest friends, who also battled depression, the trio dubbing themselves the "Blues Brothers" in appearances across the country in which they shared their own survival stories in an effort to help others.

In 2017, the letters, papers, speeches, photographs, scrapbooks, videos, interviews, and oral histories of Art Buchwald were acquired by the Library of Congress after being meticulously and diligently preserved by his son and daughter-in-law, Joel and Tamara Buchwald. Over the next two years a dedicated team of curators, archivists, and preservationists at the library processed and organized this vast treasure trove of materials—nearly one hundred thousand items in all—into a collection of 250 archival boxes and digital files that were opened to researchers in the fall of 2019. What makes the Buchwald collection so extraordinary is the richness and scope of its material, representing the full range of his life as a columnist, playwright, pundit, lecturer, political commentator, wise guy, prankster, father, husband, and friend.

While he is best known for his columns, books, and plays, Buchwald is less recognized for his extensive and lifelong correspondence, much of which is published here for the first time. The selection of letters woven into the narrative of this book reflect a rich and colorful Who's Who of political, journalistic, literary, and Hollywood legends from the early 1950s to the first years of the twenty-first century. They are filled with warmth, gossip, thoughtfulness, wisdom, heartbreak, and, of course, humor. Here are letters to and from Ethel Kennedy, Ted Kennedy, Katharine Graham, Bob Woodward, John Steinbeck, P. G. Wodehouse, William F. Buckley, Jr., Christopher Buckley, Maureen Dowd, Russell Baker, Erma Bombeck, Charlton Heston, Hugh Hefner, Irwin Shaw, Herblock, Ben Bradlee, Tom Brokaw, John Glenn, Gary Hart, Anthony Newley, and even a song from Carly Simon.

One of the pleasures of working on this book has been the joy of reading Buchwald's letters to this wide circle of friends, all providing a wonderfully nostalgic glimpse into a time gone by and an era and way of life drifting more and more into the past, when letter writing was not only a means to bind and heal friendships, but an art form in which thought, charm, humor, and civility guided a correspondent's pen or typewriter carriage. How unlike today's digital world of social media in which impulsive, brusque, and, at times, ill-mannered dialogue govern so much of our daily lives.

In addition to his correspondence, the Art Buchwald Papers include a rich assortment of his newspaper columns and magazine pieces. Many of his best-known columns are included here simply because they are Buchwald classics. But others, less well-known, are also included to provide a sense of the political and social issues he cared about.

In *Funny Business*, I have adopted an approach to Buchwald's life that weaves together his correspondence, articles, speeches, toasts, and selections from some of his best columns into a collection of humorous and poignant scenes, vignettes, and comic capers, all designed to capture the life and times of one of America's greatest humorists. It is by no means a definitive biography of Art Buchwald, but I hope it will provide both old fans and new an enjoyable look at his remarkable sense of good old American humor and decency.

If this collection brings a hearty laugh or brief smile to even one reader during our own "uptight" times, Buchwald would rejoice. Near the end of his life, as his health was failing and time was running out, his good friend and journalist Mike Wallace once asked him, "What are you going to leave behind?"

"Joy!" Art bellowed.

FROM CLASS CLOWN TO OUR TRIB MAN IN PARIS

* * * * * * *

CHAPTER 1

"PLASTERED IN PARIS"

Early Years and the Comic Charms of Paris (1948-52)

It is a strange force that compels a writer to be a humorist.

— DOROTHY PARKER

In the spring of 1948, high school dropout Art Buchwald was having the time of his life. After being discharged from the U.S. Marine Corps at the end of World War II, he had enrolled at the University of Southern California in Los Angeles as a "special student" under the GI Bill. "I'm having a ball," the new college man wrote his sisters, Alice, Doris, and Edith, back home in New York. "All your predictions about what would happen to me if I goofed off in high school have not proven true. USC sees something in me that you girls never did—a promising brain surgeon, a future member of the Supreme Court or, at the very least, a Nobel Laureate in literature." Art took great pleasure in writing to his father and sisters about his "charmed life" in California. "I have never been happier in my life. . . . I wear a cotton sweater that could be taken for cashmere, and nobody gives me a bad time or tells me what to do," he wrote home with glee. "As soon as I mail this letter I am going out to buy saddle shoes and get a date with a Trojan coed— Jewish, of course."

Art lived with thirteen other students in an off-campus boarding-house run by an odd woman named Mrs. Liebschen, who, according to Buchwald, seemed to possess a deep-seated hatred for anyone not of the Aryan race. Although she never displayed any open hostility toward Buchwald as a Jew, he always found her fondness for a "German newspaper with a swastika on the front page" a bit unsettling.

As a "special" non-degree student, he was the "envy" of his class-mates since he could enroll in any course that caught his fancy. "When asked what I intend to do with my life," he told one of his sisters, "I reply, 'I'll probably be a writer for the cinema, or start a book on the corrupt athletic programs in our university system.'" In an effort to hone his skills as a writer, Buchwald took courses in drama and creative writing. "Foreign languages and the sciences interested me as much as nuclear waste," he later said. In one of his writing classes he wrote a theme paper titled "A Short Report on Satire," an ironic bit of foreshadowing in which he claimed that humor and satire can act as a "civilizing agent" on society, tempering its political and cultural excesses. "The satirist is always at war with society," he wrote, "but I think it's a worthwhile fight."

When not in the classroom, Buchwald enjoyed the time he spent as managing editor of the campus humor magazine, *Wampus*, and as a columnist for the *Daily Trojan* newspaper, both of which provided an early outlet for his brand of humor and satire. "USC was my training ground before I went out into the world and stuck pins into the rich and powerful," he later wrote.

He even tried his hand at a comic theatrical production, once writing a musical play based on the "atomic experiments at Bikini Island," called *No Love Atoll*. Despite its catchy title, the play closed after a campus run of only four days.

Then, during his third year at USC, Buchwald struck gold. One morning over coffee he learned from a fellow student about a tuition benefit program under the GI Bill that would permit him to study in Paris—the "Mecca of writers" and the city of romance—where, he told friends, the "streets are lined with beds." His "dream was to follow in the steps of Hemingway, Elliot Paul, and Gertrude Stein," he declared. "I wanted to stuff myself with baguettes and snails, fill my pillow with rejection slips, and find a French girl named Mimi who believed that I was the greatest writer in the world."

After bidding goodbye to his friends and the peculiar Frau Liebschen, Buchwald hitchhiked from Los Angeles to New York, where he booked a one-way ticket to France on a former troop carrier. As the ship hit the open seas, Art had no doubts that he had made the right decision, and he was as happy as ever.

During the long ocean voyage to France, Buchwald spent evenings out on the deck reflecting on his past. "I started adding up everything that had happened to me since my birth," he later wrote. "My life had been a series of zigs and zags. Soon after I was born, my mother was confined to a mental institution, where she remained for thirty-five years. With my three sisters, I was placed in the Hebrew Orphan Asylum in New York, and then boarded out with foster parents . . . in eight different kinds of homes with God knows how many strangers."

Because his father, Joseph, a struggling curtain salesman in New York, was unable to afford the expense of his wife's hospital bills and the cost of supporting a family, he had been forced to give up the care of Art and his three sisters to foster homes in and around New York City. Although his father came to visit as often as he could, Art felt abandoned. "I didn't belong to anybody," he later said of his childhood.

While the majority of Art's school years were spent at PS 35 in Hollis, a middle-class neighborhood in Queens, his real education came from experiencing life on the streets, where he quickly developed a reputation for being a "bold and street wise" young man. Art traveled all alone on the subway into the city, where he wandered into coffee shops and hotel lobbies, fascinated by the colorful cast of characters he saw everywhere. "Later when I became a fan of Damon Runyon's, I knew better than most people what he was talking about," Buchwald would later recall.

But perhaps the most important lesson he learned during those sad early years was that the way to cope with the hard knocks of life was to be funny and to battle adversity with a smile. "I was the class clown. . . . I managed to get people to laugh. That was my way of getting acceptance. I learned very quickly that if you are a clown, people will be nicer to you." Increasingly frustrated by the loneliness and anger he felt, one day he vowed to himself, "This stinks! I'm going to become a humorist."

In 1942, a year after America entered World War II, seventeen-year-old Buchwald dropped out of high school and enlisted in the U.S. Marine Corps with forged permission papers. After basic training at Parris Island, South Carolina, he shipped out to a Marine airfield at Cherry Point, North Carolina, where he was inexplicably assigned to the base ordnance school, handling bombs and other lethal inventory—an unlikely post for someone who lacked any manner of mechanical or technical aptitude. During his off-duty hours, far from the airfield's stock of high-grade explosives, Buchwald started smoking cigars, a habit that quickly became a soothing obsession. "Cigars [were] a very important part of my life. They were my pacifier, my security blanket, even my Valium. Whenever I was feeling good, I put one between my lips, and whenever I was feeling bad, I lit one up."

After Cherry Point, his unit, VMF 113, was ordered to the Marshall Islands in the Pacific, where he saw action at Eniwetok and Engebi in 1944. In addition to his ordnance duties, Buchwald was editor of the unit's humorous newsletter, *The U-Man Comedy*. In one issue, after his unit scored several impressive aerial successes against the Japanese, Buchwald published a front-page open letter to Tojo, the Japanese prime minister and head of the Imperial army, proclaiming that it was time for him to "throw in the towel."

In November 1945, three months after the end of the war, Buchwald was discharged from the Marine Corps and returned to New York. Soon feeling restless and seeking a new adventure, he abandoned New York and headed to the West Coast, setting his sights on becoming a comic screenwriter in Hollywood and, during his off-hours, making "love to Ginger Rogers." When both dreams were quickly dashed he applied for admission and matriculated at USC. But after three carefree years of college life he was ready to move on.

Now, here he was on his way to Paris, "every young writer's dream," he declared to himself one night as the "ship sailed smoothly through the water" to the port of Le Havre. He "felt an unbelievable surge of happiness" about the great adventure that lay ahead. But not even in his "wildest dreams" could he have foreseen "how wonderful the future would turn out to be."

Shortly after his arrival in Paris in late June 1948, Buchwald wrote a letter home to a former high school classmate:

I am in Paris and I got a great buy on a French beret. The sidewalk salesman told me that it had belonged to his grandfather, who posed for Van Gogh's most famous self-portrait.

My money is still holding out. The secret is French bread and cheese. It is a banquet and all I need to keep me going. I haven't fallen in love yet, as I've decided to play hard to get. If a French baroness drives by and asks me to jump into her car, I will tell her, "I prefer to walk." And then add, "Just because I am an American student, I have no intention of going to Maxim's and drinking a bottle of champagne with you and letting you take advantage of me in the back of your limousine."

I am constantly in touch with the arts. I have been to the Louvre and the Rodin museums, and Napoleon's tomb. Because of my French beret, no one knows I am an American. As a matter of fact, I have been stopped by tourists who were lost and wanted to find their way. I deal with them in the same way as the French—I refuse to answer them.

From the moment he arrived, Buchwald was captivated by everything Paris had to offer: the street vendors and streetwalkers, black-market peddlers, lively music, the ubiquitous sound of taxi horns, but above all the noisy and colorful cafés. It was "like a stage setting from a Broadway musical," he later said.

Although he knew no one and didn't speak a word of French, he "savored every moment," getting by on what he described as mangled "Franglais." Several weeks after he arrived he wrote again to friends back home about the progress on his great American novel:

Just a short note to . . . let you know I haven't been deported as yet. . . . Ah Paris, what a place. It isn't a city—it's a way of life. I have never enjoyed myself as much as I have in this city. The women are beautiful, the food is exquisite, the sidewalk cafes are restful, and everyone knows how to talk French. Paris is nice now because all the American tourists are going home. Hah, I spit on you, American tourist. Go home, you fat-bellied cigar-chewing chowder head—go home you full hipped, many chested, and many chinned wife of a cigar-chewing chowder head, and leave Paris to the people who love it. They will be gone in a month for sure and Paris will be ours.

I've started a book since I've been here. I have the preface, the dedication and the title. The tentative masterpiece will be simply titled, "Plastered in Paris." It will contain all sorts of things that I've seen and done in Paris. Naturally it can't be finished till I'm ready to leave (a year maybe two), but in the meantime I just wanted you to start saving for it. . . .

I go to school. I'm learning the French language. Last month I was in a class with the backward students that possessed speech impediments. I have been promoted and am now in a class just for backward students. I learn a lot in the daytime but when I go out at night and drink wine I forget it. . . .

Your boy,
Art

During his first few months in Paris, Buchwald drifted from one cheap, seedy hotel to the next before finally moving into an apartment in a colorful, noisy working-class section near the place de Clichy. At first, his Parisian neighbors were cold and standoffish because he was American, but, as he later joked, they finally warmed up after he assured them he didn't want to "start a nuclear war, or force France to drink Coca-Cola, or abolish the French August vacation."

Soon he moved to another hotel, the Hotel des Etats-Unis, where he found a seven-dollar-a-week room with a "sink, a bed, a desk, and a very weak light bulb . . . so low in wattage that the mice went blind trying to find something to eat." To Buchwald's delight, the hotel had a café next door where he spent many a lively and raucous evening mingling with other Americans.

When not at school studying French, he worked as an eight-dollar-a-week part-time stringer for *Variety* magazine, reporting on new films at the cinema, new plays at the Paris theater, and the gay and colorful nightlife at the city's cafés and posh hotels. Although his stint at *Variety* provided him a lively taste of the city and helped pay bills, Art wanted something more and set his sights on landing a position with one of the greatest newspapers in the world, the *New York Herald Tribune*. As a reader of the Paris edition of the *Herald Tribune*, he noted that the paper lacked a nightlife and entertainment column, something Americans in Paris would love to read because, as Buchwald knew, tourists "always wanted to know where to go, and I was prepared to lead them." Years later he would say that he had "impeccable credentials" for reviewing French restaurants. "I had dined for three years in the U.S. Marine Corps mess halls, then for three years I ate in the school cafeteria at the University of Southern California."

Buchwald knew that getting a job at the *Herald Tribune* was a long shot, but he was determined to give it a try. "Every young journalist's dream was to work on the *Tribune*," he later said. "I yearned to work on the paper more than anything I had ever wanted in my life."

"GET THE HELL OUT OF HERE!"

When Art Buchwald arrived in Paris in the summer of 1948, the mighty *Herald Tribune* was at the "apex of [its] power and prestige," wrote Richard Kluger in *The Paper: The Life and Death of the "New*

York Herald Tribune." In "quality of content . . . range and depth of news coverage, and the soundness and care of its editing, the *Tribune* had only one other rival in the world: *The New York Times,*" Kluger wrote. The *Trib*'s reporting staff included some of the greatest writers and commentators of the twentieth century: Sportswriter "Red" Smith, war correspondent Homer Bigart, music critic Virgil Thomson, and columnist Walter Lippmann. Its flagship Paris bureau, in particular, gave it an international reach and status that even the *Times* didn't possess.

The bureau was run by Harvard-educated editor and publisher Geoffrey Parsons, Jr., who had worked for the *Tribune* in Chicago and London, and by managing editor Eric Hawkins, a tough, no-nonsense "feisty Englishman" who had been a boxer before becoming a journalist. Hawkins had been with the Paris bureau since 1924, overseeing the work of journalistic icons such as Eric Sevareid, Henry Miller, and William Shirer, author of *The Rise and Fall of the Third Reich.* Staff and colleagues knew he was gruff, curt, and never to be trifled with. And his reputation was the stuff of legend. In June 1940, as German troops rushed toward Paris, Hawkins boldly insisted on publishing a final one-page edition of the *Tribune* as an act of defiance against the Nazis.

With the paper's prestige and status and the pedigree of its editorial and reporting staff, it seems almost unimaginable that Art Buchwald could ever believe—or dream—that he had the slightest chance of landing a job at the *Herald Tribune.* He had no high school diploma or college degree; he had no family connections or contacts in the world of newspaper publishing; and his skills as a journalist consisted entirely of a three-year stint as a college reporter at USC and several months working as a part-time stringer for *Variety.*

But with typical Buchwald chutzpah, in December 1948 he decided to drop by unannounced at the *Tribune* bureau located on the rue de Berri just off the Champs-Elysées. He made his way up to the third-floor editorial offices and strolled up to the desk of Eric Hawkins. Surprised and taken aback, the stern Hawkins quickly gave Buchwald the once-over, glancing with disdain at the "tubby little fellow in a loud checkered jacket and tortoiseshell glasses." When Buchwald spoke up and proposed his idea for a new column, Hawkins abruptly cut him off. "The paper isn't interested in an entertainment column," he told him, "and if it was, you wouldn't be the one to write it. Now get the hell out of here!"

Although downcast, Buchwald was undeterred. "Some people might have considered that a rejection," he later said. "But I considered it a challenge." Two weeks later, in early January 1949, he learned that Hawkins was away on vacation. Seizing the opportunity to make another run at the *Tribune*, he rushed over to the bureau and made his way to the desk of the bureau's more easygoing editor and publisher, Geoffrey Parsons. With nothing to lose, he boldly told Parsons that he and Hawkins had recently discussed the possibility of Art writing an entertainment column for the paper. Parsons, who assumed that what Buchwald told him was true, said he liked the idea—especially since café reviews might bring in more advertising revenue for the paper— and hired him on the spot. He would be paid $100 a month for two columns each week: one writing restaurant reviews and a second on the French cinema. The *Trib*'s new column would be called "Paris After Dark." Art was thrilled. "I was on the staff of the greatest newspaper in the greatest city in the world."

When Hawkins returned to the office, he was furious, astounded that Buchwald had gone behind his back. Although angry and frustrated, he deferred to Parsons and let the decision stand, but for the next several weeks he was cold and distant toward Buchwald.

To make matters even worse, the first columns Art submitted were almost unusable. "He wasn't exactly a whirlwind in the beginning," Hawkins said decades later:

In fact, his copy was impossible. He was a complete novice at writing. He had the ideas, but he didn't know what to do with them. Also, his bad French didn't help. I remember some of his first pieces consisted of rewriting menus. When he wrote about the cinema, a typical Buchwald review in those days might wind up with the comment, "This is a good film if you understand French."

For weeks, whenever Buchwald handed Hawkins a column, the editor "flinched." Sensing he was in serious trouble, Art prepared "for the ax to fall." But the realization that he might be fired was also liberating. With nothing to lose, he loosened up and started writing more freely, blending his instinctive sense of humor into the column. "I cast myself as a Charlie Chaplin character," he later said with delight, "the hapless tourist who couldn't shoot straight."

And it worked. Hawkins at last saw something promising in Art's style and "encouraged" him to stay in the new Buchwald "groove." "His naivete served him well," Hawkins later said. "Gradually, he developed an identification with almost every American tourist in Paris. He was constantly fighting waiters or being baffled by wine lists. He became the typical bumbling American in Paris."

In short order Buchwald was writing not only about French films and cafés, but also about taxis, perfume, cigars, caviar, escargot, and art exhibits at the Louvre. In letters to friends back home he said he was a "busy bastard" but wouldn't change a thing. "Boy, when I made the decision to come to Paris," he wrote to one friend, "I really made the best decision of my life."

Pleased with the success of "Paris After Dark," Art's editors assigned him a second column, "Mostly About People," and then a third, "Europe's Lighter Side," both providing readers with "whimsical" accounts of Buchwald's colorful escapades in Europe. Soon, Art was one of the most popular journalists in Paris, hobnobbing with visiting American politicians and dignitaries, movie stars, film producers, and some of the most celebrated American writers of the 1950s.

One of the notables Buchwald was most excited to meet in those early years was his idol Ernest Hemingway. The two met one night at the Ritz Hotel when Art found the novelist at the bar drinking Bloody Marys with John Ringling North, head of the Ringling Bros. and Barnum & Bailey circus. Art was fascinated by Hemingway's stories about the bullfights he had seen during a recent trip to Spain and his impressions of the new crop of daring young matadors he saw perform in the arena. Hemingway told North and Buchwald that he was headed to Africa for his first vacation in a decade. "Been working steadily for three years," the novelist said. "Finished three books since *Old Man and the Sea*. Going to let them lie for a year and then go back over them."

While enjoying his fourth Bloody Mary, Hemingway disclosed to Buchwald that whenever North brought his circus to Cuba, the owner let him "work out with the bears." As Art listened intently, Hemingway paused, fixed his eyes on Buchwald, and asked, "Kid, have you ever wrestled a bear?" When an astonished Buchwald responded "What the hell?" Hemingway—without missing a beat—pressed on with his tale, telling a still-dumbfounded Buchwald, "If the books didn't sell, I think I'd be a bear trainer. I like to wrestle with the bears. I talk with 'em too."

Several years later, a less starstruck Buchwald wrote a wickedly funny satire of Hemingway's novel *Across the River and into the Trees*, a column that prompted Hemingway to call Buchwald "a smart-assed son of a bitch." Buchwald, greatly amused by Hemingway's comment, told a friend, "I was very happy, because this meant he was reading me in the *Herald Tribune*."

By 1952, Buchwald's columns had become so popular in Europe that his editors decided to syndicate his work back in the United States, a move that quickly made him a journalistic celebrity on both sides of the Atlantic.

One of Buchwald's most memorable early columns was his famous—or to some detractors infamous—"Le Jour de Merci Donnant," a satirical explanation of the birth of America's Thanksgiving Day holiday, all with a bilingual twist. In Buchwald's version, the "Pelerins" (Pilgrims) arrive at Plymouth via the "Fleur de Mai" (*Mayflower*), to eat "dinde" (turkey) and "mais" (corn) to "their heart's content." Buchwald's Thanksgiving Day column became such a favorite with readers that it was published every November for the next fifty years.

His columns were now a must-read for visiting tourists, dignitaries, or adrift and adventurous Americans passing through Paris. They relied on him for tips about cafés, plays, and art exhibits. One of those visiting Americans was a twenty-year-old art student named Robert Redford, who was studying in Paris in the late 1950s. When not attending art classes or reading French political history, Redford read the columns of Art Buchwald and Walter Lippmann. Years later, Redford thanked Art for having played such an important part in his early life. "Before I became an actor I wanted to be an artist. I went to Paris to study. I was young and very lonely," he told Buchwald. "I read your entertainment column in the European edition of the *Herald Tribune*. In those days, you wrote about restaurants and bars that tourists might want to go to. Believe it or not, your 'Paris After Dark' columns were a lifesaver to me."

CHAPTER 2

RAISING THE STATURE OF INK

Funny Business at the Herald Tribune *(1953-60)*

It sure beat the hell out of living in Cleveland.

—ART BUCHWALD ON HIS YEARS SPENT IN PARIS

"Hey there, McGarry!" bellowed Art Buchwald one night from a table at Le Colisee on the Champs-Elysées. The McGarry in question was Ann McGarry of Warren, Pennsylvania, who was working in Paris as publicity director for one of the most famous fashion designers in France. Art and Ann had first met several weeks earlier when a mutual friend introduced them to each other. "He wore a sporty brown hat which was pulled down over his horn-rimmed glasses," an unimpressed Ann recalled of their first encounter. "His shirt looked rumpled. . . . His feet [were] halfway out of his loafers and [he] made no attempt to stand up. He merely pushed up the brim of his hat, looked at me, and said 'Hi.'"

Twenty-nine-year-old Ann McGarry first arrived in France in September 1949. Although she had no job, she had plenty of ambition and a "firm intention" of making it in the city she had dreamed about for years. Coming from a large family with devoted parents who had suffered hard times during the Depression, Ann was strong, independent, resourceful, and determined to succeed. She began her career in public relations, working for department stores in Pittsburgh, Memphis, and New York City before landing a job with the prestigious Neiman Marcus corporation of Dallas, Texas. But after two years Ann realized that Texas was not for her and decided to pursue her dreams and move to Paris. When she arrived in France she was initially overwhelmed by her new surroundings—"the biggest, loudest, wildest city" she'd ever seen—but she soon made her way to the offices of Pierre Balmain, one of the world's most creative and successful postwar fashion designers, creator of outfits for such celebrities as the Duchess of Windsor, Marlene Dietrich, and Katharine Hepburn. As luck would have it, Balmain had dismissed his public relations director just before Ann walked through the door, and after a brief interview, during which he learned about her experience with Stanley Marcus and her connections at *Vogue* and *Harper's Bazaar*, he hired her on the spot.

Although Ann had not been particularly impressed with Art during their first meeting, he, on the other hand, was charmed by her from the very beginning. "I found her extremely attractive. Many things about her appealed to me. She was pretty and very bright, and after she decided I would not harm her, she laughed at all my jokes." Over the next two years, Art and Ann had an on-again, off-again romance. Although they thoroughly enjoyed each other's company—dining with film stars, going to movie premieres, and visiting the "lavish country homes" of the "international set"—there was little talk of marriage. Part of it was Art's unwillingness to commit. "He vacillated between wanting to get married and wishing he were free," Ann later recalled. Although he hemmed and hawed about settling down, Art never wavered in his affection for her. "You've got them all beat," he once told her in a letter. "I'm so lonely for you—to hear your voice or see you—I can't keep interested in anything." Finally frustrated by Art's reluctance to make any kind of serious commitment, Ann told him she was thinking of taking a new job back in New York City. Art was stunned, torn between holding on to his freedom as a bachelor and the worry that if she left he would "never find anyone like her again."

Ann was torn, too. One night while having drinks with actress Lauren Bacall, shortly before they were to join Art and Humphrey Bogart for dinner at the Ritz, Bacall told Ann she would be making a big mistake by going to New York and not giving Art another chance. "Bogey and I have watched you two together for over a year, good times, rotten times, and you're perfect for each other. Furthermore, you may not know it yet because Art is young and roly-poly and a funny man about life, but he's the best guy you'll ever meet, kid!"

Ann accepted Bacall's advice and gave Art one more chance. And she didn't have to wait long. After spending a week in Morocco on business, Buchwald returned and proposed. In early October 1952, they were married in London at Westminster Cathedral and held a reception at Claridge's, attended by a host of celebrity friends, including Gene Kelly, Rosemary Clooney, and film producers John Huston and Sam Spiegel. After the wedding, they honeymooned on the island of Majorca and then returned to Paris, where novelist Irwin Shaw and his wife, Marian, hosted a party for the newlyweds. Both Ann and Art were thrilled to be settling down. Years later Art would joke with Lauren Bacall about the fateful night at the Ritz when she persuaded Ann to stay. "Listen, buster," Bacall told him. "It was the best thing anyone [ever] did for you."

Shortly after the couple returned from their honeymoon and settled into their new life together, it was time to start thinking about a family. Over the next four years—despite a seemingly endless series of legal, immigration, cultural, and political hurdles—they succeeded in adopting three children: Joel from Ireland, Connie from Spain, and Jennifer from the American Hospital of Paris. (The Buchwalds decided to adopt after learning that Ann could not get pregnant. "I was the problem," Art wrote decades later. "I had a very low sperm count.")

"So in no time we had gone from being a childless couple to a family of five," Buchwald remembered. For her part Ann was absolutely thrilled to have a family of her own. "I'd been ready for motherhood all my life," she later wrote, and Joel, Connie, and Jennifer "filled our lives even more than we did theirs."

. . .

Buchwald would always say that the fourteen years he and Ann spent together in Paris were "the scene of our happiest moments." Part of the thrill was the extraordinary circle of friends and acquaintances they kept company with. Art played chess with Humphrey Bogart, played gin rummy with Ben Bradlee, and roamed the Left Bank with Orson Welles and Peter Ustinov. They mingled with Ingrid Bergman; Audrey Hepburn; Lena Horne; Mike Todd and his beautiful young wife, actress Elizabeth Taylor; and the Duke and Duchess of Windsor. Ann and Art spent one bizarre evening with the Windsors when the Duke played recordings of "patriotic German songs" and sang along with great delight. "He was a dimwitted man," Buchwald later wrote, "and I always believed England [owed] Wallis [Simpson] . . . for making him give up the crown." Art thought the Duchess, however, was "a very sharp lady and knew what was going on." Knowing he was a restaurant critic for the *Tribune*, the Duchess once asked him to let them know about "any new restaurants [in Paris] you think we'd like—but none with garlic, please."

They spent evenings with writers Janet Flanner and James Thurber of *The New Yorker*. (Buchwald once asked Thurber, who was nearly blind from an injury suffered as a child, what it felt like to lose his vision. In typical Thurber fashion, the humorist replied, "It's better now. For a long while, images of Herbert Hoover were the only thing that kept popping up in front of me.")

One evening the Buchwalds attended a dinner with British novelist and biographer Nancy Mitford, who was "one of the most anti-American people" Art ever met in Europe. "I once asked her what American she disliked the most," Buchwald later recalled. "She replied, 'Abraham Lincoln. I detest Abraham Lincoln. When I read the book *The Day Lincoln Was Shot*, I was so afraid that he would go to the wrong theater. What was the name of that beautiful man who shot him—John Wilkes Booth? Yes, I like him very much.'"

On other nights Ann and Art dined and shared gossip with the likes of novelist W. Somerset Maugham (who Art called "one of my favorite British people of all time"), or with legendary journalists Edward R. Murrow and Walter Lippmann, or with novelist John Steinbeck and his wife Elaine.

Art had long been an admirer of Steinbeck's work—especially *The Grapes of Wrath*. In 1946, while still a student at USC, Buchwald got a job picking fruit on a farm in Northern California in hopes of gaining enough experience to write his own version of Steinbeck's masterpiece. His planned adventure, however, quickly turned into a frightening misadventure. Guarded by men with shotguns during the day when out in the fields, then herded into filthy bunkhouses at night; it was a terrifying experience for Buchwald. Although he eventually escaped, he never forgot the terror he felt during the whole ordeal, later writing that he had nightmares about it for the rest of his life.

Now the opportunity to spend time with Steinbeck in Paris was a dream come true for Buchwald. And soon, to his great delight, the Pulitzer Prize- and Nobel Prize–winning novelist became an admirer of Art's charm and his unique brand of humor:

JULY 27, 1953

[New York]

Dear Art:

Have been wanting to tell you for a long time how much I am enjoying your pieces we get in the Trib *here. You are getting a fine humorous form and also you are about the only man living who is setting down our ridiculous time in proper and good natured terms. You are developing very rapidly and it is a joy to read. And it's in the real sturdy tradition of American humor too. At once most deadly and the most ingratiating.*

Although the *Herald Tribune* was one of the most prestigious newspapers in the world, its Paris bureau offices at 21 rue de Berri were notable for their "scruffy" appearance. The whole setting "could not have been better designed by a movie-set director," Buchwald once joked:

> The floors sagged, and when the presses were running, the entire building shook. . . . The elevator creaked in pain. . . . The limited space allotted to me could have gotten the *Tribune* in trouble with the Geneva Convention. . . . Reporters' desks were from the Clemenceau period and the lighting had been designed by Thomas Edison.

Ben Bradlee, the Paris bureau chief of *Newsweek* magazine, which shared space with the *Tribune*, remembered the offices as being "wonderfully ratty" and "grungy." During cold months, a lack of heat was always an issue, requiring reporters to sometimes wear gloves while they typed. Buchwald's typewriter and "cluttered" desk "faced a blind window which overlooked a soot-covered air shaft." In such cramped quarters, his habit of chain-smoking cigars and laughing out loud at his own columns was a constant source of annoyance to his editors and fellow reporters. And to help put out each edition of the paper there was an odd assortment of staff on hand. According to Buchwald, the French typesetters in the composing room (none of whom spoke a word of English) sang the Communist anthem "The Internationale" every twenty minutes and, to make matters even worse, the office mail clerk was almost blind, and the phone receptionist nearly deaf.

Despite the close quarters and dingy conditions at 21 rue de Berri, Buchwald loved being a *Trib* man. His weekly columns were now read and talked about nearly everywhere, and his readership was constantly on the rise. By 1955 his reputation had grown to such an extent that a mock Buchwald column titled "The Cat Prowls Again?" made a cameo appearance in the opening scene of Alfred Hitchcock's film *To Catch a Thief*, a romantic thriller about a retired jewel thief named John Robie, starring Cary Grant and Grace Kelly.

After only seven years in Paris, Buchwald had become a journalistic celebrity, prompting American radio personality Fred Allen to remark that Art's column had surely "raised the stature of ink."

The key to Buchwald's style of humor was to "treat light subjects seriously and serious subjects lightly," he once said. That formula was on full view in two of his greatest satirical successes while in Europe. The first was an offbeat and fanciful account of one of the most talked about weddings of the twentieth century; the second a comical roast of a powerful yet unwitting presidential aide who was no match for the Buchwald treatment.

"THE GREAT GRIMALDI FEUD"

During the spring of 1956, a fairy-tale story of royal romance took Art Buchwald and his friend Ben Bradlee on the road to Monaco. Earlier that year, American actress Grace Kelly had announced her engagement to Prince Rainier Louis Henri Maxence Bertrand Grimaldi of Monaco, generating a larger-than-life love story covered in newsreels and newspaper headlines around the world.

Just days before the royal wedding, Buchwald, Bradlee, and Crosby Noyes of *The Washington Star* left Paris and rushed to Monaco to cover the ceremony, despite the fact that none of them had an invitation. Leaving Paris by overnight train, the "Three Musketeers" (as Bradlee dubbed them) headed south, in the hope that their resourcefulness would get them some kind of inside scoop at the wedding. When they finally arrived at the Monte Carlo train station, there was not a cab in sight. After a bit of scrambling, Bradlee spied a small taxi and waved it down, but he immediately realized that the portly third Musketeer, Buchwald, would never fit in the cab. "There's no more room, Artie!" Bradlee yelled. Casting all honor aside, Bradlee and Noyes jumped in and ditched Buchwald, both laughing as they sped off to their hotel. However, as in most cases throughout Buchwald's life, he would have the last laugh. After making his way to the hotel, Art sat down at his typewriter and, as Bradlee described it, "pulled a rabbit out of his hat, with what I have always believed was the best column he ever wrote."

In a piece filed with the *Tribune* later that day titled "The Great Grimaldi Feud," Buchwald wrote a spoof column claiming that the reason he had been "snubbed" and had not received an invitation to the wedding was that the Buchwald and Rainier-Grimaldi families had been feuding since the thirteenth century, and that the bitterness of the rivalry had prevented him from being invited. "The reason for the feud is lost somewhere in the cobwebs of history," Buchwald facetiously wrote. "You won't find a page in the history of Monaco where a Buchwald hasn't offended a Grimaldi or a Grimaldi hasn't offended a Buchwald." A year earlier, Buchwald wrote, he had tried to heal the bickering between the two families by coaxing his aunt Molly to invite Prince Rainier to attend his cousin Joseph's wedding to a "nice girl from Flatbush." But his proud and defiant aunt would have none of it. "No Grimaldis!" she told Art.

Now stuck in Monaco with no invitation to the royal wedding, Buchwald playfully declared that he was the latest victim in the seven-centuries-long feud. Sadly, he said with feigned amusement, "the Grimaldis still had it in for the Buchwalds."

Art's column was a stroke of genius. The next morning, shortly after the daily edition of the Paris *Herald Tribune* reached the Royal Palace, an invitation to one of the most magical weddings of the century was hand-delivered to Buchwald at his hotel.

"ADULTERATED ROT"

A year after his on-the-road-to-Monaco adventure, Buchwald's satire enmeshed him in a colorful public spat with President Dwight D.

Eisenhower's press secretary James Hagerty. In mid-December 1957, President Eisenhower arrived in Paris for a NATO summit conference. Some 1,700 reporters from around the world descended on the French capital to cover the meeting. Hagerty, who had a knack for annoying journalists with his overly protective and "very sophisticated control" of the press, generally filled his daily briefings with a mind-numbing "glut of informational trivia." While covering the NATO summit, Art Buchwald decided to write a tongue-in-cheek column for the *Tribune* satirizing Hagerty's tiresome briefing style. In his spoof column, Buchwald related this fanciful colloquy between Hagerty and reporters as Eisenhower retired after a long day of NATO summitry:

Q: Jim, whose idea was it for the president to go to sleep?
A: It was the president's idea.
Q: Do you have any idea what the president is dreaming right now?
A: No, the president has never revealed to me any of his dreams.

Pursuing the state of Eisenhower's sleeping habits further, Buchwald's imaginary press corps wanted to know *exactly* how many blankets the president used when he bedded down each night. "Maybe two or three," Buchwald's Hagerty responded. Quickly challenging the press spokesman's figures, a reporter wanted to know if it was "possible" that Hagerty was misinformed, and that the chief executive had actually "kicked off" one of his blankets in the middle of the night. "Possible, but it's highly unlikely," Buchwald's cagey presidential spokesman asserted.

Reading the column in the *Tribune* the next morning, the president, who always enjoyed Buchwald's cleverness, "laughed out loud." But his no-nonsense press spokesman was outraged. Ignoring Eisenhower's advice to "simmer down," Hagerty, who felt publicly humiliated, decided to strike back. At his daily press briefing that morning, a stern and straight-faced Hagerty informed the 1,700 correspondents that what Buchwald had written was simply untrue, totally fabricated, and nothing more than "unadulterated rot."

Like any great satirist or comic, Buchwald knew not only how to throw a good punch, but how to take one—and throw one right back. Hagerty's temper tantrum and "unadulterated rot" quote were reported in newspapers around the world. It was all that Buchwald needed. When asked for a comment on Hagerty's charge of "unadulterated rot," Art casually responded that he had never written "unadulterated rot"—only "adulterated rot." The following day the White House press corps, who for years had been frustrated by Hagerty's style, had a field day gleefully reporting how Buchwald had "aroused" the ire of the president's press secretary.

The Hagerty episode, Buchwald later claimed, "was a glorious, unexpected moment of fame and gave me notoriety beyond my wildest dreams."

But not all *Tribune* readers were thrilled with Buchwald's style. One elderly resident living at the chic Le Meurice hotel in Paris complained in a letter to Art's editors in June 1955 that although Buchwald's columns were "occasionally amusing," all too often he was "too snide for his britches." Apparently Buchwald had been "bitten" by the "bad Hollywood movie" image of newspapermen as tough guys, the reader wrote. "You don't have to be tough to be a great newspaperman. I'm afraid Mr. Buchwald needs to be spanked and stood in the corner."

If it wasn't the style or slant of Buchwald's wit that irritated his readers, it was something else. In early 1955, when *Tribune* editors decided to include a photo of him alongside his weekly column, little could they have imagined that a glimpse of the man behind the humor would quickly shatter a young girl's dreams. "Why, oh why did you do it?" a heartbroken admirer wrote Buchwald's editors. For years she had dreamed of Art as a "tall, slender blond . . . with a romantic smile" and the "attitude [of] a subtle swashbuckler." But now, after seeing what he truly looked like, she and "ten other girls" in her "poetry class . . .

[were] thinking of disfiguring themselves after finding out the truth. Just think—he's a little fat man with glasses and a silly grin."

Although Buchwald was not quite the "swashbuckler" of a young girl's dreams, there were plenty of touches of Hemingway and Walter Mitty in his life. "The trick of the column," he once wrote, "was to keep moving and try to mix up the subject matter as much as possible. . . . If I stayed in Paris I would dry up."

He ran with the bulls at Pamplona alongside Irwin Shaw, George Plimpton, and Peter Matthiessen; sang Irish songs with John Huston and Gregory Peck at Linehan's Pub during the filming of *Moby Dick* in Youghal, Ireland; and traveled to Africa to write a piece for *Collier's* magazine called "Coward in the Congo"—a satirical Hemingway-esque "spoof" piece about his comic exploits as a big-game hunter on the subcontinent. And in the spring of 1958 he embarked on one of the most colorful and far-fetched adventures of his years in Paris. Having read in the newspapers "that the Soviets had announced the opening of their roads for the first time," thereby permitting foreign visitors to drive directly into the Soviet Union, Buchwald decided that a road trip was in order: He would travel by car from the center of Paris to the heart of Communist Russia. Determined at the outset not to be part of any Cold War intrigue or clandestine expedition, he made arrangements to be driven to Moscow in a chauffeur-driven Chrysler Imperial. "My plan was to travel as a rich American plutocrat and ride in the backseat with hampers of caviar and foie gras, just as the Party members imagined all of us traveled." His traveling companion on the trek would be his friend, screenwriter Peter Stone, best known for the films *Charade* (1963), starring Cary Grant and Audrey Hepburn, and *Mirage* (1965), starring Gregory Peck.

Buchwald's Russian expedition left Paris on March 30, 1958, "loaded down with food, vodka, jerrycans, spare parts and long underwear." Their adventure took them east through Vienna, Czechoslovakia, and Poland, and at every stop along the way their car was mobbed by gawking Iron Curtain bystanders fascinated by the Chrysler Imperial. "People gathered around the car, inspecting the engine, kicking the tires, and crawling underneath the suspension," Art wrote. Once in Russia, however, the slick, powerful, capitalist Imperial was no match for the brutal Soviet weather and treacherous terrain. Twice Buchwald's Chrysler got stuck in the snow and had to be towed back to safety by groups of peasants with farm horses. "We found out why Napoleon turned back," Buchwald joked at the time. "We hit the same kind of snow he did."

After finally arriving in Moscow, the weary traveling party checked into the Hotel Metropol and promptly made their way to the restaurant with high hopes of some savory Russian hospitality. But their hopes were soon dashed as they quickly realized that "all the cooks left in 1917 and all the waiters left after they took our order."

Their greatest coup in the Russian capital, however, was breaching Soviet security and making their way into a mass meeting presided over by the blustery Soviet leader Nikita Khrushchev. With an American flag planted on the front of their Chrysler Imperial, Buchwald's car whisked past Soviet guards and made its way into the arena where, through a mixture of quick talking and Buchwald bravado, they gained admittance to the rally and introduced themselves to an astonished Chairman Khrushchev, who responded with profanities and "some uncomplimentary things about" America. "But we couldn't very well complain," Buchwald quipped, "since we weren't formally invited."

For days, Western readers were entertained by a running chronicle of Buchwald's exploits, but in Russia the official Soviet newspaper, *Pravda*, was outraged by the accounts of his antics. "Before his departure, Buchwald vowed to write only the truth," the propaganda arm of the Soviet regime bitterly complained, "but he wrote only lies, which he sucked out of his finger in the office of the *New York Herald Tribune*."

When Art was not out on the road he maintained a hectic business and social calendar back in Paris, his schedule increasingly filled by colorful encounters with some of America's greatest stars. Since he was now the man to see in Europe, press agents sought him out for interviews or meetings with their celebrity clients in hopes of landing a few gossipy tidbits in his column. "All of us became very cozy, and I dropped their name and they dropped mine," Buchwald later boasted. "I felt like I was riding a horse in a steeplechase. I could hardly catch my breath after finishing a conversation with J. Paul Getty before starting a new one with Truman Capote."

He once spent an amusing evening with legendary crooner Frank Sinatra, who explained to Buchwald the basics of "Sinatra-speak." A fun person was a "gasser, a big leaguer, the best," Old Blue Eyes told Art, but a "Harvey" was a "square," and a "Fink" was a "loser." And in 1959 he had an exclusive interview with Army Specialist Fourth Class Elvis Presley, who was on leave in Paris for seven days. When Art asked the teen idol if the Army was requiring him to do any "personal appearances" while in the service, Presley said no, but he occasionally sang for some of the men in his outfit, who mostly preferred to hear songs like the old ballad "I'll Take You Home Again, Kathleen." When Buchwald asked Presley if he would consider reenlisting after his tour was up, at first Presley "shuddered," but then admitted that the Army hadn't been all that bad. "I guess the thing I liked the least was sleeping in the snow," Elvis told Buchwald. "It's not something you enjoy."

In 1958, after nearly ten years at the *Herald Tribune*, Buchwald published a collection of his columns in a book titled *More Caviar*. After its release, Buchwald's publisher received a letter from another celebrated literary admirer. Much like John Steinbeck's note five years earlier, it was a thrilling tribute to Buchwald, this time from one of the greatest British humorists of the twentieth century:

P. G. Wodehouse
Remsenburg
Long Island, N.Y.

APRIL 14, 1959

Thanks so much for the Buchwald book. I read him every morning, of course, and generally clip his piece out, but it's wonderful having him in book form.

How about this for a slogan:—

"There is only one Art Buchwald, and if you think I am going to say 'That's plenty,' you are wrong, witty though it would be. I could do with a dozen."

. . . I have always thought Buchwald simply terrific.

Yours sincerely
P. G. Wodehouse

Election Day, November 8, 1960, signaled the beginning of a new age in American politics. The charismatic young president-elect John F. Kennedy and his charming and elegant wife, Jacqueline Bouvier Kennedy, were about to bring a new style and glamour to the White House. Art Buchwald knew that with a new president came a new press secretary. James Hagerty, Eisenhower's spokesman, who had unwittingly done so much to boost Buchwald's prestige three years earlier, would soon be leaving, and the *Tribune*'s man in Paris was concerned. So, shortly after the election results were in, Buchwald wasted no time in letting the new president's press secretary, Pierre Salinger, know what was to be expected of him. He told Salinger in a letter he had high hopes that the new president and his administration would do their best to provide him with new material to keep boosting his circulation numbers.

It was only natural that Buchwald would reach out to Salinger, since both men had a lot in common: a portly physique, a keen sense of humor, and a penchant for fine cigars. So, following a few postelection pleasantries, Buchwald's letter to Salinger turned to what was really on his mind: his concern that Kennedy's promise of a get-tough policy on Fidel Castro and Communist Cuba might have a calamitous impact on one of his most essential writing tools:

New York Herald Tribune
21 rue de Berri
Paris

NOVEMBER 18, 1960

Dear Pierre:

Let me take this opportunity to congratulate you on your new appointment as Press Secretary to the President of the United States. It is my understanding that you will pick up where Hagerty left off and attack me in your first year in office. I'm counting on this, because I usually pick up several newspapers when the Press Secretary of the United States attacks me....

Hope you'll be getting over here soon, as with your French and my money we could make quite a team. Or is it your money and my French. But whatever you do, don't let the President put an embargo on Havana Cigars. If he does, neither one of us will be able to work.

Sincerely,
Art

During his time in Europe, Buchwald had certainly raised "the stature of ink." In the early 1950s his column had appeared in twenty-two newspapers in nineteen countries, but by 1957 his circulation had more than doubled, with his column running in forty-six newspapers worldwide; by the end of the decade his readership had nearly doubled *again*, his column appearing in eighty-five newspapers around the world. He was making a salary of $50,000 a year, had a seven-room apartment on the Right Bank in Paris, and, on any given day, had his choice of "luncheon companions ranging from movie stars and authors to visiting congressmen." But as the new decade opened he was feeling restless and growing tired of writing columns about Americans and celebrities in Paris. "I had literally exhausted all the humor about tourists . . . and the International set. I knew I had made it in Europe but I felt I was repeating myself over and over again."

He needed a change of scenery, but most of all he needed new material.

Buchwald was intrigued by what he heard of the political celebrity and star power that the Kennedys were bringing to Washington. He wasn't ready to make a move yet, but it just might be what he was looking for.

"DOWN THE SEINE
AND UP THE POTOMAC"

CHAPTER 3

"SALINGER'S FOLLY" AND "BOUNTIES OF THE BANNED"

With the Kennedys on the New Frontier (1961-63)

Basically I deal in a very serious commodity—humor.

—ART BUCHWALD, 1967

On January 20, 1961, John F. Kennedy was inaugurated as the thirty-fifth president of the United States. It was a cold, windy day with temperatures well below freezing. The day before, Washington had been hit by a blizzard that blanketed the city with eight inches of snow.

For Kennedy's swearing-in, the celebrated poet Robert Frost had intended to read an original poem proclaiming the onset of a new Augustan age "of poetry and power." But as Frost started to read, "the breath of the old poet congealed in the freezing air," and the glare of the sun on his text made it impossible for him to continue. Instead, he recited from memory his poem "The Gift Outright."

Less than two months later, Ann and Art Buchwald were passengers on the same flight as Frost, who was flying to Tel Aviv to deliver a series of lectures. Finding the aging poet in "fine spirits," the Buchwalds struck up a conversation on the state of modern poetry in America. When Art finally got around to asking him about the new generation of "beatnik poets," a bewildered Frost paused and replied,

"I feel sorry for them. I keep trying to read them hoping I've missed something. Maybe there's something the matter with me. I recently read [Allen] Ginsberg's 'Howl' and the best part of that poem was the name of it."

At the end of the flight, when Ann asked Frost for his autograph, the poet graciously complied and wrote: "To Mrs. Buchwald, who must admire her husband, from someone else who does."

"PRE—PEARL HARBOR MACY'S BASEMENT SPECIAL"

Within days after First Lady Jacqueline Kennedy entered the White House, she initiated plans for a complete restoration of the executive mansion. "We've got a lot of work ahead," she told chief usher J. B. West. "I want to make this into a grand house!" Her ambition was to refashion the mansion in a Jeffersonian style, and to that end she quickly gathered together an illustrious group of curators, scholars, and patrons of the arts who would help with the renovation work and the acquisition of period furnishings, antiques, and artwork.

On Valentine's Day, February 14, 1962, Mrs. Kennedy unveiled the new White House to the American people with a one-hour tele-vised tour, broadcast live on CBS and hosted by Charles Collingwood. Some 46.5 million Americans were given a unique and intimate look inside the newly refurbished presidential home by the First Lady, who provided an entertaining commentary with historical details and charming anecdotes. The program was a huge hit. *The New York Times* praised Mrs. Kennedy for her "verve and pleasure," and the *Chicago Daily News* said it was "television at its best."

Like most Americans, Buchwald was impressed and delighted by Jackie's tour, and with it he saw an opportunity to write something fresh, funny, and charming about the new first family. Only days after Mrs. Kennedy's up-close and personal look at the White House, Buchwald wrote a column about an imaginary tour given by his sister of her home in Kew Gardens, Long Island. During the tongue-in-cheek visit, his sister showed Buchwald the "East Room," so called because "it overlooks the Eighth Avenue Subway and Queens Boulevard." The historic purposes of the East Room, she explained, were to serve "as an audience room where we could meet our in-laws, our insurance agent, and our son's teacher when he got in trouble." The room's furnishings included an "early Franklin Roosevelt" couch "with the stuffing coming out" and a lamp, which, she noted, "is a rare pre–Pearl Harbor Macy's Basement Special," one of only 65,900 in existence. In her "Blue Room"—designated as such because, as his sister explained, it is the room that "depresses her the most"—was an "early Truman Gimbel's Four Poster" bed and a "President Monroe television set," which required a repairman to come in once a week to "restore it."

The column was Buchwald at his best. Decades later, in a letter to Jackie Kennedy, he reminded her of the 1962 piece, and although she admitted she had not read it at the time, she told him that if she had, she would have been amused and "never would have forgotten it."

Later that same month, Art and Ann returned to America for one of Buchwald's lecture tours. During a stopover in the nation's capital, their friend Ben Bradlee, who was now in Washington with *Newsweek* magazine, hosted a party in their honor. It was a "glitzy affair," Buchwald later recalled, with some of the most powerful people in Washington on hand: the new attorney general Bobby Kennedy and his wife, Ethel; historian and Kennedy adviser Arthur Schlesinger, Jr.; and Eunice and Sargent Shriver. The following day, at the invitation of Pierre Salinger, the Buchwalds visited the White House to attend a press briefing and to meet the new chief executive in the Oval Office. Both Buchwalds were charmed by the charismatic president, describing their visit with Kennedy as "electric."

After a "week of political stargazing," Buchwald was clearly captivated by the energy and spirit of the New Frontier. "It seemed in those days as if the whole country had rediscovered youth and love. It was a country brimming with excitement," Buchwald later wrote. "Everyone around the world want[ed] to know what [was] going on with the Kennedys."

As the couple flew back to Paris, Art admitted to Ann, "I think it's time to go home." When Ann asked "Why?" he said he was convinced his column was "running stale." Although she understood, she also told him frankly that he had a lot to lose by such a move. "You own Paris," she said. "Washington is full of newspapermen and columnists who could eat you for breakfast." But Ann wasn't the only one who cautioned Buchwald about such a move. When he arrived back in Paris he raised the possibility with a number of friends who advised against it, telling him that "it's perfectly all right to make fun of the French but it's another matter making fun of Americans." Others were more blunt: "You'll get massacred," he was told. After all, how could he, Arthur Buchwald, a high school dropout, compete with the likes of Walter Lippmann (Harvard), Joseph Alsop (Groton and Harvard), and Drew Pearson (Phillips Exeter)? But Buchwald knew that he offered readers something more than the brilliant, incisive, and penetrating commentary the others did; indeed, he offered all this, but with an indispensable twist of satire and humor.

But it wasn't just the competition that concerned him; he was worried about the effect on Ann and his young family. "I knew we'd all be in for a culture shock," Buchwald later wrote. "Our standard of living in Paris was hard to give up." Paris had been their home for fourteen years, and they loved everything about the city: the sights, the food, the company they kept; dancing with Gene Kelly in Montmartre and singing songs with Edith Piaf as they walked under the bridges of the Seine.

Although they both had doubts, Ann and Art finally reached a compromise: They would "leave everything in Paris as it is" and rent a house in Washington. It was an arrangement that permitted them to return to France if things didn't work out. As to Art's fears of falling flat in Washington as a political columnist, Ann had a "clever" solution. "Announce you're only going back for two years," she told him. "Then if you fail you can always return to Paris without your tail between your legs."

Once the decision was made, they felt happy, relieved, and excited. But upon their arrival in Washington in August 1962, things got off to a rocky start. "Art and I tried to be cheerful, but had our own problems," Ann later wrote. "He was haunted by the warnings his pals had offered in Paris.... [But] he didn't mention his worries, because he knew I was as shaky as he was. The city seemed cold and scattered. I didn't drive and had to keep taxis waiting outside the Giant and Safeway [grocery stores]."

Over the next year and a half, however, things steadily improved, and as they became increasingly settled in their new life in Washington, they abandoned any plans of returning to Paris and bought a house in the Wesley Heights section of Washington, D.C., a home they would own for the rest of their lives.

And Art's fear of failure had been unfounded. Within a year he was one of the hottest new journalists in Washington, D.C. His column of "adulterated rot," which he had fine-tuned in Paris, was now being read by the president of the United States, Washington bureaucrats, key figures on Capitol Hill, and readers in nearly two hundred newspapers around the world. His brand of humor and satire was just what the country needed as the 1960s got under way, prompting one relieved reporter for *The New York Times* to write that before Buchwald had arrived in America, humor columnists were "as hard to find . . . as epic poets."

But now with Buchwald on the scene, the search was finally over.

"BOUNTIES OF THE BANNED"

"The fifties had constituted probably the most humorless period in American history," presidential historian Arthur Schlesinger, Jr., once wrote, but with John F. Kennedy in the White House, Americans were dazzled by a young, charismatic chief executive who captivated television audiences with his charm, wit, and quick sense of humor. In particular, Kennedy's masterful handling of the media during his televised news conferences quickly became a national phenomenon. But, like Buchwald's, the brilliance of Kennedy's wit came not only from his quick and sparkling repartee, but from an appreciation of good political satire. "For Kennedy wit was the natural response to platitude and pomposity," Schlesinger once said. "His whole personal bearing communicated a delight in satire; and in his wake came an exuberant revival of American irreverence."

Although Kennedy always enjoyed reading Buchwald's pieces in the *Herald Tribune*, he was less than enamored with Art's news editors. "He invited me to his office once," Buchwald later recalled, "and told me, 'The only reason I read your (expletive deleted) paper is because of your (expletive deleted) column.'"

By the spring of 1962, however, not even Buchwald's column was enough to calm Kennedy's exasperation with the *Tribune*. "We read enough shit," the president privately grumbled to his friend and bureau chief of *Newsweek* magazine, Ben Bradlee. "We just don't have to read that particular brand." Finally, in a fit of temper, Kennedy ordered the cancellation of all White House subscriptions to the *Tribune*. (Bradlee would later write how surprised he was that the media-savvy Kennedy appeared "oblivious to the criticism of his act as demeaning and petty.")

When Buchwald got word that his column would no longer be read in the White House, he was undismayed. As with James Hagerty's temper tantrum in Paris in 1957, he was thrilled at the prospect of new material for his column, all made possible by Kennedy's self-inflicted domestic news management crisis. Within days, James Reston of *The New York Times* gave Kennedy a public scolding, reminding him that by canceling the *Tribune* he was also losing Buchwald and his weekly column of political satire. The burdens of the Oval Office might be lessened by a daily dose of his humor, Reston advised the president. "It's a hard life, all right," Reston wrote in his column, "but the thought here is that he'd [Kennedy] still feel better if he read Buchwald."

To Buchwald's great delight, the White House ban on the *Tribune* went on until late summer, when the newspaper's subscription was finally reinstated. Art received the news with a humorous "lament," telling readers how disheartened he was that he would no longer be able to live off the "bounties of the banned."

"Other newspapermen bought us drinks, Republicans sent us money, disgruntled Democrats showed us their diaries," a facetiously brokenhearted Buchwald wrote. "In Washington, if you're not banned by the White House, you're nobody and after all these months of being somebody, it's a bitter pill to swallow." Kennedy may have had his reasons "for resubscribing to the *Herald Tribune*," Buchwald wrote. But if it were up to him, he'd "rather be dead than read."

"SALINGER'S FOLLY"

While Buchwald had been thrilled by the attention he received from Kennedy's news management crisis, he was overjoyed by "Salinger's Folly." It all began in February 1963 when Kennedy, a national symbol of energy and vigor, decided to mount a public effort to get Americans physically fit. And, as an example to the country, he announced that each member of his administration, including the commander in chief's rotund press secretary, Pierre Salinger, would be required to prove his own fitness by completing a fifty-mile hike along the Chesapeake and Ohio Canal within a period of twenty hours.

Salinger, of course, was less than enthused by the idea, having settled comfortably into a bit of a non-fitness rut of his own. He was never "without a cigar, a thirst, or an appetite," he shamelessly conceded. Fitness just wasn't on his daily press schedule. He told anyone who would listen that the only robust physical exercise he had undertaken since coming to the White House was "contests of strength with stubborn wine corks; an exhausting Bach arpeggio on the piano; and weekly weight-lifting exercises with the ponderous Sunday edition of *The New York Times.*" The mere thought of a fifty-mile hike made Salinger shudder, particularly since even a walk across Lafayette Square for lunch at the Hay-Adams hotel caused sores on his feet. He pleaded with Kennedy to allow him to be exempt, but the president refused to make exceptions: Salinger was to take the hike.

"Salinger's folly," as it quickly became known among White House insiders, was scheduled for Friday, February 15, 1963, at seven A.M. But to Salinger's great relief, three days before the hike was set to begin, Art Buchwald came to the rescue, writing a column chastising the president for his bad political instincts:

> To many of us who weigh in about the same as Mr. Salinger . . . he has always appeared to have the perfect American physique. . . . When Salinger waddles, we waddle with him; when he huffs and puffs, we know how he feels. . . . If the President does anything to harm him, Mr. Kennedy will lose the support of every . . . anti-exercise constituent in the country.

The same day Buchwald's column appeared, Kennedy gave in and granted Salinger a presidential fitness pardon. A relieved and delighted Salinger immediately drafted a statement to the press announcing Kennedy's decision along with a grateful nod to his friend Art Buchwald:

IMMEDIATE RELEASE   February 12, 1963

Office of the White House Press Secretary
THE WHITE HOUSE
STATEMENT BY THE PRESS SECRETARY

The President's Council on Physical Fitness this morning issued a statement commending those in the Nation who are successfully attempting 50 mile hikes but warning that those who are not in good shape should not attempt such a feat.

My shape is not good. While this fact may have been apparent to others for some time, its full significance was pressed upon me as the result of a six-mile hike last Sunday. I have done no walking since—except to go from my office to the White House Dispensary. Even that trip required the use of an elevator. . . .

I am grateful to the many citizens who have taken the time to wire or write me their support. I am grateful to Mr. Art Buchwald of the *New York Herald Tribune* for his moving and eloquent defense of the role of the fat man in our society. The essence of the message of the President's Council on Physical Fitness to fat men was: moderation should be the rule in all things, including exercise.

DARK SECRETS

Despite being in Washington, D.C., and at the center of Kennedy's glamorous New Frontier, during the first few months after he arrived from Paris, Buchwald was occasionally overwhelmed by a sense of melancholy; at times feeling "exceedingly dull," sad, and gloomy. Buchwald's feelings at the time, however, were not just a case of homesickness for France, but a manifestation of something much more serious: a painful and difficult lifelong struggle with periodic episodes of severe, deep, dark depression.

The first signs of his illness "crept up" on him in late 1962 at which time he underwent treatment from Washington psychiatrist Dr. Robert Morse. However, after a year of counseling his condition worsened to such a degree that in early spring of 1963, Dr. Morse had Buchwald admitted to Sibley Memorial Hospital in Washington. For several weeks, while under Morse's care in a psychiatric ward, Buchwald went "on a crying jag," racked by painful memories from the past, especially the "scars" of his youth as a foster child and the loss of his mother. He was crippled with despair. "When you have depression the darkness closes in on you and all the things that you love work against you," he later said. "And it exposes you to dark trees, dark people. It's a terrible thing."

At first nothing seemed to work. "I didn't ask God to help me. I was sure that it was the devil's work and that I was already in hell and would never get out." His first bout with depression was so severe and debilitating that it required a month of hospitalization. "I was certain I would never laugh again, nor would I ever be able to make people laugh again," Buchwald later admitted.

Then to his great relief, the darkness lifted and Buchwald was well enough to be discharged from the hospital. But once at home he was still "listless and sad" and unable to work. "The normal things that you do in a day seem impossible," he later said. "Getting your breakfast, going downstairs and reading the newspaper. And that scares the hell out of you because you've been doing it all your life, and suddenly you can't even read a newspaper."

But then it all came back. "I found myself sitting at my desk a week after being discharged . . . tapping nothing particular on the type-writer":

Then I pulled open the center drawer of my desk and saw a cigar there. I hadn't smoked the entire time I was depressed. I stared at it for a moment, and then unwrapped the cellophane and stuck it in my mouth. Finally, chewing on it for ten minutes, I lit it, and suddenly my fingers moved across the keys as if I were playing a Chopin sonata. I wrote a column about Jackie Kennedy getting pregnant, which meant all the women who wanted to be in fashion had to get pregnant as well. Everything had come back. The connection between the cigar and writing was so strong I couldn't do one without the other. That afternoon I walked into Dr. Morse's office puffing on a Dunhill with a big grin on my face.

Buchwald had survived, but the painful memories and the "scars of childhood" would always be with him. And he knew that at any moment his whole life could suddenly be thrown back into a dark chasm of despair. But he kept all that had happened to him in the spring of 1963 a closely held secret. "It wasn't easy to admit that such a thing could happen to me—after all, I made people laugh," he later said. "You are ashamed of yourself. You lose all self-respect. You feel worthless. You are sure everyone knows your dirty, dark secrets."

It was a dark secret he would keep hidden from the public for nearly three decades.

"WELCOME, COLONEL BUCHWALD"

By the beginning of May 1963, Buchwald was back in the funny business. On May 4, he attended the eighty-ninth running of the Kentucky Derby in Louisville, where, upon his arrival, he was presented with a "mint julep, a colonel's hat, a colonel's tie, four cigars," and a certificate declaring him an "honorary citizen of Louisville." After recovering from his painful bout with depression, he was in an upbeat mood, in good spirits and thrilled to be back at his typewriter, his cigars, and his column. "I love my work," he told one reporter. "I wouldn't do anything else."

He was also hard at work on another book, *I Chose Capitol Punishment*, a new collection of his columns on "taxes, expense accounts, guided missiles . . . the Pentagon, Cuba, modern art [and the] Kennedy family." After its release in October 1963, Buchwald sent a copy to the president prompting a response from Kennedy's personal secretary, Evelyn Lincoln, thanking Art for his "thoughtful interest in seeing that your latest book reached" the president's desk.

And he was elated by the positive notices the book received, with one reviewer telling readers that Buchwald's book had the "magic to set you laughing almost right away." But Art wasn't taking any chances in the promotion of his new book. When the editors at *The Washington Post* offered him the opportunity to write his own book review, he jumped at the chance, telling readers that he had read it "from cover to cover with relish and delight." "I am amazed how I have managed to capture on paper the drama, the mystery, the heartbreak that is Washington," Buchwald wrote with cheeky delight in his November 1963 review. "*I Chose Capitol Punishment* is in this reviewer's humble opinion the best book to be published this year. I couldn't put it down."

"WE WEEP"

Later that same month, the joy and charm of the Kennedy Camelot legend came to a tragic end.

During the summer and fall of 1963, all political indicators showed that John F. Kennedy would be reelected president in 1964. A Harris Poll conducted in mid-August showed that "no Republican candidate for the Presidency . . . is even within hailing distance of seriously challenging John F. Kennedy." By early November 1963, Kennedy's popularity was holding steady with a 59 percent Gallup Poll approval rating.

Less than two weeks later, however, everything changed. On Friday, November 22, 1963, President Kennedy was shot dead in Dallas, Texas. At the time of the shooting, Buchwald was on his way back from delivering a speech in Charleston, West Virginia. When his taxi pulled up in front of the National Press Building in Washington, he saw people rushing in and out of the lobby screaming "Kennedy's been shot!" Buchwald hurried upstairs to the *Newsweek* offices on the thirteenth floor, where he found his friend Ben Bradlee "staring at the T.V. set yelling, 'Fight, Jack. Fight.'" Then came the announcement that Kennedy was dead. Buchwald and Bradlee "hugged each other" and "broke into tears."

Later that day, a bewildered and distraught Buchwald sat down to write a tribute poem to Kennedy for his column. Two years earlier the promise, glamour, and charm of the Kennedy era had begun with Robert Frost's inspirational poetry.

The column ended with lines from Art Buchwald's poem "We Weep":

> We weep for our President who died for his country.
> We weep for our children and their children and everyone's children for he was charting their destinies as he was charting ours. . . .

The next day, in the midst of the tragic and surreal atmosphere overwhelming the country, Buchwald had another idea for a column, one that would honor the memory of Kennedy with an appreciation of his celebrated wit and sense of humor. Despite the sorrow that enveloped the White House, Buchwald was able to get a brief meeting with Kennedy's chief speechwriter, Ted Sorensen, to discuss one of the fallen president's greatest gifts. "Mr. Sorensen was very kind and spent one hour with me going over President Kennedy's speeches and pointing out the highlights of President Kennedy's humor lines," Buchwald later wrote to historian William Manchester, author of *The Death of a President*. "We were both in a great state of shock and I believe there were tears rolling down my cheeks as I was talking to him."

Three days later Buchwald's tribute to the president was published. He spoke of Kennedy's "magnificent sense of humor," which he displayed so often at his press conferences and on the campaign trail, always with "the timing and touch of a master comedian." But the column ended on a solemn note: "One of the late President's lines which today has lost all its humor, was: 'It has recently been suggested that whether I serve one or two terms in the Presidency, I will find myself at the end of that period at what might be called an awkward age— too old to begin a new career and too young to write my memoirs.'"

Years later, Buchwald would write of that dark weekend in November: "It did not make any sense then, and does not make any sense now."

CHAPTER 4

BRUMUS, BATMAN, AND BUCHWALD "BUCHSHOTS"

A Satirist in a Mad, Mad World— The Tumultuous 1960s

Think of the trouble the world would save itself if it would pay some attention to nonsense!

— E. B. WHITE

HOOVER WHO?

In late 1964, Buchwald wrote a piece that was not only one of his best columns of the 1960s, but possibly one of the best satirical pieces of his entire career. In a December 8, 1964, spoof titled "J. Edgar Hoover Just Doesn't Exist," Buchwald asserted that Hoover, perhaps one of the most powerful and feared men in America, was nothing more than a "mythical person first thought up by the *Reader's Digest*" magazine. The myth had started, Buchwald wrote, in 1925 when the magazine printed "an article on the newly formed Federal Bureau of Investigation and as they do with many pieces they signed it with a nom de plume. They got the word 'Hoover' from the vacuum cleaner—to give the idea of a clean-up; Edgar was the name of one of the publisher's nephews, and the J. stood for jail."

Brilliantly funny "fake news" indeed, but no one, including Buchwald, could have predicted the reaction from readers across the country. People everywhere started to think that it might actually be true. Perhaps J. Edgar Hoover *didn't* exist, despite the fact that he was a very *real* person, still alive and presiding over the FBI as he had done for four decades and would under eight presidents, starting with Calvin Coolidge and ending with Richard Nixon. In the 1950s and '60s he had been "prominently mentioned" in Gallup Polls of the "most admired Americans," had twice been featured on the cover of *Time* magazine (1935, 1949), and most recently had appeared on the cover of *Newsweek*—the day *before* Buchwald's column ran.

Newspapers across the country were deluged with calls of "alarm" and letters to the editor wondering whether Buchwald's column was true. Fears that Hoover didn't exist even filtered into high schools. One young girl in Springfield, Missouri, "almost cried when the column was mentioned in history class," and Democratic senator William Proxmire, greatly amused by the piece, wrote Buchwald to tell him that a high school class in Waunakee, Wisconsin, wanted to know "the truth" of what he had written.

One infuriated reader told the editor of the *Gazette* in Emporia, Kansas, that it was simply disgraceful that "such a fable should be circulated," while another from Missouri insisted that Buchwald be fired. For days, editors everywhere tried calming readers by reminding them that Buchwald was a satirist, while also conceding that perhaps, in this case, his "foolish tongue" had "too much cheek."

Other papers took a different approach, running their own spoof columns claiming that Art Buchwald *himself* didn't exist, with one editorial in the *Arizona Republic* claiming that they had spoken with an FBI agent who declared that the columnist was, in fact, a "mythical person first thought up by *Mad* magazine."

Although the FBI director never spoke publicly about the piece, he clearly was not amused, privately telling one associate that Buchwald was nothing more than a "sick alleged humorist." The furor over the Hoover piece went on for weeks, and whenever Buchwald appeared publicly he was asked about it. Perhaps the most perplexing response he received was during a visit to the Midwest when a woman asked him where he got his "facts" that Hoover did not exist. Buchwald replied, "I made it up."

After a brief pause, the inquiring lady persisted, "I know that, but where did you get the facts?"

THE SAM DOMINO THEORY

From the moment he assumed the presidency after the assassination of John F. Kennedy, Lyndon B. Johnson left no doubt as to who was in charge. By pursuing a policy of "guns and butter"—the butter being increased spending on social programs for his "Great Society," and the guns an increased military commitment to a war in Southeast Asia—LBJ showed he was determined to leave a lasting mark on the presidency and American society. But almost from the start his dreams were frustrated and overshadowed by the nightmare of Vietnam and what inevitably became known as "Lyndon Johnson's War."

The geopolitical strategy underlying America's commitment in Southeast Asia was the so-called domino theory, the belief that if the United States did not resist Communist aggression abroad, nation after nation would topple until a Communist red wave reached the shores of the United States. While many hard-line "hawks" were true believers in the theory, others argued that such a policy was unsound or foolish.

Buchwald saw the domino theory as an opportunity for a bit of political satire, not mean-spirited humor poking fun at a tragic war, but satire intended to open people's minds about a policy that was being used to justify such a war. "The satirist has his job laid out," Buchwald once wrote. "He must wake people up so they will wake themselves. It's a great task, but a necessary one."

In one Vietnam-era piece titled "He Thought Up the Domino Theory," Buchwald mocked the origins of the celebrated Cold War strategy, by facetiously claiming to have tracked down the very architect of the policy. "His name, it turns out, is Sam Domino," Buchwald wrote, "and he lives in Forest Hills, New York." When Buchwald asked the mythical Mr. Domino how he came to discover the theory, he told the story of one remarkable evening at a family buffet:

> There were about twenty people lined up.... When my uncle, who was first in line, slipped and fell backward, he knocked over my aunt . . . and so on until all twenty people were on the floor. It suddenly occurred to me that if this could happen to people, it could happen to countries.

Out of a sense of patriotism, Mr. Domino forwarded a complete report of his findings to Secretary of State John Foster Dulles, who conducted his own experiment by lining up twenty employees in the State Department cafeteria. When the same result ensued as had occurred at the Domino family buffet, it was "proof enough" for Secretary Dulles, and from that day forward, Buchwald mused, American foreign policy at the highest levels of the Eisenhower, Kennedy, and Johnson administrations was governed by Sam Domino's remarkable theory.

MY FRIEND BATMAN

By the spring of 1966, with some two hundred thousand American troops in Southeast Asia and weekly U.S. casualties on the rise, there seemed no end in sight to the Vietnam quagmire. On March 3, *The New York Times* reported that in the first two months of the year the United States had suffered 4,300 casualties—already well more than half the 7,000 casualties suffered by American forces during *all* of 1965. Like many Americans, Buchwald was increasingly alarmed by America's involvement in the war. As the president, Congress, and policymakers struggled for a solution, Buchwald, armed with his typewriter and gift for satire, proposed a new course of action.

On January 12, 1966, a new series premiered on the ABC television network. The show, *Batman,* starring Adam West in the lead role and Burt Ward playing his sidekick, Robin, was a phenomenal overnight success. During the week of its debut, one out of every three viewers in New York City tuned in, giving it the highest ratings of any show since the Beatles appeared on *Ed Sullivan* in September 1965. With a beleaguered President Johnson overwhelmed by his troubles in Southeast Asia, Buchwald crafted a column depicting an imaginary scene from a *Batman* episode in which LBJ decides to use the ultimate "secret weapon" from America's military arsenal—the Caped Crusader:

> Lights up—we see a phone and hear it ringing. Suddenly Batman comes out on the stage and walks over to the phone. He picks it up. "Yes, chief."

The dynamic duo, in Buchwald's fictional tale, are asked by LBJ to join the fight in Vietnam. "He must be out of his mind," Batman whispers to Robin as the two scramble for a way out of their predicament. Finally, out of sheer desperation, Buchwald has Batman tell the president, "Yes, chief, but . . . I'm 4-F. I've got psychological problems. Why else would I be wearing leotards?"

Within days after the column appeared, West, who feared that ex-Marine Arthur Buchwald might now be in danger, sent a reassuring note from his secret hideaway:

ADAM WEST

APRIL 1, 1966

Dear Mr. Buchwald:

I've finally emerged from the Batcave long enough to write this note to you, and to tell you how much I enjoyed the enclosed piece, which appeared in the Los Angeles Times.

Reading your most apt columns in the Times *is one of my regular morning activities, and it always amazes me that you can sustain your high tone of humor behind your observations.*

If President Johnson gets out his axe after you, please rest assured that Robin and I will superjet to your aid in our multi-multi-powered Batplane and do our stuff in full Technicolor.

Should you be out this way at any time, it would be a great pleasure to meet you.

> *Sincerely,*
> *Adam West*
> *"Batman"*

A FREE HOME, FREE EDUCATION, AND FREE COLOR TV FOR EVERY VIET CONG SOLDIER

Art Buchwald was never at a loss to offer President Johnson unwelcome advice on how to win the war in Southeast Asia. On New Year's Day 1967, he proposed a series of measures that, to his mind, made both strategic and economic sense. In a column called "Price Per Head: Vietnam War Is Costing Us Too Much," Buchwald cited a recent government study that estimated it cost the Pentagon $332,000 to kill one Viet Cong soldier—an unsustainable expense, Buchwald contended, to an increasingly skeptical American public. To assist the president, Buchwald recommended a number of sensible cost-effective solutions: Instead of dropping bombs, he suggested dropping American automobiles that had been recalled for manufacturing defects. Once the North Vietnamese took to the highways, Buchwald argued—or at least on those highways not already destroyed by U.S. B-52 bombers—the unsuspecting North Vietnamese motorists "would proceed to kill each other" in droves. Another Buchwald idea was to drop pamphlets over Viet Cong strongholds offering to give any soldier who defected to U.S. forces a free "$25,000 home, free education for his children, a color TV, and a paid-up membership to the country club of his choice."

Much like his "J. Edgar Hoover Just Doesn't Exist" column of two years earlier, this particular piece, according to archival researchers William Burr and Matthew Aid of the National Security Archive in Washington, D.C., had unintended consequences that Buchwald could never have imagined. In September 2013—six years after his death—Burr and Aid disclosed that the National Security Agency had spied on Buchwald, beginning in the mid-1960s. In their report, Burr and Aid suggested that "perhaps some humorless FBI or White House official put Buchwald on the watch list . . . because of his satirical writings about the Vietnam War." Specifically, Burr and Aid surmised that it may, in fact, have been the New Year's Day column of 1967 that touched too raw a nerve in high government circles and provided the catalyst for secret government surveillance of Buchwald.

K-A-T SPELLS CAT

As LBJ struggled to win an increasingly unwinnable war in Vietnam, back at home he faced an equally troubling struggle to secure justice and civil rights for millions of African American citizens. During the years 1964 and 1965, when racism and violence against Blacks was on the rise, systematic efforts to block African Americans from voting in the South persisted, with many Southern states using a variety of discriminatory practices such as unfair and biased literacy tests to disqualify ballot applicants. Estimates were that some three million out of five million eligible Black voters in the South were disenfranchised during those years.

In response, in January 1965, Dr. Martin Luther King, Jr., announced a massive protest effort to focus national attention on the need for legislative action to guarantee the right of African Americans to vote.

On March 7, 1965—a day forever known as "Bloody Sunday"—a group of six hundred nonviolent demonstrators embarked on a protest march from Selma to Montgomery, Alabama, in support of their cause. Governor George Wallace issued an order prohibiting the demonstration, but the protestors refused to yield, leading to a bloody confrontation with Sheriff Jim Clark and a well-armed group of policemen on the Edmund Pettus Bridge, where they beat, tear-gassed, and bull-whipped the marchers. Images of the brutal encounter, captured by news photographers and television crews, were broadcast around the world. In response, eight days later President Johnson went before a joint session of Congress to call for the speedy passage of comprehensive federal voting rights legislation "to eliminate illegal barriers" to a citizen's right to vote.

Although it would take another six months before the federal Voting Rights Act was finally signed into law, during the congressional debate over the bill, Art Buchwald wrote a satirical attack on the use of literacy tests in the South. In a column that appeared in newspapers around the world in April 1965, Buchwald spun a tale about a fictitious African American scholar named George Abernathy who embarked on a hopeful journey to register to vote at the courthouse in his hometown of "Bull Whip, Alabama." After making his way through a phalanx of sheriffs, a veil of tear gas, and a barricade manned by police with cattle prods, Abernathy finally makes his way into the registration office. When he arrives at the registrar's desk, Abernathy, a Rhodes scholar with a BA from Columbia University, a master's from Harvard, and a PhD from MIT, is informed by the official in charge that he will have to pass a literacy test:

Official: "Would you please read somethin' from this here newspaper."
Abernathy: "It's in Chinese."
Official: "That's right."

After translating three stories written in Chinese, Abernathy is asked to decipher some hieroglyphics from the Rosetta stone. When he complies, the flustered election official asks him to interpret the first fourteen articles of the Finnish national constitution. When Abernathy complies, the thoroughly agitated official tells him it's now time for Part 4 of the test. After pulling out a jar from the back office, he asks Abernathy, "Would you be so kind to read for me any two of these Dead Sea Scrolls?" After reading the first one perfectly, the Harvard-educated Abernathy "stumbles" on the second. "Ah'm sorry, George," the relieved official says. "You've failed the literacy test." As a dispirited Abernathy departs, he passes a white applicant who approaches the desk and is asked by the registrar, "Would you please spell CAT for me?" "K-A-T" the white applicant replies. After a pause, the voting official calmly replies with encouragement, "Try it again. You're getting warm."

It was a classic Buchwald column, sharp, cutting, laced with wit, and filled with sarcasm. Decades later, Richard Kluger, in his history of the *Herald Tribune*, singled out this particular column for praise, applauding Buchwald for his use of "excoriating satire" to boldly confront social injustice and "diehard bigotry" in the South.

BUCHWALD, BOBBY, AND BRUMUS THE OVERDOG

Art and Ann Buchwald had casually known Robert Kennedy and his wife, Ethel, since the winter of 1962, but after the death of John F. Kennedy in 1963, they grew to be much closer friends. The Buchwalds were frequent guests at Hickory Hill, Bobby's home in McLean, Virginia, for parties, birthday celebrations, luncheons, charitable events, and the annual family pet show, which Buchwald once described as a "pretty wild affair." As the presiding "ringmaster," Buchwald—decked out in a red hunting jacket, black top hat, and black leather riding boots—would hand out awards to pets in a variety of categories. (Most years Buchwald was the center of attention at the annual pet show, but in May 1977 heavyweight boxing champion Muhammad Ali stole the limelight from Art when he pitched in as co-judge of the event and helped pin ribbons on the winners—including one award for a "basset hound dressed as Buchwald.")

Awards were given for pets with "the longest tail, the shortest tail, longest nose, [and] the shortest nose." The "most unusual pet" division, however, always brought the most surprises. One year, when a skunk was proudly entered in the "most unusual" category, Buchwald quickly awarded it first prize, then yelled, "Get him out of here!" Other times, a child's entry required a bit of quick thinking on Buchwald's part. "I remember during the judging of the reptile class, a very small girl brought up a glass jar to the judge's stand," journalist and Kennedy friend George Plimpton recalled after attending one of the shows. "Buchwald looked in and poked around in some grass at the bottom, and finally asked, 'Well, what's in here?' 'It's a dead snake,' the girl said. 'It died on the way here in the car.'" Perplexed at first, Buchwald paused, then gathered himself and in a solemn voice asked the astonished crowd "for a short period of silence . . . and [then] awarded the dead snake's owner a consolation ribbon."

The Buchwalds were even on hand for one of the most celebrated Kennedy family adventures: a 1967 raft trip down the Colorado River with mountaineer Jim Whittaker, George Plimpton, and singer Andy Williams. Art later wrote a column about the excursion that included a pre-trip warning from his father about undertaking such an expedition. "It's all right for Kennedy to go down the rapids because he can walk on water," Buchwald's father reportedly said. "But you're going to have to swim."

From the very beginning of their friendship, Bobby Kennedy was fascinated by Art Buchwald's life story. "I was an orphan, and I was raised in foster homes, and I had a Jewish upbringing," Art later recalled. "And he was very fascinated with this because this is something that he had never experienced. . . . He was very interested in other people's lives, particularly if they weren't Harvard, Yale or Princeton."

Although a frequent guest to Hickory Hill, Buchwald was keenly aware that there was always a polite distance between him and Bobby. "He was sort of a Hamlet figure, in a sense. He was polite enough, but you never knew if you were intruding on his time or on him." And unlike some Washington reporters, Art knew that as a political columnist he had to maintain a certain distance from the Kennedys, so as not to blur the lines of friendship, journalism, and politics. "I refused to become part of his political life. . . . I wasn't a confidante, and I didn't want to be," Buchwald later said. "I wrote a column, and I didn't want to know the inside of things because it would inhibit me in my own appraisal of them." Buchwald admired the fact that whenever he wrote an unflattering column about the Kennedys, they usually brushed it off. "They had a good enough sense of humor to know what I was doing, and they really didn't get mad, at least not enough to not talk to me again." Sometimes, however, if Bobby felt Art had gone too far, he wouldn't hesitate to show his irritation. Once, after Kennedy read Buchwald's playful column about RFK's role in the settlement of the 1966 New York subway strike, Bobby was irked—and he let Art know it. "I really cut him up pretty badly," Buchwald later recalled. "So about a week later, I was at a party at Hickory Hill dancing or something, and Bobby yelled, 'I didn't invite you. Ethel invited you.'"

But as Buchwald got to know Kennedy better there was much more about him that Art grew to admire. He was a "fantastic" father and had a strong, deep-seated compassion for the underdog, Buchwald fondly remembered. But he also saw another side of Kennedy: his intense feelings for the "Overdog."

The Overdog in question was Kennedy's beloved three-hundred-pound black Newfoundland named Brumus, who, in Bobby's eyes, could do no wrong. But Buchwald knew better. "Brumus is a legend in his own time," Buchwald joked in a column. "He is a large, friendly looking, furry animal with sad eyes and drooping ears who sits around on the back porch of Hickory Hill wondering whether he'll bite a dog or a child next." At times Kennedy's dog could be irritating to friends and bystanders. "He [was] known to attack mailmen, police, diplomats and even priests, not necessarily in that order," Buchwald wrote. "Brumus is much misunderstood," he quipped. "Underneath all that growling and barking lies a mouth of real teeth."

Brumus even provoked the ire of J. Edgar Hoover. When Bobby Kennedy served as attorney general under President Kennedy, he routinely brought Brumus into his office at the Department of Justice to spend the day with him at work. Brumus suffered from "abandonment anxiety," Robert F. Kennedy, Jr., wrote in his family memoir, *American Values*, "and my dad couldn't bear to hear all the whining and crying when he tried to take leave of Brumus most mornings." An irate Hoover was so incensed at RFK, he once convened a meeting of his top legal advisers to try to find a "legal justification to ban Brumus" from the Justice Department.

And to his great chagrin, Buchwald was on hand at Hickory Hill one day to witness a particularly warm greeting by Brumus to two elderly guests who were enjoying their lunch on the lawn. "Bobby and I were sitting, relaxed on the stoop, watching everybody having a nice time and everything, and suddenly Brumus wandered down," Art later recalled. "And there were these two ladies that were, I guess, around sixty each, sitting eating their lunch. Suddenly Brumus lifted his leg and peed on one of them." But, as was often the case with RFK's beloved Newfie, that was not the end of the story. After Kennedy and Buchwald fled the scene, George Plimpton, who was also on hand that day, watched in amazement as Brumus promptly reappeared for a repeat performance. "These two women wandered around for awhile and then sat down again . . . and [then] Brumus came ambling out of the house—and did it again . . . to those same two!"

Brumus the Overdog struck again in 1965 shortly after Kennedy was elected to the Senate. After being sworn in at the U.S. Capitol, RFK sought advice from legendary Virginia senator Harry Byrd as to what accommodations could be made for bringing Brumus to his Senate office. Buchwald recalled that one day Kennedy said to Byrd, " 'How long do you have to be here before you can bring your dog to the office?' Harry Byrd said, 'Bring him anytime; we'd be very happy.' So Bobby brought Brumus to the office. He called up Harry Byrd, and he said, 'I've got my dog here.' And Harry Byrd said, 'Gee, that's great, bring him down; I've got my dog.' I don't know what [kind of dog] Harry Byrd had; it must have been some little spaniel or something. So Bobby and Brumus went down to Harry Byrd's office. Brumus went over to the little dog, and the little dog was so frightened that he peed on the rug, at which point Brumus raised his leg and he peed on the dog. And that was the last time Bobby said that he had been invited into Byrd's office."

Peeing on fragile old women and the cowering puppy of a powerful U.S. senator was one thing, but Brumus crossed the line in the summer of 1967 when he took on the wrong man. After being accosted by Brumus on July 26, Buchwald turned to an old friend, the preeminent Washington lawyer Edward Bennett Williams, for assistance in a potential "lawsuit" against Brumus's protector and die-hard defender Robert Kennedy. Williams and Buchwald, unfazed and undaunted by the prospects of a messy legal battle with the powerful Kennedy clan, issued a tongue-in-cheek demand for damages inflicted on the defenseless Buchwald:

Law Offices
Williams and Connolly
Washington, D.C.

AUGUST 7, 1967

Honorable Robert F. Kennedy
United States Senate
Washington, D.C.

Dear Senator:

I have been retained by Mr. Art Buchwald to represent him in the matter of the vicious and unprovoked attack made on him on Wednesday, July 26, by the large, savage, man-eating, coat-tearing black animal owned by you and responding to the name, Broomass (phonetic).

Mr. Buchwald has been ordered to take a complete rest by his physician until such time as he recovers from the traumatic neurosis from which he is suffering as a result of the attack. He will be in isolation at Vineyard Haven, Martha's Vineyard, Massachusetts for an indefinite period at a cost of $2,000 a month.

He is concerned about the effect of exposing this ugly episode on your

political future. Accordingly, he has asked me to handle it so as to attract
a minimum of attention until such time as our demands are rejected.

  Since Broomass is black, the case is fraught with civil rights under-
currents.

Very truly yours,
Edward Bennett Williams
Cc: Art Buchwald

A NIGHT OUT AT THE PLAYBOY MANSION

In the fall of 1967, Art Buchwald was offered a chance to fulfill the
great American Dream when he received an invitation to stay overnight at Hugh Hefner's Playboy Mansion in Chicago. Hefner, the
founder and publisher of *Playboy*, one of the most successful maga-
zines of the late twentieth century, was born and raised in the Midwest
in a devout Methodist family. In 1953, Hefner, then only twenty-seven
years old, founded *Playboy* with $600 of his own money and $10,000
from stock sold to family and friends. The first issue, featuring a calendar photo of Marilyn Monroe, sold more than fifty-three thousand
copies. *Playboy* was an instant success, and by 1960 had a circulation
of over one million. The stunning success of the magazine was in no
small part due to Hefner's "shrewdness"—some called it "genius"—in
sensing the coming of a new age; a new and rebellious America with its
"changing attitudes about sex and a steadily more candid view of sexu-
ality," wrote David Halberstam in *The Fifties*. "Hefner was fighting
that part of the Puritan ethic that condemned pleasure. He thought
hard work and sexual freedom were not incompatible in this ever
richer society. In the broader sense as well, *Playboy* shepherded a generation of young men to the good life."

  Expecting to catch his own personal glimpse of the good life, Art
Buchwald was thrilled to be invited to Hefner's home, and, afterward,
chronicled the visit in his column on November 9, 1967. Upon his arrival at the Chicago airport, Art was whisked away to the Playboy

Mansion in a limousine, where he was greeted by Hefner's butler, who escorted him to his overnight accommodations in the "gold room." After a swim, a steam bath, and dinner, Buchwald's host finally arrived on the scene at nine o'clock sharp. "He was dressed in pajamas," Buchwald wrote. "'Oh boy,' I thought, 'now the action begins'":

> "What would you like to do?" Hefner asked.
> "Anything you'd like to do," I said, chuckling.
> "What about a game of gin rummy for a penny a point?"

With all hopes of achieving the American Dream dashed, Buchwald made the best of his men's night out by playing gin rummy with Hefner until the wee hours of the morning. In the end, Art was no match for the lord of the mansion. He lost $33.00.

Shortly after Buchwald's column was published, his host and fellow gin rummy partner sent Art a note:

PLAYBOY
Hugh M. Hefner
Editor-Publisher

NOVEMBER 22, 1967

Dear Art:

Thanks for your nice note and special thanks for your delightful piece on your evening here at The Playboy Mansion. The more articles written about our puritan existence here at PLAYBOY, the more certain America becomes that the Hefner hacienda is actually the center of all the sexual excesses conceived by contemporary man. And the more curious people become about the private world of PLAYBOY, the more the magazine and Clubs prosper. It's a good life!

Meanwhile, I've got to improve my gin game, if I'm to stay ahead of the competition hereabouts.

All best,
Hef

"A BAD ELIZABETHAN DRAMA"

At times, the decade of the 1960s had an eerie Shakespearean quality to it all. "The whole thing...seems a little like a bad Elizabethan drama," wrote historian and Kennedy speechwriter John Bartlow Martin, "where the curtain comes down on a stage filled with dead bodies."

On March 16, 1968, after months of soul-searching and political squabbling with advisers and family members, Senator Robert F. Kennedy announced he was running for president in an uphill primary challenge against the incumbent president, Lyndon Johnson.

For over a year Kennedy had been torn about whether to make the challenge. The passions of his heart told him to run; but the hard, cold political realities in his head told him to wait. "He was fighting a battle with himself about what role to play," Buchwald later recalled. "There were people who said, 'Run.' And then there were other people who said, 'Don't run.' So here again he was a Hamlet figure; he didn't know what to do." Once asked by Kennedy for advice, Buchwald told him to wait. "I thought Johnson was going to run and it was just going to be a hopeless cause."

But after Senator Eugene McCarthy of Minnesota, who entered the race while Kennedy remained on the sidelines, made a strong showing against Johnson in the March 12 New Hampshire primary, Kennedy decided to run. Although LBJ's stunning withdrawal from the campaign several weeks later appeared to boost Kennedy's candidacy, he still faced a strong and bitter fight from McCarthy, along with the likely entrance of another contender, LBJ's vice president, Hubert H. Humphrey.

The prospects of Kennedy's candidacy looked promising at first as he scored back-to-back primary wins in Indiana and Nebraska, but then his campaign stalled when McCarthy defeated him in Oregon in late May. A stunned but determined Kennedy then moved on to California, where he regained his momentum by defeating McCarthy in the June 5 primary.

But then Kennedy's triumph turned to tragedy when he was shot just after his victory speech at the Ambassador Hotel in Los Angeles. He never regained consciousness and died the next morning.

On Saturday, June 8, Kennedy's funeral was held at St. Patrick's Cathedral in New York City, where his brother Ted delivered the eulogy and singer Andy Williams sang "The Battle Hymn of the Republic." Kennedy's casket was then taken by train from New York on an eight-hour, 225-mile journey to Washington, D.C. Along the way thousands of mourners, young and old of all races, gathered silently along the railroad tracks or on the station platforms to pay final tribute to the fallen senator. Rows of policemen, firemen, and veterans offered proud salutes, while groups of nuns watched in tearful silence, their hands folded in solemn prayer. Stunned onlookers held makeshift banners with the words "Farewell Bobby," while other mourners stood and stared, slowly waving American flags.

Gathered on the funeral train that day was a vast assemblage of Kennedy family members, politicians, celebrities, and friends, including Art and Ann Buchwald, who occupied the same compartment as Ted Kennedy, his sisters Pat and Jean, and Bobby's flag-draped casket. As the hours passed, Buchwald felt increasingly uncomfortable and ill at ease by the surreal nature of the whole tragic scene. "I didn't know what to do," he later said. "So I went out on the platform where the [Kennedy] children were."

> And that was the first time . . . that I really had a feeling of what was going on outside the train. . . . On the platform, you could hear the cheers, and the people crying. At several places along the way, I noticed kids running out after the train would go by, and pick up things off the rail. I asked one of the Kennedy kids what that was about. They said that people were laying things on the rails, and when the train ran over them . . . they were souvenirs.

When the funeral train finally arrived at Washington's Union Station just after nine P.M., Art and Ann stood together with actress Lauren Bacall as the next grim scene unfolded. "I dreaded the removal of the coffin from the train," Ann later said. "Teddy and everybody lined up, and they pulled the casket off the rear end of the car. . . . I was almost delirious."

After Kennedy's coffin was loaded into a black hearse, the funeral procession slowly made its way through the dark night to Arlington National Cemetery for a final graveside ceremony. Twelve pallbearers, including RFK's seventeen-year-old son, Joseph Kennedy II, and former astronaut John Glenn, slowly carried the coffin up to the burial site, where a simple service was held in the darkness of night, the gathering spotted with flickering flames from candles held by many of the Kennedy children. At the end of the ceremony, John Glenn slowly folded the flag that had been draped over Kennedy's coffin and handed it to Senator Ted Kennedy, who passed it on to Robert Kennedy's widow, Ethel.

Two days later, a grieving Buchwald sat down to write his weekly column—another tribute to another martyred Kennedy. But unlike the poem "We Weep," which he had written for JFK in 1963, this was a eulogy of more personal memories: "hazy film sequences" that flashed through Buchwald's mind about his fallen friend. It was a montage of scenes of Bobby "walking alone in deep thought" at Hickory Hill; then out on the campaign trail "talking intensely" about the poor, the future of the country, and the "plight of the Indians"; then relaxing at Hyannis Port with his family playing a spirited game of touch football; then far out West fearlessly rushing through the Colorado River rapids.

After the column appeared, Buchwald sent a copy of his tribute to future U.S. senator John Glenn, who had also been a friend of both John and Robert Kennedy. Several weeks later, on July 5, 1968, Glenn sent a poignant letter of thanks to Art. "I guess we all have a feeling of unreality about the past few weeks," Glenn wrote. "There are so many daily reminders that I guess it is impossible to accept the finality of what has happened." With his note, Glenn described a sermon he had heard recently which "touched on the subject of death":

One of the stories used to illustrate one approach to death involved trying to explain what had happened to a child after a loved one had died. The mother explained this by asking the little girl if she remembered the night she had fallen asleep on the couch and her father had come in later, lifted her in his arms and took her to her own room where she awakened the next morning, wondering how she had arrived in this location, for she remembered going to sleep on the couch the night before. The little girl said yes, she remembered that time. The mother likened death to that experience in that we are taken from one room of our existence, or life as we know it, to another without really understanding how we got there or understanding completely what happens in the other room when we arrive, but that doesn't make it any less enjoyable or less wonderful when we get there. There will be good and happy times in the "next room" also.

Best regards, Art, and thanks again.

> Sincerely yours,
> John H. Glenn, Jr.

Less than a year after Bobby Kennedy's assassination, Buchwald reflected on the impact of his death, and that of his brother Jack, in an oral history for the John F. Kennedy Presidential Library:

> I think that the tragedy of Bobby Kennedy—as it is with Jack Kennedy—is we really don't know what he could have done, and what kind of a man he could have been; what kind of a president he would have been. We don't even know if he would have won [at the Democratic Convention] in Chicago, or had he won in Chicago, would he have beaten Nixon. . . . These are things that I think people think about—what kind of a world it would have been. . . . So I just think that for history we have half a history . . . of a man who might have been. And this is the second tragedy in a row because Jack Kennedy was the same kind of a man.

With the death of Robert Kennedy, the battle for the 1968 Democratic nomination was now down to two candidates: Senator Eugene McCarthy and Vice President Hubert H. Humphrey, known to many as "the Happy Warrior" for his buoyant and optimistic approach to politics and campaigning. (Buchwald once joked that the reason President Johnson didn't send his vice president to Winston Churchill's funeral in January 1965 was that Hubert Humphrey couldn't "look sad.")

On the Republican side the clear front-runner was Richard Nixon, who had beaten back an early challenge from Governor Nelson Rockefeller of New York. During the campaign Buchwald had quipped that Nixon was "lucky" the New York governor had gotten in the race. "Without Rockefeller," he said, "Nixon would have had to run against himself and that would have been one of the dirtiest campaigns in American history."

In early August, the Republicans held their convention in Miami Beach to formally nominate Nixon for president. The gathering was a dull and tedious affair. "Boredom lay on the convention like a mattress," presidential historian Theodore H. White wrote. However, the four days of lackluster television coverage were periodically "brightened" by Art Buchwald, who, according to *The Washington Post*, provided "excellent" spot appearances on the CBS-TV network.

Three weeks later the Democrats gathered in Chicago for their convention. Even before the opening gavel sounded, politicians and journalists were predicting a chaotic affair. Weeks before, some eighty anti-war groups had announced they would occupy the city with some one hundred thousand protestors in an effort to disrupt the convention. In response, the city's defiant and tough-minded mayor, Richard J. Daley, prepared for the worst, turning Chicago into an "armed camp."

On the evening the Democrats gathered to nominate their candidate for president, the political battle inside the convention hall quickly became a sideshow to the riots and bloodshed occurring outside in the streets of Chicago. For hours, televised images of violent clashes between protestors and Chicago police were broadcast around the world. "The whole world is watching! The whole world is watching!" protestors chanted as the battle raged between police and demonstrators.

Eighty-nine million television viewers watched in shocked disbelief as the convention inside descended into turmoil, with shouting matches breaking out between some of the delegates and Mayor Daley. In the end, Humphrey was nominated on the first ballot, but it was a Pyrrhic victory. "The Democrats are finished," Theodore White wrote as the convention drew to a close.

"Everybody over reacted—except me," Buchwald said of the riots in Chicago. And in the days following the convention he had plenty of dark humor to offer his readers about the disturbances. One of his more comically mordant pieces was a column published only two days after the convention in which he suggested that a new organization, the "Veterans of Democratic Wars" (VDW), be formed for all of the "battle hardened" journalists and Democratic delegates who had survived the fighting in Chicago. The returning VDW members, Buchwald suggested, should receive "welcome-home parades" (complete with confetti), benefits under the federal GI Bill, adequate housing, and free healthcare. But the true mission of the VDW, Buchwald wrote, would be to ensure that the 1968 gathering—and the sacrifices made by the VDW veterans in Chicago—would be the "convention to end all conventions."

"THEY CAN DO WHAT THE HELL THEY WANT FOR FIVE YEARS"

Shortly after the Republican convention in Miami Beach, Art received a letter from novelist Irwin Shaw, an old friend of Buchwald's from his Paris years, who was now living in Switzerland. "The convention was a gas, wasn't it? Nixon, yet!" Shaw wrote. "If I could vote, I would go for William Jennings Bryan. Government by ouija-board is the only logical system these days."

During their years in France, Art and Ann Buchwald had many friends, but one of their closest was Shaw, who lived in the same apartment building as them at 24 rue de Boccador.

Shaw was born in 1913 in the South Bronx, but spent much of his youth in Brooklyn. After graduating from public school he attended Brooklyn College, where he wrote for the school newspaper and played quarterback for the football team, an experience that provided the colorful backdrop for one of his best-known short stories, "The Eighty-Yard Run." He spent time as a scriptwriter for radio serials, and then in 1936 had his first big break with the production of a play, *Bury the Dead*. Like Buchwald, Shaw served in World War II; in 1948 he used his war experiences for the setting of his first commercially successful novel, *The Young Lions*, later made into a movie starring Marlon Brando, Montgomery Clift, and Dean Martin.

For nearly forty years, Shaw was "one of the heroes" of Art's life. "He was a big bear of a man who laughed a lot, drank even more and lavished much-needed encouragement on young writers," Art would later say. The fondness he felt for Shaw was shared by other writers of his generation, including Southern novelist Willie Morris, who described Shaw as "one of the most generous and kind-spirited men I ever knew. One doubts if any writer had more admiring friends."

Throughout their lives, Buchwald and Shaw maintained a close and regular correspondence, their letters filled with gossip, politics, and updates on work. During the summer of 1968, Shaw was hard at work on a new novel, *Rich Man, Poor Man*, the story of three German American children, Rudy, Tom, and Gretchen Jordache. It was an extraordinarily ambitious work for Shaw, tracing the lives of the fictional family from the final days of World War II to the late 1960s. Although struggling with the new novel, Shaw took time to write Art with a progress report:

Chalet Mia
Klosters, Switzerland

AUGUST 16, 1968

Dear Art,
... The summer's been quiet, but productive. I have about 110,000 words done on my new book and there's only another 200,000 to go. In despair about how detailed I was getting about my characters, I have just now arbitrarily left out five years of their lives. Between [pages] 450 and 451 they can do what the hell they want for five years....

I am writing this at 8 in the morning, to delay the awful moment when I have to put the piece of yellow paper in the machine and type pg. 451 in the right-hand corner. But it can't be put off indefinitely. So that's all for now.

> *Love to you all,*
> *Irwin*

Absorbed by his work on the new book, it would be over a year before Shaw sent another report to Buchwald on *Rich Man, Poor Man:*

Klosters, Switzerland

OCT. 19, 1969

Dear Art,
... I wanted to finish my book and I did. This week. It's a monster— 1265 pages. Of course, this is the first draft and I'll have an awful lot of revising and editing to do. I'm taking a few days off before tackling it. I'm leaving for Paris tomorrow morning and will stay there indefinitely....

I've never worked as hard in my life as I have the last two months, but this place is made for hard labor and I don't feel any the worse for it.

As usual, the first thing I read in the Tribune *is your piece. You've really been hitting a great average. I don't know how you find the time to do it all....*

Now I've got to start packing. My book is in 8 volumes so I have to go everywhere by road.

My love to Annie and the kids.

Yours,

Irwin

Three weeks later Shaw sent another update from Paris:

NOV. 2, 1969

Dear Art,

. . . I'm hacking away at my book. My publishers love it, they say, but I don't love it quite enough to let it go out just as it stands now. At this moment I'm writing a new opening. If I continue like this, the book will certainly be ready for publication in 1980.

Love to all,

Irwin

In the words of *The Wall Street Journal,* by the end of the 1960s Art Buchwald was a "humor conglomerate." In 1962, when he first arrived in Washington, his six-hundred-word column was syndicated in nearly 200 newspapers, but by the end of the decade his circulation had more than doubled to more than 450 newspapers; and by the mid-1970s his column ran in more than 550 newspapers, including those in such cities and towns as Pocatello, Idaho; Paducah, Kentucky; Fairbanks, Alaska; Cedar Rapids, Iowa; and Ironwood, Michigan.

His fear of failure in competing with the likes of Lippmann, Alsop, Pearson, Arthur Krock, and others had been unfounded. Columnist Russell Baker of *The New York Times* told Buchwald in an admiring letter, "I think you're going to do all right in Washington, now that you've got the feel of it." Even the staid and most sober-minded of them all, Walter Lippmann, admitted that he was "one of the best satirists of the time."

Buchwald was about to publish his twelfth collection of columns and was hard at work on a Broadway play. He was also host of his own radio show, a "guest columnist" on the hit CBS news series *60 Minutes*, and one of the most sought-after lecturers in the country.

The political funny business was getting mighty good for Artie Buchwald.

CHAPTER 5

BUCHWALD AT LARGE

A Day in the Life of a Humorist

Art Buchwald is a small, chunky, roly-poly man, of swarthy complexion, black hair and eyes, glasses like goggles, and a sort of cocky rolling gate, like a sailor just come ashore and up to no good.

—ALISTAIR COOKE, BBC COMMENTATOR
   AND HISTORIAN, SEPTEMBER 1971

He made it all seem so easy. "The column's a snap. I love it," Buchwald would respond in a breezy manner when asked how he went about his work. Colleagues, competitors, and friends were amazed at his ability to churn out a column three times a week, each one as fresh and lively as the last. "I read your columns three times a week in the *Trib*," his friend novelist Irwin Shaw told Art, "always with the greatest admiration for their wit and your fecundity."

And he always made it *sound* so easy, declaring that he could write a column in about an hour, or even faster "if I get lucky"; and he never worried about overwriting. "My typewriter practically stops at six hundred words automatically," he once joked.

Part of why he made it look so easy was that he loved doing what he did. "It's a beautiful business because you can make people happy and there are very few people in this world that have a chance to make other people happy," he told an interviewer.

By the 1970s, Buchwald had achieved a power and prominence that was nothing less than remarkable, something he could never have imagined when he left Paris. Nearly every year he published a collection of his best columns, selling up to 35,000 hardcover copies and another 150,000 in paperback. He was a radio and television celebrity and a much sought after speaker. (One of his standard talks was titled "The CIA for Fun and Profit.") It was estimated that by the early 1970s Buchwald earned an annual income of over $200,000 a year.

His reputation as a world-renowned humorist was second to none, with one magazine dubbing him America's funniest and most successful newspaper columnist. "In a city awash with self-important journalists, hyperserious analysts and determined deep thinkers, his column is perhaps the most widely read of all," wrote *Newsweek*. But his success and the relaxed and unhurried way in which he seemed to have achieved it, rested on a deceptively easygoing style and discipline. "Buchwald is incomparable," fellow columnist Russell Baker once said. "And he is brave, too, doing one of the hardest things in the world to do—to be funny, in exactly the same sort of way in regard to tone and technique, three times a week. I know I couldn't do it."

Author and essayist E. B. White once wrote, "A writer should concern himself with whatever absorbs his fancy, stirs his heart, and unlimbers his typewriter."

From the moment Buchwald woke up each morning at seven-thirty A.M., he was on the prowl for something to "unlimber his typewriter." (He often joked that his children had standing instructions to come up with at least several ideas each week "or out they go.") While still in bed Buchwald would scan *The New York Times* and *The Washington Post* for ideas. "We have a golden rule that he's not to be talked to while he's reading the papers," his wife, Ann, once reported. "He has breakfast in bed so he'll be spared the maid who always feels obliged to tell him what's in the news or on the *Today* show." If fortunate enough to find anything to catch his fancy, Buchwald would tear the items out of the paper and then, like a veteran beat reporter from a B movie, gather his set of hot tips for the day, set them aside in a pile, and begin to dress for the office.

Once downstairs he would chat briefly with his wife and family and then at eight-thirty A.M. grab the phone, dial the Diamond Cab Company, and request a taxi to take him to the office. Because he had no driver's license, taxis were his primary means of transportation. It was estimated that Buchwald spent nearly $800 a year on D.C. taxis. (Just over $5,000 a year in today's dollars.) When the cab arrived, usually around nine-fifteen, Buchwald would say goodbye to his family, hop inside the waiting taxi, and, after settling in, begin to pore over more newspapers on his way for the fifteen-minute drive to his office at 1750 Pennsylvania Avenue, NW, just one block from the White House.

After arriving at nine-thirty he would take the elevator and head up to his office on the thirteenth floor, where he would greet his assistant and then make his way into his book-lined office, where he got down to work.

After settling in—and with his first cigar of the day already under way—Buchwald would resume his search for column ideas by flipping through more daily newspapers and a selection of newsmagazines, including *The Wall Street Journal*, *The Washington Star*, *The Boston Globe*, *Newsweek*, and *Time*, clipping or ripping any item that caught his interest. "That," one reporter for *The New York Times* wrote after spending a day with Buchwald, "is the extent of his research."

Then, after leisurely sorting through his assortment of clips and deciding on a topic, Buchwald would sit down at his Olivetti electric typewriter, pause to gather his thoughts, take a puff on his cigar, and start pecking away briskly, with "amazing speed and seeming ease." "I don't stew over it," Buchwald told an interviewer, and within an hour he could "bang out" a column that usually ran around six hundred words and covered about two and a half pages of news copy.

When writing his columns, Buchwald lived by a set of rules. He was never "preachy" or mean-spirited and always tried to keep his emotions in check. "I don't come into the office and scream and say, 'Oh my God, did you read this story?' I don't lead parades or picket the White House. I'm not a columnist with every-day explosions. I don't get all shaken up. I guess maybe I'm lazy, but I find going off like an atom bomb exhausting. I just do what I do because it makes me feel good. I write for myself."

Although Buchwald's satire could sting, it was never vicious, something he learned early on, years before he became a celebrated journalist. While still at the University of Southern California, he wrote an essay about the nature of meaningful satire:

> It is criticism with a difference. You don't satirize innocent weaknesses, sufferings or misfortunes, nor would you criticize a man for being born lame or losing a child through some act of nature. Some satire is designed to knock the wind from your sails. Other satire will reduce the object to ruin. The trick of satire is to unmask the victims and show them as they really are. But the trick in satire is to do it cleverly so the intended victim will not be able to protest without giving himself away.... A satirist may use custard pies or pointed quills to get over his point. One satirist may be a clown, a Falstaff, while another may be Satan laughing from Hell at the serious little people who inhabit the earth. Another satirist may be the friend of all mankind, slyly sticking in his barbs through flattery and commendation of the system he is attacking.... [But] the writer must be careful he is not accused of being a hater of mankind. The best way to do this is to abuse people and make them laugh while you're doing it. It indicates that the writer is just having a good time and he's really your friend. The abuse will stick.

To be truly effective as a columnist, Buchwald knew that being a good-natured rebel was part of the job. "I've always been against the establishment, whatever it is, and I think most humorists should be against the establishment, whoever is in power," he told journalist Patricia Marx in a radio interview in 1964. "Because I have a feeling we always get a little too serious about our establishment and we take them too seriously and you have to keep putting pins in these balloons to bring people back down to earth and it's the job of the humorist to stick the pin in the balloon."

Although never afraid to mock or haze any political figure or any wing of the political spectrum, he knew that "making fun of the Left" always meant trouble. "The extreme Left is very ridiculous now, just as ridiculous as the extreme Right," he told an interviewer in the summer of 1969. "But when you make fun of the Left you find all the people who believed in you suddenly turn against you and say you sold out and everything. That's where it takes a little more guts."

After nearly an hour of typing away at a first draft, Buchwald would snap the copy out of his Olivetti and give it a first read, making changes, fixes, cuts, and rewrites. "A lot of times," he once said, the column "turns out a lot different than I imagined when I started . . . because I will get an idea and then I'll see it doesn't work or I'll get one line in the column which will just send me off on another tack which is much better."

Once satisfied, Buchwald would run it by his longtime assistant Cathy Crary. "He would give it to me to read and gauge my reaction to it," Crary would later recall. If she hesitated or seemed puzzled by a phrase or, most important, didn't laugh at the proper moment, Buchwald would ask, "What's wrong?" Crary would point out to him what was confusing or which jokes fell flat. Once her critique was over, Art would return to his typewriter for final revisions and edits until he felt it was just right. Once done, the latest Buchwald creation was sent off to *The Washington Post* and his syndication service for distribution across the country and around the world.

Then, unless he had a morning tennis match with a friend, Buchwald would turn to the day's mail, which inevitably brought in a lively batch of letters and notes from fans, admirers, cranks, and crackpots. On any given day, messages from friends in the entertainment industry

arrive from such notables as film director John Huston, a friend
in the Paris years; composer Richard Rodgers, who on one occasion wrote to thank Art for attending a tribute dinner in his honor; comedian Phyllis Diller, wanting to know his favorite joke of all time;
actress Joan Crawford, complimenting him on his "special brand of
humor," or filmmaker Frank Capra, heaping praise on Buchwald's satirical skill. "I burn incense to a talent who can come up with a humorous column day after day," he told Art in one letter. The daily mailbag
often contained notes from other VIPs, such as former president
Dwight Eisenhower, praising a column Art wrote about Senator Barry
Goldwater that made him "chuckle," or from columnist Anthony
Lewis of *The New York Times*, applauding a column Art had written
about life on Martha's Vineyard.

At times, he would take a moment to shoot off a quick letter to one
of his Washington, D.C., friends, such as Ben Bradlee, now managing
editor of *The Washington Post*. After attending a dinner party with
Bradlee and actress Lauren Bacall at the Georgetown home of Katharine Graham, Buchwald sent this good-natured dig to his friend:

Dear Ben:

*I didn't want to tell you this the other night at Kay's, but Betty Bacall
told me at dinner that she likes me a lot more than she likes you.*

Art

And there was always the steady stream of correspondence with
the Kennedys. After Buchwald sent a glow-in-the-dark football to
young Christopher Kennedy, the son of Robert and Ethel Kennedy,
Art received this letter of thanks:

Hyannis Port

Dear Art,

*Thanks a lot for the football. At last we can play at night. There just
isn't time to play all the football we want during the 12 hours of light but*

thanks to you we can finally fulfill our lives. Also, it'll be great for scaring little kids: telling them it is a UFO.

> *Thanks,*
> *Love,*
> *Chris*

And he was always happy to write a letter of recommendation for one of the Kennedy children, such as this for Maria Shriver in 1971:

AUGUST 12, 1971

... Hundreds of prep schools have been after this brilliant, delightful and beautiful girl. ... You are in fact getting a rare jewel. Maria lights up a campus better than 100 searchlights. She brings joy and laughter wherever she goes. At the same time she is a leader, an athlete, a scholar, and a stateswoman. ...

I don't want to build her up too much, but I would be less than honest if I didn't tell you what I thought of her. Oh, she does have her faults. She's too honest, too kind, too trusting for the world we live in; but you wouldn't want anyone who is perfect, would you?

I very rarely write letters of this sort. ... To me the school comes first and if I thought you were getting a lemon I would not hesitate to tell you.

If I can be of further help don't hesitate to write to me. My mail's been terrible anyway.

> *Sincerely,*
> *Art Buchwald*

One of his most cherished correspondents from the Kennedy family was Ethel Kennedy. "My mother's best friend through the years was the warm, rotund, and gentle humorist Art Buchwald," Robert F. Kennedy, Jr., wrote in his family memoir, *American Values*. Ethel regularly sent the Buchwalds notes about family matters, upcoming summer vacations at Hyannis Port, the Hickory Hill Pet Show, or the Robert F. Kennedy Memorial Tennis Tournament.

Ann and Art could always count on a card or letter offering a warm birthday wish or holiday greeting, such as this Christmas note to the Buchwalds in December 1975:

For Ann and Art—

Who make everyday seem like Saturday—and who always make me feel like I'm sailing.

With Christmas love,
Ethel

In addition to letters from friends and colleagues there was the never-ending stream of correspondence from fans, schoolchildren, and inquiring readers. One editor of an educational magazine wanted to know what role science played in Art's life when he was a child. Buchwald responded:

Science played no part in my life. I never understood how to boil an egg in test tubes or how to look at frog's legs through a microscope. I veered towards liberal arts. Frankly, I did so poorly in science I still don't know how to make a hydrogen bomb.

When asked by a high school teacher in Michigan what historical figure from the past he would most like to have met, Buchwald wrote:

I have a hard time thinking about who I want to meet in history. My first thought is Joan of Arc, but I read up on her and it seems she never talked too much. She was really tight-lipped and I understand she didn't say anything when they burned her, like, "Put out that match," or "Can I have one last cigarette before I go?"

I would like meeting Nero because he always had good parties and provided transportation for those who drank too much. I don't think I would want to meet any of the saints. They were too serious and were always getting into trouble.

I guess I would like to meet Louis Armstrong because wherever he is right now I'm sure he has picked up a great orchestra and I would rather listen to him than Herbert Hoover.

Although he enjoyed receiving letters from admirers and school-children, Art took special delight in the "hate" or "crank" mail he received. On his office wall he always posted a selection of the twenty *best* hate or crackpot letters that had come his way. The ever-changing montage contained such letters as one from an incensed Beatles fan who, after Buchwald wrote a column lampooning the rock and roll band, chastised him by writing, "You should be ashamed of yourself for hurting our darling Beatles. I hate you, you dirty old man." One angry reader called him "a Socialist slob," while another advised him to "take a good long look at yourself in a mirror and then bang your thick skull into it." When Buchwald once used the word "damn" in one of his columns, he received a nasty letter from an outraged reverend who said he would pray for him despite his use of "cheap, cross, crude [language] lacking in good taste." In response, Buchwald wrote back, "I guess you are going to have to continue to pray for me because I don't consider damn a cuss word. Nor do I consider it vulgar or cheap. Damn is a fine English word and it makes me happy to say it." And one brief note from a reader certainly must have given Art some pause, telling Buchwald that if Art sent him some money, he would surely "remember" him on "Judgment Day."

Unfortunately, there was also the inevitable sampling of vile anti-Semitic correspondence. One letter from a reader in the Midwest greeted Art with "Hello Schnook! Buchenwald!" while another referred to him as a "Pink Kike" Socialist. Although Buchwald could always take his share of intelligent criticism, he drew the line at ugly, hateful anti-Semitic mail. Upon receipt of any such letter, Art would reach into his desk and pull out a custom-made rubber stamp containing one word: "BULLSHIT." After applying this pithy response, the offending letter would be returned to the sender.

After devoting thirty to forty minutes to the mail, Buchwald would stroll out of the office and begin "prowling" the halls of the thirteenth floor because, he once quipped, he couldn't "stand the cigar smoke" in his office. (He was now up to six to eight cigars a day.) While roaming the hall, he would often pop his head into the offices of fellow columnists Rowland Evans and Robert Novak, where he would pepper them with a flurry of one-liners and wisecracks.

Then, it was off to lunch.

The Sans Souci restaurant on Seventeenth Street, NW, was a short stroll around the corner from Buchwald's office. In its stylish glamour years of the 1960s and '70s, the Sans Souci was one of the most exclusive and expensive French restaurants in Washington. (It was so difficult to get a table at the restaurant that Mick and Bianca Jagger were even turned away at the door when they showed up unannounced without a reservation.) But, as a frequent guest, Art had his own permanently reserved spot: table number 12 on the right side of the dining area.

A "savvy Frenchman" named Paul Delisle was the maître d' and overseer of a waitstaff outfitted in "white jackets with gold-braid epaulets." Each table was covered with a white cloth and decorated with a colorful arrangement of fresh-cut flowers. At noon each day the restaurant was "the epicenter of D.C.'s midday schmooze scene," *Washingtonian* magazine wrote. It was the gathering place for the most powerful and influential in the city. "Before Sans Souci there was no power lunch," Buchwald said. "No important decision was made in the government without it first being discussed at our restaurant over rognons de veau and Dover sole, served with either a respectable Mouton Rothschild or a chilled bottle of Pouilly Fuisse." On any given day, one might catch a glimpse of celebrity out-of-towners such as Andy Warhol, Elizabeth Taylor, Frank Sinatra, John Lennon and Yoko Ono, Walter Cronkite, Warren Beatty, or Jack Nicholson. Sans Souci's regulars included Ted Kennedy, Henry Kissinger, Ethel Kennedy, Russell Baker, Eppie Lederer ("Ann Landers"), Ben Bradlee and Katharine Graham of *The Washington Post*, and legendary attorney Edward Bennett Williams and his law partner Joseph Califano. It was the place to be and the place to be seen.

Lunch with Buchwald at table 12 was always a lively affair with rich French food, gossip, teasing, and, for several of his guests, a cocktail or two—but none for Art. "Buchwald never drank," Joe Califano recalled, "but the rest of us drank at lunch, and ate and laughed." On one occasion, before an especially power-laden lunch, Buchwald drafted a briefing memo for the owner and publisher of *The Washington Post*:

Memorandum to Kay Graham
Subject: Luncheon Tomorrow at Sans Souci
Date: December 15, 1966

This is a list of guests at the luncheon tomorrow which will help you know who they are and what is to be talked about.

1. Benjamin Bradlee is the Managing Editor of the *Washington Post*, which is a very influential newspaper in the nation's capital. Bradlee's interests are football and girls—not necessarily in that order—but if you wish, you can talk to him about the newspaper business.
2. Edward Bennett Williams is a leading criminal lawyer in Washington who has defended such diversified clients as Milwaukee Phil, Arizona Pete, and Three Finger George. He is a very strong Catholic, so I suggest you discuss religion with him—particularly birth control and if priests should get married.
3. Art Buchwald is a columnist for the *Washington Post*. He is terribly charming and can talk on any subject. I think of the three, you will find him the most interesting.

And Buchwald was, indeed, always "charming." After a lunch with Eppie Lederer, he received this thank-you:

FEBRUARY 13, 1969

Art Baby:

Lunch at Sans Souci was tres elegant. Merci beaucoup. Now you've heard all the French I know.

It was muy simpatico of you to bring su esposa, Ann. Now you've heard all the Spanish.

Ich lieb dere—that's my Yiddish, Doll.

Eppie

After lunch—usually ending about two-thirty P.M.—it was back to the office to attend to more Buchwald-at-Large business: returning phone calls, answering more mail, tinkering with an upcoming lecture or speech, making plans to attend a charitable event (sometimes with a member of the Kennedy family), lining up a group of friends for a Sunday outing to a Washington Redskins football game, scheduling an upcoming poker game with friends at his home on Hawthorne Street, or perhaps doing a scheduled interview with a newspaper or magazine.

One such interview appeared in *The Washington Post Book World* in the fall of 1969, "Portrait of a Man Reading," which featured a particularly enlightening examination into the literary mind of Art Buchwald. When asked what he read for pleasure, Art responded, "All sorts of things . . . but I'm a half-a-book reader. . . . It's not a bad practice. When someone asks if I read a book, I can say, 'Oh yes, I'm about halfway through it.'" As to how he selected his reading, "Weight plays a big part in what I read. If the book is too thick and heavy, I get frightened."

When asked what his favorite "war book" was, he responded, "*Catch-22*. I think that's one of the funniest books I've ever read. I laughed out loud more while reading that book than almost any I can remember." (Even before *Catch-22* was published in the fall of 1961, Buchwald knew there was something remarkable about the book. "Please congratulate Joseph Heller on masterpiece *Catch-22*. I think it is one of the greatest war books. So do Irwin Shaw and James Jones," Buchwald wrote in a telegram to Heller's editors.)

When queried about whether he was "diligent with certain types of books," the satirist responded, "Possibly. Take pornography for instance. I'm very selective about my pornographic reading. In fact, I have a new project: I'm thinking about putting out a *Reader's Guide to Pornography.*"

Once work in the office was complete, Buchwald might wander the halls outside his office for a bit, popping in here and there to chat with someone from one of the other Washington news bureaus, or just pack up for the day, stroll downstairs, and head to Doc Dalinsky's Georgetown Pharmacy, where he would catch up on the latest gossip or play a few spirited games of gin rummy; or he might make a quick stop at a local jeweler's to buy a new watch. "He was obsessed with watches," Cathy Crary later recalled, "and bought them constantly" for himself and for friends.

By four-thirty P.M.—whether he was at the office or out on the town visiting friends—Buchwald would hail a cab for the trip home to his house on Hawthorne Street.

Unless Buchwald's schedule required that he attend an in-town dinner that evening to deliver a speech at a charitable event, or to do an in-studio television interview, Art would sit down to dinner with Ann and his children before heading up to his in-home office for more work: chatting with friends on the phone (always looking for a fresh tip for a column); working on the draft of an upcoming speech or magazine article; or continuing work on a new collection of his columns. After several more hours of "Buchwald-at-Night," he would call it quits, thus ending another day in the life of a humorist.

After seven years in Washington, Buchwald was at the top of his game. Nothing seemed out of his reach, not even the bright lights of Broadway. "Everyone thinks I have one of the best jobs in the world," he told one inquiring reporter. "But if you look at it objectively and examine it from all sides, I do."

THE WORLD
ACCORDING TO ART

THE GREAT JOE MAYFLOWER FEUD

Buchwald on Broadway (1969-70)

We're in show biz!

—ART TO ANN BUCHWALD, SPRING 1969

The decade of the 1970s opened with a very public, very bitter feud between two of America's most celebrated columnists, a quarrel that divided the Washington political and social establishment for nearly three years—and at the center of it all was Art Buchwald. "The Great Grimaldi Feud" of 1956 may have been pure fantasy, but for Buchwald "The Great Joe Mayflower Feud" of 1970 was pure nonsense.

Despite the demands of his three-times-a-week newspaper column and a very busy and very lucrative speaking schedule, during the spring and summer of 1969 Buchwald found time to write a script for a Broadway play called *Sheep on the Runway*, a political satire set in a fictitious Asian country called Nonomura, located in a remote region of the Himalayas. The main characters in the comedy are an inept U.S. ambassador; a naïve and unsophisticated monarch named Prince Gow; and a devious, at times maniacal, Washington journalist by the name of Joe Mayflower who, after his arrival on the scene, brings political chaos to the Nonomuran nation through his manipulation of the ambassador, the prince, and the American military.

The financial backing for the play came from Buchwald's friend Roger Stevens, a wealthy real estate magnate, a philanthropist, founding chairman of the John F. Kennedy Center for the Performing Arts, and the producer of more than two hundred Broadway plays, including such hits as *West Side Story, Cat on a Hot Tin Roof,* and *Death of a Salesman.* The play's co-producer was Bob Whitehead, creator of the Broadway hit *A Man for All Seasons,* and its director Gene Saks, whose credits included film versions of Neil Simon's *Barefoot in the Park* and *The Odd Couple.*

Despite the play's stellar production team, when *Sheep on the Runway* first hit the stage during the traditional out-of-town pre-Broadway performances, it was met with mixed reviews. In New Haven, Connecticut, Buchwald was so disheartened by the audience's initial response that he considered booking a flight out of town. "I found out from a friend that they can't extradite you from Brazil if you've written a flop," he said at the time. But after several grim all-night sessions of fixes and rewrites on the script, things began to turn around, and by the final night of its New Haven run on December 27, *Sheep* was playing to a full house.

Despite the encouragement they had received from the final performances in New Haven, the opening night reviews in Philadelphia were dismal, requiring another round of script rewrites by Buchwald. The long days and long nights of working on the play were starting to take their toll on Art, leaving him in such a "daze" that at one point he told a reporter, "All I know is that Yale is located in Philadelphia, but I don't know what part of town."

Soon Saks and Whitehead were forced to bring in seasoned "play doctor" Joe Stein, whose hits included *Fiddler on the Roof* and *Zorba the Greek,* for a consultation to see if *Sheep* could be fixed in time before moving on to New York for opening night. Stein bluntly told Buchwald, Saks, and Whitehead that while the play had promise, it needed one more "major rewrite." The biggest problem, he told them, was with one of the major characters, Joe Mayflower, the cynical political columnist. His role was "too straight," Stein said. Mayflower instead needed to be "completely paranoid" and portrayed as "an absolute madman."

Over the next several days, Buchwald, Whitehead, and Saks were encouraged by many of Stein's last-minute revisions to the script in Philadelphia, but there was still some uneasiness about *Sheep* as they prepared for opening night on Broadway. And then, adding to everyone's anxieties, just two days before departing for New York, one of the major actors became too ill to go onstage. Art was tired and disheartened by it all. "One gets the feeling that the Gods are angry, but why me?" he confided in his diary.

But as the play prepared to open in New York, more trouble was on the horizon back in Washington, D.C., as a feud between Buchwald and one of the most influential columnists in the world was about to erupt.

As Joe Stein's revisions for a more deranged Joe Mayflower were being feathered into the play at Philadelphia, word began to filter back to Washington that Joe Mayflower was *actually* based on the character and personality of columnist Joseph Alsop.

Joseph Alsop and his fellow columnist and brother, Stewart Alsop, were the epitome of the Washington establishment. In background and pedigree they were everything that Art Buchwald was not. Both Alsops had been born in Avon, Connecticut, and were distantly related to the Roosevelt family. Both attended the prestigious Groton School. Joe went on to Harvard, where he wrote for *The Harvard Crimson,* and Stewart went on to Yale. Starting in 1945, the Alsop brothers cowrote a column for the *New York Herald Tribune* that provided incisive commentary on domestic politics and international affairs. In 1958, however, they parted ways professionally: Stewart moving to *The Saturday Evening Post* then on to *Newsweek;* Joe writing his own syndicated column for *The Washington Post.*

At first, when Alsop's friends suggested to him that he was the model for Joe Mayflower, he brushed it off with a laugh. But after a Philadelphia newspaper referred to the play as a "libelous spoof" on Alsop, and his Washington friends continued to tease him about the similarity, Alsop had had enough and flew into a rage.

Feeling publicly humiliated by the gossip about Joe Mayflower, Alsop spread word throughout Washington that "anyone who went to the opening of *Sheep on the Runway* would no longer be considered a friend of his." (Alsop's brother Stewart thought Joe might have a valid point about the character in Buchwald's play. "It must be my brother he's written about," Stewart said. "Otherwise, why would everyone be calling me Stewart Mayflower?")

Like any good bit of social or political gossip in Washington—particularly gossip that had the promise of stirring up trouble—notice of Alsop's "declaration" of war against Buchwald made its way into *The Washington Post* style column of Maxine Cheshire. Cheshire, in her column, disclosed that "Alsop has not been amused to find himself satirized so recognizably and so unflatteringly" and that for the Washington establishment "the decision to attend opening night in New York or stay away has become 'a litmus test of loyalty.'"

As word of Alsop's fury quickly spread up and down the East Coast, Buchwald, who was trying to keep focused on last-minute script problems before opening night, was deluged with calls asking for comment on the Alsop social ultimatum. At first Art tried to make light of the rumored rift, joking with one reporter that he had, indeed, heard that "Joe Alsop was sticking pins in a doll of me." But when the rumors and gossip persisted and grew more ominous, an agitated Buchwald issued a public statement denying that Joe Mayflower was Joe Alsop, telling reporters that the character in his play "bore no resemblance to my dear friend" and that he was "hurt and appalled that Mr. Alsop would think I would put a character on the stage that in any way would look or sound like him."

However, the Joe Mayflower gossip wouldn't let up. Sensing that things were quickly getting out of hand, Buchwald took the unusual

step of sending a letter to the editor of *The Washington Post* to deny
Cheshire's story about the Mayflower-Alsop comparison:

Dear Editor:

*I haven't been home in some time, but I understand . . . that someone
is trying to build up a feud between myself and my esteemed colleague
Joseph Alsop. The misunderstanding seems to be based on a play I
wrote which opens on Broadway sometime within the next few weeks. In
the play I have a character named Joe Mayflower who happens to be a
political columnist. I have continually denied, and I will to my dying day
(which could be after the critics get through with me) that my character
is not based on Mr. Alsop.*

*I am naturally upset that people might think I would use a live per-
son as a basis for a character in my play. Anyone who reads my column
knows there isn't an ounce of truth in anything I write.*

Art Buchwald

Alsop, however, was unconvinced and dug in his heels, telling
friends that he intended to do something about it—even if it meant
suing Buchwald. After discussing the matter with Bob Kintner, an old
friend and former president of NBC, Alsop hired entertainment lawyer William Fitelson to look into the matter. During a preview performance of *Sheep* in New York, Fitelson showed up unannounced at
the Helen Hayes Theatre to see whether Alsop might have a case. No
doubt Fitelson's ears quickly perked up when he heard the main character, U.S. ambassador Raymond Wilkins, describe Joe Mayflower as
a "prissy newspaperman" and someone who can be a "mean son of a
bitch."

Although Buchwald wasn't on hand at the rehearsal that day, Bob
Whitehead was. After seeing the performance, Fitelson approached
Whitehead to tell him that he represented Alsop and demanded that
Buchwald not only change the name of the character in the play but
also write letters to *Newsweek, The New York Times,* and *Life* "stating
that there was no resemblance between" Joe Mayflower and Joe Alsop.

Only after Buchwald had done that, Fitelson said, would Alsop decide whether or not he would go ahead with a lawsuit. Then in a final twist of the knife, Fitelson reportedly told Whitehead that he wasn't really concerned about it all "because he understood the play was a bomb and wouldn't last a week."

When word reached Buchwald about Fitelson's conversation with Whitehead, he was upset and alarmed. He immediately contacted two old friends, attorney Edward Bennett Williams and his law partner Joseph Califano, to tell them about Alsop's demands. Rather than express concern, Williams and Califano told Buchwald that he should be "elated" by the news. Having seen some of the bad notices *Sheep* had received on the road, they told Art that any publicity—even bad publicity—from a lawsuit might actually help. "Alsop might save your show after all," Williams told him. But when a clearly troubled Buchwald pressed Williams and Califano further about whether they thought Alsop would *really* sue, Williams responded, "No chance. But if he wants to sue, we must not look a gift horse in the mouth."

Knowing that Williams and Califano were in his corner gave Buchwald some measure of relief, but back in Washington, Alsop just wouldn't let up. Bothered by the continuous stream of calls from reporters, Alsop called Ben Bradlee at *The Washington Post* and told him he was "sick and tired of the publicity" being generated in his paper by the feud. Concerned that the matter was spinning out of control, Bradlee offered to mediate.

He first contacted Ann Buchwald and told her that he was concerned about Art's reputation. Since arriving in Washington in 1962, his name had been "unblemished" by any hint of scandal. But now, Bradlee told her, the town was rife with gossip about what a "rat" and "slanderer" Buchwald was. Concerned about the implications of it all, Ann called Art in New York and told him about her conversation with Bradlee, then pleaded with him to change the name and be done with it. Buchwald told her that while he wanted to change the name he couldn't do it at this late date because the "actors had a great deal of trouble learning their lines and I could never change Joe's name without lousing up" the play. When Bradlee learned that Art wouldn't give in, he decided to make one last attempt to resolve the dispute by scheduling a meeting with Edward Bennett Williams. In the meeting at Williams's law office, Bradlee expressed concern about their mutual friend. "Eddie, I am worried about Artie," he told Williams. "All his friends in Washington are furious at him for maligning Joe Alsop. We've got to save him." Listening intently, Williams asked Bradlee what he thought Buchwald should do. "You've got to talk Artie into changing the name of his main character," pleaded Bradlee, "because Artie's reputation is at stake." Williams, the brilliant, fearless, legendary lawyer, responded, "Benjy, if Artie were only a friend, I would certainly do everything in my power to persuade him to make the necessary changes. But Artie isn't only my friend. He's my client. And as my client the only thing I can advise him to do is to take the demands and tell Joe to—"

Before Williams could finish, the phone rang in his office. It was Katharine Graham, owner and publisher of *The Washington Post* and Buchwald's close friend, wanting to know how Bradlee's efforts to resolve the impasse were going. Bradlee told her Williams wasn't "buying any of it" and wouldn't budge.

While the quarrel with Alsop remained unresolved in Washington, back in New York, Buchwald was doing everything he could to keep his attention focused on opening night. And things were not going well. On January 16, nearly two weeks before the play was set to open, Art was in an anxious and gloomy mood. The cast seemed lethargic and the reaction of audiences at preview performances had been erratic. "Things are really going lousy," Buchwald wrote in his journal.

On January 25, 1970, only days before opening night, Buchwald was given a much-needed boost when he received a letter from seven-year-old Christopher Kennedy, the son of Robert and Ethel Kennedy.

On behalf of all the Kennedy children (known to Buchwald as "the Blue Meanies"), Christopher sent best wishes to Art—along with a hand-drawn sketch—for the opening night of his play:

Hickory Hill

JAN. 25 [1970]

Dear Art,

Light up your cigar, your eyes, and your nose on Opening Night by pushing the tummy of yourself. The little blue man is you. . . .

This little blue man is to cheer you up if the people don't like your play. If they do like your play . . . it's yours for keeps anyway.

We want you back here. . . . And this letter is from all the Blue Meanies.

Here is a picture of a Blue Meanie drawing by Christopher. . . .

Chris

[P.S.] Sock it to 'em

With *Sheep on the Runway* about to open, Buchwald was torn. "I want the play to be right, but I also want the agony to be over with," he wrote in his journal. "I don't think I could stand another week of waiting for the ax to fall." The "ax" was what the theater critics would say when it premiered, especially Clive Barnes of *The New York Times.* "Please, Clive, like my show," Buchwald pleaded privately in his diary.

On opening night, scores of friends and other "Buchwaldians," as *Washington Post* reporter Sally Quinn noted, flew in hour after hour on the Eastern Air Lines Shuttle from Washington. The bitter feud about the play and Alsop's threat about social banishment and legal action were on everyone's mind. "The interesting part of this evening," columnist Joseph Kraft told a reporter, "is to see who's not here rather than who's here." Rumors had circulated for days that several Washington politicians and socialites loyal to both camps had agonized about whether to go for opening night. It was reported that one prominent journalist had scheduled a trip to Europe on the night of the premiere to avoid having to make the decision.

Feud or no feud, a celebrated cast of Art's loyal friends and colleagues flocked to the city that night. On hand were Edward Bennett Williams, Ben Bradlee, Russell Baker, Ethel Kennedy, Arthur Schlesinger, Jr., playwright Lillian Hellman, Averell Harriman, Walter Lippmann, David Brinkley, George Plimpton, Franklin D. Roosevelt, Jr., and Buchwald's own father, Joseph. "I never saw my father happier than that night," Buchwald later wrote. "He hadn't met many of my friends, and they were pleased to shake hands with him and say nice things about me out of earshot."

Only an hour before the show was to begin, Buchwald and his wife, Ann, who looked "beautifully coiffed" that night according to Quinn, gathered with friends and admirers for drinks in the lobby of the Algonquin Hotel. As the time to depart for the theater arrived, Art admitted that he was a bit nervous, but was also glad it would all be over soon. When they arrived at the Helen Hayes Theatre on Forty-sixth Street, they were greeted by a mob of reporters, autograph seekers, and photographers. Finally making their way inside the theater, the Buchwalds got to their seats just before the curtain rose.

During the first act the audience was "sharp and attentive," laughing and applauding as if on cue. But during intermission, the offstage play—the Alsop-Buchwald feud—was on everyone's mind. Journalist Sally Quinn noted that the break "was spent ticking off names of those who were there and speculating on who had chickened out and why."

When the curtain rose after the interval, the audience appeared more relaxed and at ease, their laughter mixed with an occasional howl or "loud guffaw." As the final curtain came down the audience erupted in applause, prompting three curtain calls and cries of "Author! Author!" After the cheering and clapping ended, the Washington and New York glitterati made their way to Sardi's restaurant for the traditional opening night gathering for drinks, dinner, and the long, anxious wait for the early reviews to come in.

The Buchwalds were greeted by a wild scene as they arrived at the restaurant. "My God. This is the most glamorous group I've seen at a theater opening since I can remember," exclaimed one of the waiters at Sardi's. Everyone was in good spirits, all pleased that it had all gone so well. "I thought it was great, just great," Ethel Kennedy told a reporter.

Shortly after eleven P.M., Buchwald and others hurried upstairs to watch the television reviews on the late news broadcasts. When Art returned downstairs he greeted his guests with welcome relief: "Four out of four good ones," he told the crowd. Then came more good news: "Five out of five," Buchwald reported. While everyone breathed a bit more easily, they all knew it would be the newspaper reviews the next day—especially from Clive Barnes of *The New York Times*—that would really matter.

After spending a nervous morning walking the streets of New York, Ann and Art returned to the Algonquin Hotel to await the verdict of the newspaper critics. He tried to keep his mind focused on the previous evening: "No matter what the critics say, I had a wonderful time," he wrote in his journal. Then, the phone rang with news about the Clive Barnes review, and the news was good. "Art Buchwald's 'Sheep on the Runway' is an always endearing, often very funny play," Barnes began his critique. "Despite its mild-sounding exterior, it is at heart far more politically savage than I recall Mr. Buchwald's columns being.... The tone of the play resembles Woody Allen more than anyone else ... and the individual lines are a lot funnier than the play itself." Although he chided Buchwald for some structural problems, Barnes concluded, "It remains a rattling good first play.... I wholeheartedly recommend 'Sheep on the Runway,' warts and all. It may not be perfect, but who is perfect?" Buchwald would later write of the *New York Times* review, "Good old Clive Barnes. He's a great man, a kind man, a truthful man."

In the end, the play received generally favorable reviews from most major newspapers. One of Buchwald's favorites was from Martin Nolan of *The Boston Globe*, who wrote, "The only people who couldn't enjoy Buchwald's play are those who think the Vietnam war was a swell idea."

Sheep on the Runway went on to have a run of 105 performances in New York and then moved on to Washington, D.C., where Buchwald's luck finally ran out. The play had a sad and somber opening at the National Theatre on May 4, 1970—the same day four students were killed at Kent State University by National Guard soldiers during a protest against the Vietnam War. As if that wasn't enough, the theater critic for *The Washington Post*, Richard Coe, wrote a scathing review of *Sheep*, calling it "a thin little comedy which, after a promising first act, grinds quickly, very quickly, downhill in the second." Ben Bradlee, who had grown accustomed to rough treatment of his colleagues by *Post* critics, took Coe's critique of Buchwald in stride, saying that his friends always got "lousy reviews in the *Post*."

Despite the disastrous opening night, *Sheep* had a three-week run and then closed its doors on May 23, 1970. (At one point, as the play limped on, Ann Buchwald offered some advice to her husband. "I told Art that the only way he could keep such a political play going was to have nude ushers.")

Buchwald had taken a huge professional and personal risk in his bid to become the next Neil Simon, and it had taken its toll, but he had survived. "When I look back on it, I consider my first experience in the theater worth every moment," he said. "Besides, Clive Barnes in his review said he hoped I'd write another play."

Although *Sheep* was a hit, the Joe Mayflower feud was not over yet. Unbeknownst to Buchwald, the day after the Clive Barnes review, Joseph Alsop's friend Robert Kintner, who months before had advised him to retain counsel for a potential lawsuit, wrote to Joe with some sage advice about the quarrel that had caused so much bad blood between the two. In his letter, Kintner suggested that Alsop refrain from making any further statements to the press or friends about the affair and henceforth "treat the matter, both publicly and privately, as one of those things" and let it go. He cautioned that the more angry the columnist appeared to colleagues and the press, "the more the publicity will continue," resulting in more embarrassment to Alsop. In response Alsop thanked Kintner for his counsel. "That was an exceedingly nice letter. It came at a bad time. It gave good advice. And I am very grateful for it."

Alsop took Kintner's counsel to heart and refrained from filing suit or making any more inflammatory statements about the play. But "hard feelings" toward Buchwald remained, and for nearly three more years Washington society hosts and hostesses were forced to abide by the terms of the silent feud and avoid putting either of them on the same guest list. It wasn't until November 7, 1972, when both Buchwald and Alsop accepted invitations to attend a party hosted by Joseph Califano, that Maxine Cheshire could publicly and safely announce in her *Washington Post* column that a truce had been reached and that "one of Washington's most publicized feuds had ended."

"The Great Joe Mayflower Feud" of 1970 was finally over.

CHAPTER 7

"CRUISE DIRECTOR ON THE *TITANIC*"

Buchwald in the Nixon Years (1969-74)

Watergate is the glue that keeps the nation from falling apart.

—ART BUCHWALD, FEBRUARY 1974

Goodbye, Broadway. Hello, Nixonland.

The years of Kennedy's "New Frontier" and Johnson's "Great Society" had furnished Buchwald with a bounty of rich material for his weekly political columns, but when Richard Nixon arrived at the White House in January 1969, Art knew he was living in a satirist's paradise. For five years, Nixon provided Buchwald with prime targets for his wit and special brand of political humor.

Once asked if he ever read Art Buchwald, Nixon replied:

Nixon: "No, no I don't think he is funny. He is certainly not serious."
Q: "Where does that leave him?"
Nixon: "That leaves him . . . irrelevant."

While Nixon had only mild disdain for Buchwald, Buchwald had nothing but affection for Nixon. "As a humor columnist, I needed

Richard Nixon a lot more than he needed me," Buchwald once said. Art's delight began during the 1968 campaign when Nixon was pitted against Hubert H. Humphrey, the Democratic nominee, and independent candidate George Wallace, former governor of Alabama. As usual, Art played no favorites. "Nixon [looks] like someone you wouldn't buy a used car from and Humphrey like a guy who had bought one, and Wallace, like a guy who would steal one."

Within days after Nixon was declared the winner, Buchwald was off and running. Disregarding the age-old tradition of a political "honeymoon" for an incoming president, Buchwald wrote a column only five days after Nixon entered the White House, lampooning his failure to log any significant achievements since becoming president. He satirized Nixon for making no "gains in the fight against crime"; for his failure to reach a peace agreement in Vietnam ("How much time does he need to get the ball rolling?"); for his inability to "resolve the Middle East crisis"; and, lastly, for his failure to land a man on the moon.

Some of Buchwald's readers, however, didn't take too kindly to the weekly barbs directed at the new president. One reader from New York wrote:

> I have come to the conclusion that you are what they call in the theatrical world, A SICK COMEDIAN! . . . How come you are always writing those snide and sarcastic humorous so-called columns about Mr. Nixon? . . . Believe you me . . . most of us really only buy the papers who use your daily writings, just for the cross word puzzle.

Another "disgusted reader" was equally direct. "I wouldn't think of wasting the ink in my pen to call you Mister. In plain words, you and your column stink. You are a sarcastic, no good stinker. Why they let your crap get into print, is beyond me."

When Buchwald wasn't taking aim at the president, he went after Vice President Spiro T. Agnew, Nixon's "attack dog," who labeled the liberal establishment an "effete corps of impudent snobs," and the liberal press "nattering nabobs of negativism." When Art learned that Nixon was going to give Agnew an office right next to the president's, Buchwald said, "Now this could mean one of two things. Either Mr. Agnew is going to have a strong voice in Nixon's decisions—or he's under White House arrest."

At times it seemed as if anything Nixon or Agnew did was fair game for Buchwald. When the president and Henry Kissinger made the historic move to normalize relations with Communist China in February 1972, cigar aficionado Buchwald wondered why the president had normalized relations with China but not Cuba. "Nixon is going to Red China, and I still can't get Havana cigars," Buchwald grumbled.

As a political humorist he had never had it so good. Being in Nixonland, he told friends and readers, was "like going to Las Vegas for a year and rolling nothing but sevens."

BRUMUS LIVES ON!

On June 30, 1971, Buchwald received a black-bordered memorial card notifying him that the late senator Robert F. Kennedy's beloved yet troublesome dog Brumus had passed on to the great pet afterlife. But after reading the notice, Art was less than reassured by the announcement:

JUNE 30, 1971

Dear Art,

On the 27th of June I went to that big dog pound in the sky, but I've already been recycled so you'll still be seeing me around.

It is up to you to guess in which disguise.

Eternally,
BRUMUS

"THE BITE OF B & B"

Since 1962, newspaper readers had been entertained each week by the satire and brilliant wit of Art Buchwald in *The Washington Post* and Russell Baker in *The New York Times*. "The Bite of B & B," as one reporter called it, provided a welcome one-two punch for morning readers who were desperate for a bit of humor in the midst of a world that, at times, seemed to have gone mad. Like Art Buchwald's humor, Baker's "Observer" column in the *Times* satirized the foibles and follies of politicians and celebrities and poked fun at the daily absurdities of American culture and society.

Born in rural Virginia, Baker, like Buchwald, came from a tough and difficult childhood. His father, a stonemason, died when Russell was only five. Soon after, his widowed mother, Lucy Baker, moved the family to Baltimore, where she found work as a seamstress. When not at work, Baker's strong-willed mother concentrated her energies on making sure that her son would become a success. "She would make me make something of myself whether I wanted to or not," Baker wrote in his poignant Pulitzer Prize–winning memoir, *Growing Up*.

After attending Johns Hopkins University and serving in the Navy in World War II, Baker got a job as a local reporter for *The Baltimore Sun*. By 1952, his reporting skills had earned him a spot in the *Sun*'s London bureau. After two years abroad he was brought home to cover the White House until he was lured away by *The New York Times* to cover national politics, including the presidential campaigns of Eisenhower and Kennedy. By 1962, however, Baker had grown bored with politics and sought a change. After *The Baltimore Sun* tried to lure him back, the *Times* offered him his own column called "The Observer."

When Buchwald arrived in Washington, he and Baker quickly became friends and amiable competitors. "His column in the *Times* was funny, witty, and erudite," Buchwald once said of Baker's column. "All the things I hated him for." They often lunched together at Sans Souci, where, in between courses, they tried "to steal column ideas from each other." For the next several decades the two carried on a humorous and playful correspondence, all in good fun but at times laced with the "Bite of B & B."

In mid-February 1970, Baker was approached by a reporter in Florida for some material to be used in an introduction of Art at an upcoming speaking engagement in St. Petersburg. Baker was only too happy to comply:

FEBRUARY 24, 1970

Mr. Robert Pittman
St. Petersburg Times
St. Petersburg, Florida

Dear Mr. Pittman:

You may, if you like, use the following as part of your introduction to Art Buchwald:

"I was greatly startled to hear that Art Buchwald was to make a public appearance in St. Petersburg tonight. I remember him well, of course. In his day he was a great jazz clarinetist who even achieved a certain fame when playing with Dogmeat Hines and his Natchez Seven in the late 1920's. I had been under the impression, however, that the old fellow had died fifteen or twenty years ago. It is wonderful to hear that he is not only still alive, but still capable of public appearances. If the old gentleman's lip has not given out, you are certainly going to hear some memorable clarinet playing in St. Pete tonight."

Sincerely,
Russell Baker

In the spring of 1975, a loyal yet befuddled fan in New Hampshire wrote Baker about the difficulties he faced each day to read the wit and wisdom of "B & B." Because he could afford to buy only the *Times* with Baker's column each morning, he was forced to "snatch" the *Post* with Buchwald's column out of the "neighbor's trash" each day. "I think he suspects I'm headed for the looney bin and I'm beginning to wonder," the steadfast reader told Baker. "So I'm writing to you for re-assurance. . . . All I want to say is that if you and Art should stop writing I'd surely end up in the looney bin."

Days later Baker wrote back with a thoughtful reply to his admirer in New England:

APRIL 23, 1975

I am sending your letter on to Art Buchwald so he can be reminded of his duty to keep you out of the looney bin. I don't know whether you can count on his going five more years, however. The poor old gentleman, as you may know, celebrated his 93rd birthday just last week and has long periods when he thinks he is Mark Twain. . . .

Sincerely,
Russell Baker

After Baker forwarded a copy of the fan letter to Art, an equally sympathetic Buchwald chimed in:

APRIL 29, 1975

Thank you so much for your letter which Mr. Baker forwarded to me.

I am sorry you have to read my column after it is thrown into the trash can. A lot of the humor is lost once it gets mixed up with the garbage.

I suggest you continue reading Baker as he is noted for keeping people from going off their rocker. He has a sobering influence on all of us.

Sincerely,
Art Buchwald

In June 1976, Baker received an unwelcome letter from a reader in Tennessee, who mocked him for trying to imitate the style of Art Buchwald. "Up until a few months ago you were a fair-to-middling columnist. No great shakes, but no worse than the average," he informed

Baker. "[But] a few months ago you started trying to write like Art Buchwald.... It can't be done.... Nobody writes like Art Buchwald, but Art Buchwald. It ain't funny, Magee—you're only making a fool of yourself."

The note did not sit well with Baker, a two-time winner of the Pulitzer Prize, who couldn't resist sending a copy of the letter to Buchwald:

JUNE 29, 1976

Dear Art:

I am getting sick and tired of getting your fan mail. I know you have a lot of fans, but why do they have to write to me?

This guy ... really pisses me off.

Cheers,
Russ

"WISEST THING YALE EVER DID"

Back in December 1969, Art had spent a miserable Christmas season in New Haven, Connecticut, trying to keep his *Sheep on the Runway* play from falling apart. The one bright moment in the midst of those bleak days was when he received an invitation to spend Christmas Day with Yale president Kingman Brewster, Jr., and his family. "No supplicant at a Salvation Army Christmas dinner is as grateful as I am for the Brewster turkey and trimmings," Buchwald wrote in his journal that day. "I am willing to pray, sing or write praises for Yale. I keep thanking everyone for passing the plates my way."

Nearly six months later, on a bright, sunny Monday, June 8, 1970, Art was back in New Haven, but this time President Brewster and Yale were singing his praises on commencement day. Among those on hand to receive honorary degrees were Swiss psychologist Jean Piaget, in recognition of his groundbreaking work in the field of child cognitive development; British theologian Henry Chadwick; and Art Buchwald, who arrived onstage sporting a lavender shirt with a lavender tie underneath his black academic robe.

In announcing Buchwald's honorary degree of doctor of humane letters, President Brewster praised Buchwald for his unique brand of humor and satire, which, he proclaimed, was "in the great American tradition of skepticism—graced with a kindly sense of the absurd." At first Buchwald was humbled by it all, telling the crowd, "Now they've got me intimidated. I'm going to have to think twice before I give Yale a hard time." But, in true form, Buchwald gathered himself and quipped, "It was the wisest thing Yale ever did." Later, as he left the ceremony, a reporter asked him if being a "Yalie" meant that he would now become a major contributor to the college. "Hell no!" he shouted back.

BUCHWALD'S BET

Whenever a feature article about Buchwald appeared in a magazine or newspaper, there was the inevitable mention of his wit, black horn-rimmed glasses, ubiquitous cigar, and, somewhat uncharitably, descriptions of his physique with words like "somewhat plumpish," "rotund," or looking like an "amiable panda."

Although Buchwald paid little attention to such descriptions, during the summer of 1972, Art and his friend Edward Bennett Williams decided it was time to trim a few pounds from the stout frames of the columnist and the counselor.

"We were sitting in the Sans Souci restaurant . . . on a hot August afternoon," Buchwald wrote in a piece for *The Saturday Evening Post.* "Williams and I had each just finished off a mousse au chocolat and as we sipped our coffee, we discussed different reasons why we couldn't lose weight":

"We need an incentive," I said. "Something that is bigger than both of us."

"I know an incentive," Williams said, eating a petit four.

"What is it?" I asked, nibbling on a sugar-coated strawberry.

"Greed," Williams replied. "Greed has been the motivating force in both our lives."

I couldn't argue with that. "We will make a bet as to who can lose the most weight in a certain amount of time . . . and the man who loses the most will be paid by the other man to the tune of $100 a pound."

At the initial weigh-in at the Metropolitan Club, Williams "tipped the scales at exactly 220 pounds," Buchwald wrote. "I weighed in at exactly 190 pounds—and the battle was on:

We both used psychological warfare tactics. One noontime I sent a tray of French pastries to Williams's office when he'd decided not to go to lunch. Two evenings later, a large chocolate layer cake was delivered to my home with a note, "I'm always thinking of you—Eddie." I sent Williams a book on ice cream. He gave me a $15 gift certificate for Fannie Farmer Candies. . . .

Since everyone knew about the bet, I kept getting intelligence reports every day. Williams, who was defending . . . a case . . . in New York City, was seen . . . at P.J. Clarke's at three o'clock in the morning, surrounded by nothing but fried onion rings. In the meantime, I worked desperately to lose weight. Since I don't drink liquor, every pound I took off was painful.

In six weeks, I had taken off ten pounds. Williams, by his own admission, had put on six.

He demanded a summit conference at Paul Young's Restaurant.

"I want to call off the bet," he said. . . .

"No chance of calling off the bet," I said.

"But I'm $1,600 behind," he protested.

"I'll tell you what I'll do," I said. "If you lose you have to give the money to the United Jewish Appeal. If I lose, I'll give it to your favorite charity. This way we won't be taking money from each other. What do you want me to give it to?"

"Cardinal O'Boyle's Right to Life Committee," said Williams. "It's an anti-abortion organization that helps pregnant girls."

On the day of the final weigh-in, Buchwald was still struggling:

I went to the Y.M.C.A. and worked out for an hour and then spent another hour in the steam room. In three months I had managed to take off sixteen pounds. I was certain this was enough. As a matter of fact, I was so sure of myself that I hired a violinist for $50 to play for the weighing-in. . . . We could have sold $10,000 worth of tickets to the weighing-in. All of Washington knew about the bet. . . .

I arrived at the Metropolitan Health Club at ten of twelve. . . . Williams was in the steam room where he had been since ten. I went into the steam room, but he refused to shake my hand.

"Let's go," he said.

"I'd like to take off another pound, if it's all the same to you," I said.

"You trying to forfeit the match?" he asked.

I followed him out of the steam room. "What a terrible loser," I said.

We both walked into the locker room where the scale was. I opened the door to the shower and out stepped my violinist playing "Hearts and Flowers." Williams was in a rage. . . . As I got on the scale the violinist played "Let a Winner Lead the Way." I weighed in at exactly 174 pounds.

Williams then got on the scale. I couldn't believe it. He was down from 220 to 199 pounds. I demanded a recount. The scale still showed 199. I had lost $500. . . .

It was one of the great upsets in diet history. Williams had lost twenty-one pounds in two weeks, probably nineteen of it in water.

My victory luncheon at the Sans Souci turned into a bitter meal of humiliation and abuse. . . . Now the only thing I have to show for my painful three months is a thank-you letter from Cardinal O'Boyle telling me how happy I made all the unmarried Catholic girls in Washington.

BUCHWALD: A THIRD TERM FOR NIXON!

On the night of June 17, 1972, a group of burglars financed by Nixon's Committee to Re-Elect the President—known as "CREEP"—broke into the Democratic National Committee headquarters at the Watergate office building in Washington, D.C. After the intruders were arrested, Nixon and his political aides engaged in an elaborate cover-up to prevent the scandal from destroying his presidency. For the next two years the White House was transformed into a bizarre and menacing theater of the absurd, with the media churning out daily reports of campaign dirty tricks, bribery, corruption, and alleged criminal activity at the highest levels of the executive branch. Each week, especially with the almost daily revelations uncovered by *Washington Post* reporters Bob Woodward and Carl Bernstein, something new and shocking was revealed about Nixon's White House and the antics of his "palace guard."

While Buchwald was outraged and disturbed by the Watergate scandal, he still wrote about the affair with his usual touch of wit and satire. In a February 24, 1974, column he presented an imaginary conversation with a psychiatrist named Dr. Sieg Fried Siegfreed, who propounded a theory on why Watergate was important to the morale of the country. "It has comedy, mystery and melodrama. I would prefer that it have a little sex as well but we can't have everything," Buchwald's imaginary Dr. Siegfreed pronounced. "Without

Watergate you would have a mass mental depression in this country. I maintain that Watergate is the glue that keeps the nation from falling apart."

As a political satirist Buchwald was thrilled by the scandalous material provided by Nixon and his aides, and he was delighted to be along for the ride. "I consider myself the cruise director on the *Titanic*," he told a crowd in Hamilton, Ohio. His greatest concern, however, as he playfully told readers and audiences around the country, was that Nixon might eventually be driven from office. "Let me make this perfectly clear," he repeated time and again during the spring of 1974, "I'm neither for impeachment or resignation. As a humor columnist, I need Nixon. He's been great for me. I'm going to run him for a third term."

By the summer of 1974, the scandal had so overwhelmed the Nixon presidency that Buchwald proposed in his column a new public relations strategy for the embattled president: "stay out of Washington as much" as possible. In a July 1974 column titled "Nixon Game Plan: A Moving Target," Buchwald concocted a conversation with Secretary of State Henry Kissinger about a possible itinerary for a presidential on-the-road strategy. When Kissinger suggested that the chief executive climb Mount Everest as part of Operation "Moving Target," Nixon inquired, "Henry, why would I want to climb Everest? To be the first president of the United States ever to hold a summit talk on a summit?—I like it."

Despite the fun Buchwald was having at Nixon's expense, some of Art's readers weren't laughing. "For the life of me, I can't understand why a newspaper would continue printing the garbage that [Buchwald] puts out," one disgruntled reader from Bloomington, Illinois, wrote. "If he ever wants or decides to leave [the country] I would gladly pay his one way ticket." Another reader, from Lexington, Kentucky, was a bit more graphic in his criticism. "I think if Art Buchwald had lived at the time Jesus was on earth that he would have unceremoniously shoved, kicked and cursed his own friends and relatives, while trying to get to be the first one to spit on Jesus Christ."

But Buchwald was undeterred, telling one reporter, in a brief moment of serious reflection about Watergate, that he had "a sense of outrage about the whole White House thing, mainly because I feel like they've taken me for a sucker," he said. "I think that's why the American people are angry with Nixon. He's taken them for patsies. He keeps giving out this junk, saying it's the whole story. But they're not stupid and neither am I. If they're going to play with me, I'll play with them."

By late July 1974, things looked bleak for Nixon's presidency. With ongoing investigations by a special prosecutor and impeachment hearings by the House Judiciary Committee, the pressure mounted on Nixon to resign—especially after the release of a secretly recorded conversation on August 5 between the president and his chief of staff, H. R. Haldeman, which showed an effort by Nixon to cover up the investigation of the break-in. It was the "smoking gun" destined to destroy his presidency.

Finally, on August 8, 1974, Richard M. Nixon resigned. On the evening he announced his decision to the American people, Art Buchwald was on hand at the White House press briefing room to watch Nixon's historic speech. "What impressed me more than anything else was that while one leader of our country was resigning and another was taking his place, I did not see one tank or one helmeted soldier in the street, and the only uniforms I saw that night were two motorcycle policemen who were directing traffic on Pennsylvania Avenue. Two hundred million people were able to change presidents overnight without one bayonet being unsheathed."

"YOU'RE OUR SON OF A BITCH"

A little over two months after Nixon's resignation, Art Buchwald attended a dinner at Antioch College in honor of his friend Edward Bennett Williams. As attorney for *The Washington Post*, Williams had incurred the wrath of Nixon and his top aides during the Watergate scandal, eventually earning him a spot on the president's notorious "enemies list." "We're going after him," Nixon once told his chief of staff. "We're going to fix the son of a bitch."

At the dinner honoring Williams on October 16, 1974, Buchwald gave his own account of his friend's illustrious career:

> Edward Bennett Williams is a legend in his own time. . . . His name is a household word in every part of America—Sing Sing, San Quentin, Lewisburg, Leavenworth, Atlanta and Allenwood.
>
> This crowd would have been twice as large tonight if the people Williams defended had been able to get furloughs from their parole boards.
>
> Edward Bennett Williams believes that every man, no matter how innocent, deserves a lawyer. To paraphrase Will Rogers: "Williams has never met a man he couldn't plead."
>
> I know what you all are asking, "How did Ed Bennett Williams become the great legal hero he is today?"
>
> Ed Bennett Williams was born in a small condominium in Hartford, Connecticut. He used to walk three blocks to school every morning. And three blocks back every evening. Education meant that much to him.
>
> One day as he was walking home from school, he saw a man being led out of an insurance company building in handcuffs, surrounded by FBI agents.
>
> "What did that man do?" little Eddie asked a policeman.
>
> "He embezzled twenty million dollars from widows and orphans."
>
> "What will happen to him?" Ed asked.
>
> "He will go to prison."
>
> That incident changed Ed Bennett Williams' life.
>
> Incensed by the injustice of it all, Ed vowed he would become a trial lawyer, and see that men who embezzled money from widows and orphans would never go to jail again.
>
> After attending Holy Cross and Georgetown Law School, Ed

opened a law office to fight for the underdog. But when he discovered underdogs don't pay their bills, he opened his practice to anybody. Although he has defended Senator Joe McCarthy . . . Adam Clayton Powell, Frank Costello, Bobby Baker, and Ben Bradlee, Williams has never forgotten his humble beginnings. Not one insurance company executive has ever gone to prison for embezzling from a widow or an orphan since Edward Bennett Williams passed his bar exam.

Many tributes have been paid to this legal giant, but I imagine the greatest honor that has ever been bestowed on him was when President Richard Nixon, in one of his more lucid moments, called Eddie a son of a bitch.

The exact quote on the tapes was, "I think we are going to fix the son of a bitch. I wouldn't want to be Edward Bennett Williams after the election." . . .

I'd just like to say, Eddie, you may be a son of a bitch, but you're our son of a bitch—which is more than we can say for Richard Nixon. And I say this for all of us. We thank God that before they got you, you were the first one to get them.

ANOTHER GLASS OF OVALTINE FOR "DEEP THROAT," PLEASE

While *Washington Post* investigative journalists Bob Woodward and Carl Bernstein were pursuing their investigation of President Richard Nixon and his top aides, one of their key informants was a clandestine source known as "Deep Throat." According to Watergate legend, for over thirty years only three people—Woodward, Bernstein, and *Post* managing editor Ben Bradlee—knew Deep Throat's true identity. However, when Bob Woodward saw a magazine photo of Art Buchwald having lunch at the Sans Souci in the fall of 1977, with a mysterious guest whose right arm only is seen reaching for a glass on the table, Woodward decided to have a bit of good-natured fun with Art about the identity of his shadowy luncheon companion:

The Washington Post
1150 15th Street, N.W.
Washington, D. C. 20071

Art,

Deep Throat asked that I pass along his deepest thanks. It was thoughtful of you to have them airbrush out his body and face. Though it looks like you are having lunch with just a hand, he thinks—in fact, is sure—no one will recognize him. Of course, the half empty glass of Ovaltine gives away something.

Woodward

SAY AMEN, ART BUCHWALD, SAY AMEN

Laughing Through the Carter Years (1976–79)

Sometimes I really believe that this entire government's only purpose is to provide me with material for my columns.

—ART BUCHWALD, OCTOBER 1977

ANN MCGARRY BUCHWALD

Although Ann Buchwald once jokingly referred to herself as "the other Buchwald," for over forty years she played an important, prominent, and lively role in the long and storied "Buchwald saga." While much of Art's rapid success as a columnist was due to the popularity of his political wit, Ann's charming personality and hard work helped pave the way for their rise in Washington's celebrity-driven society. Friends admired the fact that they were both level-headed, kept their ambitions in check, and never really took any of their fame seriously. "We're not striving," Ann said. "We're just really grateful. Art is very down to earth and I am down to earth, sort of Irish superstitious."

People were particularly drawn to Ann's winning personality. She was "charmingly unspoiled by their years in Paris," one reporter noted after an interview. Anyone who spent time with her was immediately impressed by her intelligence, "uninhibited" spirit, and "effervescent," "bouncy," and "friendly" personality. Lady Bird Johnson, the wife of President Lyndon Johnson, once praised Ann for her "blithe spirit, her lively wit and the range of her talents." She was a Washington host and hostess's dream come true, a "wonderful listener with a perky air," one admirer said. "She is the person you are happy to get placed next to at a dinner party."

As Art's stature grew, Ann had the difficult chore of balancing what she described as the "whole jazz of housekeeping" with her own yearnings for an independent career. "I don't think there is anything worse than a wife walking two paces behind her husband, wondering if he will introduce her," she once said. During the 1960s she had often helped Ethel Kennedy with fundraising events, and in 1965 became an author in her own right when she cowrote *White Gloves and Party Manners* with Marjabelle Young, a helpful guide to etiquette for children and young adults, and three years later a book of etiquette for boys, *Stand Up, Shake Hands, Say "How Do You Do,"* a book that sold especially well in Brooks Brothers department stores. Then in 1975, her third book, *What to Do, When and Why*, a handbook of advice for pre-teen girls (also coauthored with Marjabelle Young), was published. After its release she sent a copy to Rose Kennedy, the matriarch of the Kennedy family, who wrote back with a letter of thanks:

JANUARY 29, 1976

Dear Mrs. Buchwald:

Thank you very much for sending your book. . . . The article on eating asparagus particularly interested me. Before we went to England, I told my children to be especially careful about their manners and I gave them admonitions as you did about eating asparagus with forks. At one of our first embassy dinners, to my surprise and the amusement of my eldest offspring who were present, the British promptly discarded their forks and used their fingers!

The message nearest to my heart is to thank you and Art for the many occasions when you both have shown solicitude for Ethel and the children and have brought them cheer and encouragement on some of the difficult days. Ethel has often spoken of you both and all of us Kennedys certainly appreciate your thoughtfulness. . . .

My love, dear Mrs. Buchwald, to you and Art and if you are ever near do come to see me here at Palm Beach. You will receive a warm welcome.

Sincerely,
Rose F. Kennedy

In the early part of the 1970s, Ann became a Washington, D.C.–based literary agent affiliated with the colorful West Coast agent Irving "Swifty" Lazar, but parted ways with Lazar four years later after he took on former President Richard Nixon as a client. Without missing a beat, however, Ann went out on her own and quickly became one of Washington's "hottest literary agents," negotiating book deals for journalist Nancy Dickerson and Tommy "The Cork" Corcoran, lobbyist, political insider, and adviser to President Franklin D. Roosevelt.

In 1977, Ann returned to her own literary pursuits when she and Art teamed up to cowrite a memoir about their years together in Paris titled *Seems Like Yesterday*. Although written primarily by Ann, the narrative is periodically "interrupted" by Art's personal recollections of events or, in some cases, proffered "corrections." The book was well received by critics, with one reviewer calling it a "hilarious account of the Buchwalds' courtship and marriage." During the book tour, Art occasionally joined Ann along the way, including an appearance together on *Larry King Live*, and a memorable scene during a stopover in New York City when, in the middle of Ann's interview with UPI reporter Julianne Hastings, Art made a cameo appearance:

"Tell me, Mrs. Buchwald, what is it about Art that first attracted you to him?"

Bang! The door to the bathroom of the hotel suite flies open.

Out plods Art Buchwald in a sleeveless, white T-shirt and grey flannel pants, wet hair plastered back, steamed-up glasses slipping down his nose, a fat cigar hanging out of his mouth and a folded shirt tucked under his arm.

As the famed columnist pads by, stoop-shouldered, in his bare feet, his wife motions towards him with a sweep of her hand: "The great romantic figure."

While juggling her own career as a writer and literary agent, Ann still had three children to raise and a house to run. "Marriage is work," she once said, and she put up with a lot from Art, including the many difficult aspects of his life and work: his periodic bouts with depression, the move from Paris to Washington, his constant travels out on the lecture circuit, the public feud with Joe Alsop, and the months he spent away from home while working on *Sheep on the Runway*.

But there were still times when Buchwald could turn on the youthful charm reminiscent of their days in Paris. One night, in the mid-1970s, while the couple were in bed watching a Fred Astaire and Ginger Rogers movie, Ann lamented the fact that she and Art never danced anymore. After she wandered into the living room to brood, Buchwald appeared a few minutes later "having first donned full dress, top hat, tails and a pair of sneakers." With him he had a "tape recorder blaring music by Lester Lanin" and then asked Ann, "Would you like to dance?"

Living and working with a celebrated funny man had its moments of stress and strain, but the Buchwalds made it work. "Many of [Ann's] friends . . . criticized her for catering to my whims," Art wrote in the late 1970s. "Most of them have been married two and three times. We're still together, so we must be doing something right."

RICH MAN, POOR MAN

On Sunday, February 1, 1976, the television miniseries *Rich Man, Poor Man* premiered on ABC Television. Based on Irwin Shaw's bestselling novel, the twelve-part series starring Peter Strauss, Nick Nolte, and Susan Blakely was a phenomenal overnight success. It was one of the top-rated shows on television for two months and eventually went on to win four Emmys and four Golden Globe awards. Shortly after the third episode aired, Buchwald wrote his friend in Switzerland about the incredible reception the series was receiving back in America:

FEBRUARY 13, 1976

Dear Irwin:

Just a short note to tell you that I have been watching RICH MAN, POOR MAN and I thought you would like to know that never in the history of publishing has one book gotten such exposure on television. Every time they go to the commercial and come back they show the cover of the book, so in a one hour show that's about 14 times. As you probably know, you are knocking them dead in ratings. It's really a well done show. . . . Whether or not you know it, you are becoming a household word in this country now through a medium I know you hate. But God knows there is nothing like it when it comes to becoming famous.

Naturally I am very pleased when any of my friends do well and want to assure you that while you are in Switzerland, you are doing very well in the United States. I mean VERY well.

I guess I shall end this letter with a request for a loan, but I really don't need any money at this time. Maybe in the future, but not right now.

All kidding aside, I can't tell you what something like this can do for a writer. I have never seen it before. . . . It's really great.

Someone told me you felt shafted by ABC because they are using 12 hours instead of six. It may make some difference for you financially, but as an exploitation and publicity vehicle, it's unreal.

Love,

Art

On February 24, 1976, Shaw responded:

P.O. Box 39
Klosters, Switzerland

Dear Art,
... Rich Man, Poor Man has become an event rather than a book. Although as you know I live a Spartan and economical existence, and hardly need more than $100,000 every three months to keep body and soul together, I am not altogether displeased by the fact that my publishers have now put out 2 million copies of the paperback and are talking about 3 million. And they're using the cover shown on the tube, as even publishers these days are likely from time to time to show a grain of sense.

I don't think I ever complained about them showing part of the show in one hour segments. That's their business. I don't know about the artistic merits of the show, but whoever was responsible sure knows how to sell....

Something that never happened to me before happened last night. Some guy from Disneyland in Florida called up to ask me to come there just to autograph books—completely at their expense. Maybe I'll run for some political office.

Anytime you want to ask for a loan ask, I have some Israeli bonds you might be interested in....

> *Love to all,*
> *Irwin*

VINEYARD HUES

Buchwald loved spending summers on Martha's Vineyard—"Its own sort of heaven," he would say. It was a time to relax with his wife, Ann, and family, clear his head, socialize with friends, and, above all, laugh and joke far from the social and political madness of Washington. "If you like the sea, you can go to the sea. If you like sailing, you sail. If you like to look for mussels or clams, you can do that," he once said of life on the Vineyard. But for Art it was mostly a time to "read, eat spaghetti, eat lobster, do a little work and entertain." Gatherings in Vineyard Haven with old friends such as William and Rose Styron, Kay Graham, Edward and Agnes Williams, Mike Wallace, Walter Cronkite, Carly Simon, and members of the Kennedy family were a joy, especially because it was all out of the celebrity limelight.

He started going to the island in the mid-1960s upon the recommendation of Richard Goodwin, adviser and speechwriter to President John F. Kennedy. At first he rented a house next door to William and Rose Styron, but then purchased his own home in Vineyard Haven in the same neighborhood as the Styrons, Lillian Hellman, and John Hersey. (When Hersey, author of A Bell for Adano, Hiroshima, and The Wall, died in 1993, Buchwald wrote to his wife, Barbara, "What a loss we have suffered. John was my idol when I was a kid and he was my role model when I grew up. I have never known anyone as modest or as kind as John. Believe it or not, when I was in his presence I was in awe of him. He is still with us through his books—each one more wonderful than the last. His friends must rejoice in the fact that we knew him. Obviously, we all miss him very much and the Vineyard will never be the same without him.")

Each August one of Buchwald's great delights was to be the emcee—sometimes while decked out in a cowboy hat—of the annual auction to raise funds for the Martha's Vineyard Community Services program, which provided support for daycare, medical assistance, and counseling services for island residents. In the "Possible Dreams" auction, the items up for bid were once-in-a-lifetime experiences with the rich and famous, such as a sail with Walter Cronkite, a walk across the Brooklyn Bridge with historian David McCullough, tea for eight with Kay Graham, or cocktails for four with Lillian Hellman.

Members of the Kennedy family occasionally sailed over from Hyannis Port to spend time on the Vineyard with Jackie Kennedy, the Styrons, and the Buchwalds, often heading to the beach for a picnic or to Vineyard Haven for a tennis match. And, of course, there were the inevitable lively and adventurous summer sailing excursions and legendary touch football games at the Kennedy compound in Hyannis Port. During the summer of 1966, the editors of the *Vineyard Gazette* had some fun with the results of a mock Gallup Poll about "how the Buchwald family enjoyed their weekend at Hyannisport" with the Kennedys:

> When questioned as to whether they would rather play touch football with the Kennedys or go to Vietnam:
>
> 94 percent said they'd rather go to Vietnam
> 3 percent said they'd rather play water polo
> 3 percent said they'd rather play "Russian Roulette."
>
> Those questioned were then given a list of people and asked to give their preference as to whom they'd like to crew for in a sailboat race:

Senator Teddy Kennedy	2.3 percent
Senator Bobby Kennedy	1.7 percent
Joe Kennedy, Jr.	6.5 percent
Eunice Shriver	8.5 percent
Captain Bligh	56.9 percent

In late June 1978, just as the Buchwalds were preparing for their annual summer vacation on the Vineyard, Ethel Kennedy received a letter from a doctor at Georgetown University Hospital who claimed to be writing, in the "utmost confidence," on behalf of Art to inform her that Buchwald was suffering from a peculiar form of the "Mal-de-Mer Syndrome," a condition which most likely would prevent him from sailing with the Kennedys that summer. The effects of this disorder, the doctor explained, came about whenever Art swallowed "as much as one mouthful of salt water" or heard the simplest order to adjust sails on a boat. To make matters even worse, the doctor warned, the slightest tipping of a boat at sea could aggravate his weakened condition and "induce sterility and severe acne." When Ethel Kennedy received the report on Art, she wasn't buying any of it:

JULY 14, 1978

Dear Doc—

Thank you for your letter concerning Art Buchwald and his personal problems.

Confidentially, after several lunches at Sans Souci, I wondered about the state of his health. The symptoms you mentioned: bulging eyes, heightened complexion, slurred speech and the weak bladder were all there. Wishing to get a second opinion—no offense—I contacted ... a noted kidney expert at Bar Harbor, Maine. Begging your pardon, he said Washington doctors are far too inland to recognize Mal de Mer. He felt that the best cure for the patient—and here I'm afraid he mixed up his metaphors—is to get right back up on his horse....

I agree with this world renowned expert—the best cure for someone like our friend Art with his weak kidney is to wash his hands, take a large dose of alum, hop on board the Resolute, *relax and enjoy, and, if worse comes to worse, go before the mast. But not if women and children are on board.*

Something else I think you should be privy to (darn it, I don't know how that word crept in there), Artie has said that lots of times while waiting for you—he is overcome by the same anguish and has taken steps right there in your reception room to obtain relief....

I'm a firm believer that the best doctor is the one who puts himself in his patients' sheets. So I think you should accompany Artie on his next trip aboard the Resolute....

Respectfully and in deep confidence and here's to the Hippocratic oath—

Love,
Ethel

"THE STINGS OF WASP PREJUDICE"

Buchwald once described Ben Bradlee as "the perfect Renaissance man." He was "handsome, he'd gone to all the right schools, his French was perfect, and he was a straight shooter," Buchwald wrote admiringly of his friend. "He also had humor, and we took an instant liking to one another." On July 29, 1975, Art paid tribute to Bradlee at a celebration of his tenth year as managing editor of *The Washington Post*. In his remarks Buchwald offered a "mini-roast" of his friend with a chronicle of the many "challenges" Bradlee had faced while growing up as a member of the White Anglo-Saxon Protestant establishment:

> Everyone knows about Ben Bradlee as a professional man, but there is little known about his childhood. I was going through his garbage the other night and I found a biography that sheds new light on Ben and explains much of his behavior today.
>
> On a warm, hot night 53 years ago, Ben Bradlee was born to Mr. and Mrs. Frederick Bradlee in the white Anglo-Saxon Protestant ghetto on Beacon Hill in Boston, Massachusetts. Ben's father was a banker which was one of the few professions open to a WASP at that time.
>
> In those days in Boston WASPS were discriminated against everywhere. They couldn't get into Jewish country clubs; they were turned away from soul food restaurants; the Mafia wouldn't let them into their families and the Kennedys refused to let them dance with their daughters.
>
> At an early age Ben felt the stings of WASP prejudice. He applied to six public high schools in Boston, but their quota of Protestants had already been filled. So Ben's father had no choice but to bus him to St. Mark's Prep School which had been financed by the Rockefellers to educate underprivileged Beacon Hill children.
>
> Ben became a student leader at St. Mark's and formed the Anglo-Saxon Liberation Front, dedicated to eliminating discrimi-

nation against WASPS at the local Polish candy store. He edited the school paper and despite strong opposition from the administration, printed complete excerpts from the King James version of the Bible.

After graduating from St. Mark's with honors, Ben found the doors of most universities closed. . . . The only schools that would take a WASP in those days were Harvard, Yale and Princeton. Ben chose Harvard which was not the best school, but the one closest to home.

At Harvard Ben worked hard to prove that WASPS were as good as anybody else. He was the first one in the library in the morning and the last one to leave at night. But despite his efforts to be part of the school, he felt the coolness that he had experienced all his life because of his ethnic background. He was blackballed from the Hungarian Hasty Pudding Club and the exclusive Japanese-American Friendship Society. When he went to a Harvard-Yale football game at New Haven, he couldn't get a table at Mory's. The only girls who would date him were coeds from Vassar, Radcliffe and Smith.

Once he tried to march in a Sons of St. Patrick's parade and they threw him out on his ear.

All these incidents left marks on Ben. He decided if he was ever going to help his people he would go into journalism and tell the WASP story to the world.

But Pearl Harbor intervened and Ben, despite the way he had been treated, chose to fight for his country.

It's hard to believe that in that day and age the prejudice in the Navy was so strong that the only thing a WASP could become was an officer. There was an unwritten rule that a WASP could never serve as a mess boy or deck swabber or paint scraper—the things that Ben dreamed of being all his life.

But Bradlee took his commission cheerfully and never let on his bitterness at having been relegated to an officer's deck chair for the entire war.

In the South Pacific Bradlee fought bravely and won ten battle stars. It was one of these actions at the height of fearful combat, with shells whistling over his head, and torpedoes careening around him and the depth charges blowing waves over the bridge that Bradlee decided he would like to become a reporter for *The Washington Post....*

The rest is history. Thanks to Ben Bradlee WASPS can go almost anywhere in this country without being turned away because of their blond hair or their plain small noses.

They can now get into state universities, have jobs with oil companies and insurance firms, and automobile dealerships that were once closed to them.... In less than 20 years, White Anglo-Saxon Protestants have made enormous strides in the United States and they owe it all to one man: BENJAMIN C. BRADLEE.

"ASK YOUR MOTHER OR FATHER FOR A DANCE"

Although Buchwald was a master of satire, he could occasionally delight readers and audiences with thoughtful words of advice. On May 25, 1975, he delivered the commencement address at Vassar College in Poughkeepsie, New York. His speech to the graduating class was so well received that excerpts were reprinted in *The New York Times* and in newspapers around the country, including such cities as St. Joseph, Missouri; Bennington, Vermont; Butte, Montana; Burlington, North Carolina; and Canandaigua, New York:

My Fellow Americans:

... The tendency in this country is to wring our hands and say everything is rotten. But I don't feel this way. I am basically an optimist....

I don't know if this is the best of times or the worst of times, but I can assure you of this: This is the only time you've got—and you can either sit on your asses or go out and pick a daisy.

We seem to be going through a period of nostalgia now and everyone seems to think yesterday was better than today. I personally don't think it was, and I would advise you not to wait ten years from now before admitting today was great. If you're hung up on nostalgia, pretend today is yesterday and go out and have one hell of a time. I have traveled across this great land of ours and I have heard the cries of despair. People ask: "What can we do to make things better?" Even today you are probably asking this question as you sit out there in rapt attention listening to my brilliant words. Well, here are some things you can do right after graduation:

Throw a baseball to a little girl.

Ask your teacher for his or her autograph.

Take a shower with a friend.

Ask your mother or father for a dance.

Throw a kiss to a little old lady.

And, take a walk in the woods with someone you love.

There's a lot to be done. And being an optimist, I believe that somewhere out in the class of 1975 is a scientist who will develop a flip-top beer can that doesn't cut your finger. . . .

My final message is that no matter what you read in the newspapers or see on television, I assure you that we're all going to make it. For 200 years this country has muddled through one crisis after another and we have done it without changing our form of government. It seems like centuries ago, but it is less than a year, that a President of the United States was forced to resign from office under the darkest clouds and he was asked to leave the office because he lied to the American people. . . . I believe that any country in the world that can still do that, can't be all bad.

"MAKING IT IN AMERICA"

On July 4, 1976, millions of Americans celebrated the country's bicentennial with a dazzling array of loud and glorious celebrations.

In New York Harbor a majestic "armada" of 225 tall ships was on full display. And later that night a glittering spectacle of fireworks illuminated the harbor and the Statue of Liberty. In true American style it was a "day of mammoth presentations," reported *The New York Times*, "with pageantry and prayer, with games and parades, with picnics and fireworks, with the peal of bells and the chant of protests."

For Art Buchwald, however, the day was something much more personal. In a Sunday, July 4, 1976, column he wrote a remembrance of his father, Joseph, who had died nearly two years earlier. Despite the sad and painful memories of his childhood, Art had never stopped loving his dad, and in his column that day he paid tribute not only to his father but to the nation that had embraced him when he first arrived in America as an immigrant at the turn of the century. "Dear Pop," Buchwald wrote. "The thing I shall always remember is how you ... kept telling me there was no better place to live.... Well, Pop ... I don't know if all those great men in 1776 had you immigrants in mind when they signed the Declaration of Independence ... but even if they didn't, they made it possible for you and millions like you to come to a free land."

In late January 1979, Buchwald received a letter from an African American social worker who was counseling drug-addicted youths in an impoverished section of New York City. As part of their rehabilitation program the counselor required that his patients read the works of a variety of noted American authors and commentators, including Buchwald, to provide some diversion and positive inspiration while they worked toward recovery. In his letter the caseworker told Buchwald that his writings had been well received by his patients and, in fact, several had questions for him about a writer's life.

On February 6, 1979, Buchwald responded with this thoughtful letter:

It's very hard to answer your question, what gives literary work lasting importance? The only thing I can say is, it is probably that the works which survive are those that can be read by future generations and understood. For example, Romeo and Juliet *has lasted all these years mainly because the story and plot haven't changed much. Unrequited love and tragedy seem to be a universal malady.*

In answer to the second part of your question, being blessed with creativity, or whatever the hell it is—it has to be a blessing if someone will pay you for it. If you don't get published it can be very frustrating, and you can get terribly paranoid and angry if nobody is listening. I don't find it a lonely life. People talk to me all the time. I think the nice thing about the work I do, is that I am filled with hostility, and I have an outlet for it three times a week.

Your discussion group sounds very interesting and I admire the fact that you are devoting time to writing. I obviously cannot claim to know what it is like to live in Bedford-Stuyvesant, but I can appreciate how books can help you get over a lot of rough moments. My background was that I was in orphanages and then put into a series of foster homes. My salvation was the public library. Through books I was able to escape into another world where nobody could touch me. I have a feeling that is what you are trying to do, and I wish you luck in getting the people in your group to find some escape through the written word.

Sincerely,
Art Buchwald

"WALK AND CHEW GUM AT THE SAME TIME"

On January 20, 1977, James Earl Carter, Jr., former governor and peanut farmer from Plains, Georgia, was sworn in as the thirty-ninth president of the United States. Carter's 1976 long-shot presidential campaign, against many better-known Democratic party regulars, had quickly caught the attention of American voters impressed by his folksy style and Washington outsider status. From the start Buchwald knew Carter would be a good mark for satire. "He said at the beginning of his campaign that he'd never lie to us," Art said. "Any man who says that, I think, will be a very good target."

The new president and his team brought a common touch to the presidency, in stark contrast to the turbulent years of Watergate and Vietnam and the imperial-like presidency of Nixon. When Carter and his wife, Rosalynn, *walked* rather than rode from the U.S. Capitol to the White House after the inauguration, Buchwald, like many Americans, was astonished. But Art had a ready answer in his column: "When President Carter decided to take the walk, his aides and the Secret Service tried to talk him out of it. But he was adamant and told them, 'I have to show the country I can walk and chew gum at the same time.'"

But public response to the walk was nothing compared to the reaction after the new president carried his own bags. "People are actually arguing whether Jimmy Carter should carry his own luggage or not," Buchwald quipped. It was an issue which soon divided the nation's capital into two factions: the "Pro-Carter-Luggage-Carrier" people versus the "Anti-Carter-Luggage-Carrier" people. The antis, Buchwald conceded with amusement, had several persuasive points. Not only was it unpresidential for a chief executive to carry his own bags, but, in a still-wary post-Watergate America, many felt anxious and suspicious about a president carrying suitcases. "What's he hiding?" people would ask. Others, however, had more tangible concerns, worried that if such a superficial gesture was imitated by others, it could cause a spike in unemployment by putting thousands of baggage handlers and porters out of work. In the end, Buchwald was firmly in the "Pro" camp. "I side with the 'Pro-Carter-Luggage-Carrier' people on the theory that it shows the man who has his finger on the [nuclear] button is not too big to also have his hand on his own Samsonite" suitcase.

"A GUTSY EVEL KNIEVEL"

When President-elect Carter announced on December 22, 1976, that he was appointing Joseph Califano as the new secretary of the Department of Health, Education, and Welfare, Buchwald's reaction was bittersweet. Although he was thrilled that his longtime friend would soon become a part of the new administration, he was saddened by the fact that as a member of the cabinet—with his own chauffeur-driven limousine—Califano would no longer be able to serve as the designated carpool driver for Sunday football outings to RFK Stadium. As a law partner of Edward Bennett Williams, who was co-owner of the Washington Redskins, Califano had a designated parking spot near the stadium that made him the obvious choice to be in charge of the Sunday carpool. Hours before each home game, Califano would make the rounds in his green Ford station wagon gathering his crew: Ben Bradlee, Jack Valenti, Art Buchwald, and an assortment of children huddled in the back for the trip to RFK Stadium. Along the way Buchwald would inevitably tease and pester Califano with a barrage of directives and complaints about his car and his driving, wondering when he was going to trade in the old Ford, warning him about pedestrians or jaywalkers, constantly offering a host of opinions on anything that happened to pop into his head on the way to the game.

Soon after Califano's nomination, Buchwald felt it was his patriotic duty to tell the world about the Joe Califano *he* knew—the man behind the wheel. In an amusing column published in January 1977, Buchwald depicted a fictitious interview he had with the FBI during a background check on the new HEW nominee. When asked what type of person Califano was, Buchwald responded, "He's a gutsy Evel Knievel. Knievel has jumped over fourteen chartered Greyhound buses on a motorcycle, but Califano is the only man I know who has ever tried to drive straight *through* them." When queried about any "prejudices" Califano might have, Art shot back, "He hates red lights."

When asked to list one of Califano's "best traits," Buchwald proudly proclaimed his patriotic spirit. "I've seen him side-swipe an ambulance rather than miss the Redskins band playing the 'Star-Spangled Banner.'"

Years later Joseph Califano would recall with great delight the impact Art's column had on his staffing search at HEW. For days after the piece ran, whenever Califano was wrapping up an interview with a potential department employee, he would end by asking the applicant, "Do you have any questions for *me*?"—a query that often prompted the reply, "Yes, do you *really* drive the way Art Buchwald says you do?"

"THE FEMALE ART BUCHWALD"

While having lunch with Art one day at the Sans Souci restaurant, Russell Baker complained that the joy had finally gone out of their lunches. The only reason for them to get together anymore, a dispirited Baker told him, was to try and "steal column ideas from each other" and even that wasn't working anymore. In order to breathe new life into their luncheons, Buchwald suggested they form an eating club "like they have at Princeton." Not "enough prestige," Baker replied. "Why not an academy?" Excited that they now had something to justify their lunch dates, the two agreed to call their new group "The American Academy of Humor." When the question of membership arose, they mulled over the names of several humorists, but were unable to agree on any of the potential candidates. Suddenly, Buchwald blurted out, "Why not Erma Bombeck? She is very funny and makes three times as much as we do."

For nearly two decades Erma Bombeck had been a successful author and humorist with her column, "At Wit's End," which provided amusing commentary on life in suburban America. Raised in Dayton, Ohio, Bombeck got her start in journalism in high school when she was hired as a part-time reporter for the local newspaper, where she scored her first journalistic scoop by landing an interview with Shirley Temple. In the early 1960s she started writing a regular column for a weekly newspaper, the *Kettering-Oakwood Times*, that became so popular it soon went into national syndication, eventually appearing in more than nine hundred newspapers with a readership of more than thirty million in the United States and Canada. She was also the author of several bestselling books, including *The Grass Is Always Greener Over the Septic Tank*; *If Life Is a Bowl of Cherries, What Am I Doing in the Pits?*; and *When You Look Like Your Passport Photo, It's Time to Go Home.*

On May 29, 1978, *Time* magazine published a feature article, "She-Wits and Funny Persons," chronicling the recent publishing success of books by American humorists Nora Ephron, Fran Lebowitz, and Erma Bombeck. In the article, Bombeck was praised as "the female Art Buchwald," prompting a kindly note from her friend and fellow member of the American Academy of Humor:

MAY 23, 1978

Dear Erma:

I read the TIME magazine piece in which you were described by friends as "the female Art Buchwald." This disturbs me very much as I was thinking of having a sex change operation because it now turns out that women humorists are making a lot more money than men. I don't know what to do, and Ann still has mixed feelings about it.

Sincerely,
Art

SAY AMEN, ART BUCHWALD, SAY AMEN

Another Buchwald soulmate was fellow columnist Esther Pauline "Eppie" Lederer, known to the world as Ann Landers, whose question-and-answer column provided heart-to-heart advice to perplexed or troubled readers for nearly five decades. Born in Sioux City, Iowa, she and her identical twin sister, Pauline Esther Phillips (who would later become known for her own celebrated advice column, "Dear Abby"), learned their craft early on when they cowrote a gossip column for their college newspaper. In 1955, Lederer began writing the nationally syndicated "Ask Ann" column under the pen name Ann Landers, a name by which she would be forever known to some fifty million readers over a colorful forty-seven-year career.

In her October 4, 1978, column Ann Landers published a letter from an outraged reader about a twenty-five-year-old young man who was suing his mother and father for the sum of $350,000, alleging parental "malpractice" in raising their son. In response an equally incensed Landers included a quote from her friend Art Buchwald. "There are a lot more disappointed parents in this country than disappointed children," she quoted Art as saying. "After we send our kids to college and pay $40,000 to educate them, they should be able to read and write or give us our money back." To which Landers added in her column, "To that I say amen, Art Buchwald, amen."

After seeing himself quoted in her column, Buchwald wrote:

OCTOBER 6, 1978

Dear Eppie:

Thanks for the plug in your column. The reaction was immediate. Being mentioned in your column is now a higher status symbol than appearing in The New York Times *crossword puzzle.*

Less than a year later, in a June 1979 column titled "Advice to the Gas Worn: Just Ask Artie," Buchwald imitated the style of Ann Landers in a series of fabricated letters and answers between fictitious readers and a similarly fictitious advice columnist known as "Ask Artie." One of the more memorable letters was from a "Soulful Sarah":

Dear Artie:

My boyfriend uses leaded gasoline in his car, and I use unleaded gasoline in mine. He doesn't want to get serious because he says mixed marriages don't work. What do you think?

—Soulful Sarah

Dear Sarah:

As long as you respect the other person's fuel needs, love will prevail. Many mixed marriages wind up with one of the parties being catalytically converted.

—A.B.

While on a trip abroad Eppie Lederer happened to see the "Just Ask Artie" column during a stopover in Greece. Buchwald's new style prompted a quick note of warning:

Dear Artie:

Very funny—and I don't mind your getting into my act. Just don't get too good at it, honey. I need the job.

Love to you and Ann,
Eppie

"WHAT KIND OF FOOL . . ."

In the fall of 1979, Art Buchwald attended a dinner in honor of an old friend from the University of Southern California, film producer David Wolper. In the audience that night was British singer, songwriter, and actor Anthony Newley, perhaps best known for the songs "For Once in a Lifetime" and the 1963 Grammy Award-winning "What Kind of Fool Am I?," both cowritten with Leslie Bricusse and both from the 1962 Broadway hit *Stop the World—I Want to Get Off.*

After his appearance that night, Newley wrote Buchwald:

NOVEMBER 16, 1979

Dearest Art:

You were so funny last night that very few of us performers present will ever forgive you. Make me one promise. If you're not too old to mount a podium by the time it takes place, would you be the master of ceremonies at my first tribute?

> *Love and admiration,*
> *Tony N.*
> *xxx*

DECEMBER 4, 1979

Dear Tony:

Thank you so much for the nice words about my performance at David's bar mitzvah. You cannot believe what a thrill it is to get such a letter from you because I am one of your biggest admirers. Every time I strike out with a girl, I start singing to myself "What Kind of fool am I?" I haven't paid ASCAP [American Society of Composers, Authors, and Writers], for the performance rights but I assure you I owe a lot of money....

> *Cheers,*
> *Art*

"I'M DOING EXACTLY WHAT I WANT TO DO"

It's estimated that by the end of the 1970s, Art Buchwald had written nearly four thousand columns since joining the *Herald Tribune* in 1948. He had published more than twenty books of his collected pieces and was now out on the road almost once a week—giving at least forty-five speeches, lectures, or commencement addresses each year—all earning him an estimated $500,000 annually. (Just over $2 million today.)

Life was good for Art Buchwald and he was having the time of his life. "I love it. I love what I'm doin'. I love live audiences. I love the column," he told one reporter. "I'm doing exactly what I want to do in life." And the zaniness of the world—its politics and its politicians—was still treating him very well. "The world is getting crazier. It's gone absolutely mad," he told a reporter in October 1977. "Sometimes I really believe that this entire government's only purpose is to provide me with material for my columns."

JOINING THE HERTZ FIVE STAR CREDIT CARD CLUB

Goodbye Carter, Hello Reagan (1980s)

"A STRAIGHT FLUSH"

"I don't know if this made the European edition," Buchwald wrote Irwin Shaw on February 5, 1980, "but I felt you should keep up with this sort of thing." Art was referring to a column he had just written for the current issue of *Newsweek* magazine titled "Brother, Can You Spare a John?," a piece that proclaimed a national emergency for any Americans who might, in the course of a busy day, find themselves in desperate need of a public restroom. "While great strides have been made in this country to help the handicapped, the government has turned its back on people who must go to the john," Buchwald wrote in mock desperation. "In a society where everyone is guaranteed equal rights, there is no such thing as a free tinkle. . . . The time has come for the people to raise their voices in protest."

Few of the columns Buchwald wrote in his long career matched the colorful letters to the editor *Newsweek* received from readers across the country. One ecstatic reader wrote: "ART BUCHWALD FOR PRESIDENT! Tinkling isn't a right, it's a necessity."

Another praised Buchwald's courage to speak his mind: "As usual Mr. Buchwald gets a straight flush."

And finally this from a frustrated mother in Michigan:

> As a mother of a normal 6-year-old, I sympathize with you. On my last shopping trip, exactly 29 minutes and 30 seconds after leaving the house, the child's urges became noticeable. After ever so politely asking for the use of a public john, we were informed that it was "for employees only." Before the sale could be rung up, . . . the child informed everyone that the event had taken place.
>
> To my surprise, I felt no embarrassment. . . . I simply announced to my child . . . "It's alright sweetie—they don't want you to use their restroom—that's the reason they put nice carpet here." And with that, we stepped off the puddle and left!

"I WORSHIP THE VERY QUICKSAND HE WALKS ON"

On November 4, 1979, an enraged mob of more than five hundred Iranian students stormed the gates of the U.S. Embassy in Tehran. After taking control of the embassy compound, the students seized ninety hostages, including sixty-five Americans, and promptly vowed they would hold their captives until the deposed shah of Iran—who had been granted exile in America after his regime was toppled—was returned to Iran to face Islamic justice. More than just a political and diplomatic standoff, the hostage situation was quickly transformed into "television's first live Global Crisis Mini-Series," television critic Tom Shales of *The Washington Post* wrote. Soon, the "sight of chanting, fist-waving mobs" became such a part of the "fabric" of everyday life in America that Shales coined a new term for it all, calling it "Terrorvision."

As the hostage crisis dragged on, by March 1980 President Jimmy Carter's presidency—and his bid for reelection—were in deep trouble.

To many Americans he appeared weak and helpless in his unsuccessful efforts to free the American captives. And soon he faced a serious political challenge within his own party when Senator Edward M. Kennedy decided to make a bid for the 1980 Democratic nomination. On the Republican side, Ronald Reagan, a former Hollywood actor and governor of California, seemed the odds-on favorite to capture his party's nomination for president.

As the campaign got under way, Buchwald wrote to Irwin Shaw in Switzerland to assure him that the American political landscape was not as bad as it might seem from abroad. "Please don't get discouraged about the news from the U.S.," Art wrote. "As you know, Europeans never see the bright side of things over here, and tend to exaggerate Carter's ineptitude and Reagan's low intelligence."

Despite a bruising primary challenge from Kennedy, Carter was able to secure the nomination and go on to face the Republican nominee Ronald Reagan in the fall. During the campaign Buchwald pursued his long-held, self-imposed fairness doctrine of mocking both candidates. "I respect Carter," he quipped over and over again about the incumbent, "I worship the very quicksand he walks on." About the choice of candidates the voters had been presented with in November he joked, "At least 50% of the people aren't happy with either Carter or Reagan. What worries me is the 50% who *are* happy."

On November 4, 1980, Ronald Reagan defeated Jimmy Carter in a landslide victory, winning 489 electoral votes to Carter's 49. When Reagan was sworn in as the fortieth president of the United States on January 20, 1981, Art Buchwald was overjoyed, telling a packed crowd of students at Arizona State University that his "morale soared" as he watched the inauguration. "There will be some marvelous stuff for someone who has to make his living making fun of people."

And with that Art wasted little time getting down to funny business, taking direct aim at the contrasting Southern style of the outgoing Carter administration and the incoming West Coast chic of Reagan. "You can say what you will about the Reagan administration," he wrote, "but you can't deny it has turned Washington into the fashion capital of the world. All it took was a rich First Lady [Nancy Reagan] from California, and her richer friends, and suddenly this dusty, peanut-farming . . . town turned into a land of lynx and sable."

Almost immediately after Reagan took office, one of Buchwald's favorite targets in the new administration was the choice of James Watt as secretary of the interior. From the very beginning, the controversial Watt, caretaker of some 350 million acres of federal lands and parks, was a public relations nightmare, especially after he announced that under his stewardship, preservation and the environment would take a back seat to a less conservation-minded approach in his department. Finally, after two years of policy missteps and public gaffes, Reagan forced Watt to resign in the fall of 1983. When the embattled secretary stepped down from his post, Buchwald mockingly paid tribute to his departure with an imaginary dialogue between Watt and his horse Old Paint as the two rode off into the sunset:

> Well, Old Paint, our work is over. . . . I had great visions for this land. . . . I wanted every American to have a strip mine he could call his own. . . . If I'd had a few more years we would have had bulldozers down there in the valley, oil rigs in the hills, and all of that snow on the mountain could have been turned into acid rain.

NO MORE THREE-MARTINI LUNCHES

On September 23, 1981, nine months after Reagan took office, Democratic senator Gary Hart of Colorado introduced legislation to cut the federal tax deduction for business lunches by 30 percent in order to provide federal funds for "nutritionally balanced, low-cost or no-cost lunches to children." When Buchwald learned of Hart's proposal, he wrote a satirical piece titled "The Three-Martini Lunch Crowd: Let Them Eat Ketchup." In his column Art fabricated an imaginary dialogue with a Washington lobbyist named "Semple Simon" who, on behalf of the "Society to Protect the Free Business Lunch," claimed that for many corporate executives "it was the only decent meal" they had each day. "Look at [Hart's] proposal in human terms," Semple Simon said. "The minimum nutritional requirements for a business lunch include a cocktail, soup . . . smoked salmon, a main course of meat . . . dessert, coffee and a cigar. Where can you cut down on a meal like that without sending someone away hungry?"

After Senator Hart read the column, he decided to have a bit of fun with Buchwald:

United States Senate
Washington, D.C.

OCTOBER 28, 1981

Dear Art:

I've been meaning to write to thank you for your most generous and pointed column on my school lunch bill. As if that weren't enough, now you've given the proposal a further boost on the Phil Donahue Show.

I'm most flattered and grateful, and as a small token of appreciation I'd like to buy you lunch sometime. Of course, given my commitment to this bill and its principles (not to mention the fact that Senators can't claim the tax deduction for business meals anyway), we would dine on a USDA-approved school lunch, or a reasonable facsimile.

Should you prefer to go Dutch, I'd understand. In that case, our meal would look something like this:

Buchwald
3 martinis
Vichyssoise (bowl)
Spinach salad
Sauteed vegetables
Prime rib
Potatoes au gratin
Chocolate mousse
Coffee
Cigar

Hart

Water

Campbell's tomato soup (cup)

Leaf lettuce

Ketchup

Tofu patty

French fries (seven)

Water

In keeping with the spirit of things, of course, I'd expect you to claim only 70 percent of the cost of your meal on your expense account.

Thanks again, Art (in all seriousness). Let's keep in touch.

Sincerely,

Gary Hart

BUCHWALD AND BUCKLEY: "YALE MEN ALWAYS STICK TOGETHER"

By any measure William F. Buckley, Jr., was an extraordinary man who lived a *very* extraordinary life. He was an author, magazine publisher, conservative political commentator, skillful and penetrating debater, talk show host, spy novelist, avid and intrepid sailor, pianist and harpsichord player, winner of the Presidential Medal of Freedom, and patriarch of the modern conservative movement. Buckley came to national prominence in 1951 with his controversial book *God and Man at Yale.* Four years later he founded *National Review* magazine, which became one of the most influential voices in the creation of a viable and intellectually coherent conservative political philosophy. As columnist George Will once wrote, "All great Biblical stories begin with Genesis. Before Ronald Reagan there was Barry Goldwater and before Barry Goldwater there was *National Review* and before . . . *National Review,* there was Bill Buckley." Along with his singular intellect, he had a gift for humor marked by a keen, wry, satirical, and often self-deprecating wit.

Beginning in the late 1970s and into the 1980s, Buckley and Buchwald carried on a charming and entertaining correspondence. None of it concerned the political Left or political Right. It was all about mistaken identity, pride, good-natured competition, and who, in the end, could get the best credit card deal from the Hertz Rental Car Company. Their exchange first began on August 27, 1979, when Art received a note from Buckley informing him of a letter he had received from the Hertz corporation with an invitation to join its Five Star Credit Card club. The problem, however—as Buckley informed Buchwald—was that the letter *he* received had been addressed to a "MR. BUCHWALD." Art's curiosity quickly aroused, he wanted to know more:

AUGUST 27, 1979

Dear Bill:

Thank you so much for the note. The question is, who was the Hertz Five Star Credit Card made out to? If it was made out to you, I am terribly impressed, because the most I ever received from Hertz was a Three Star Credit Card. If the card was made out to you, could you get in a good word to [Hertz] for me. It's very embarrassing to go around Washington with a tattered old Hertz Card in my wallet.

Thank you so much.
Art Buchwald

Although gratified by the note from Buckley, Buchwald was riled about the obvious slight from the rental car giant. Taking matters into his own hands, he sent a letter to the top man at Hertz:

AUGUST 30, 1979

I am enclosing a letter addressed and sent to Mr. Buckley, although the salutation was to me.

This is my situation: were you offering Mr. Buckley or me a Five Star Credit Card? If you offered it to Mr. Buckley, I am deeply hurt, because I feel that I rate the same Five Star credit as he does.

Is Hertz discriminating in favor of conservative columnists?

I assure you that we liberals pay our bills just as fast—even faster than the conservatives. Also, liberals need the 30% discount far more than conservatives. It's true that I don't have a private aircraft, so you don't have to send a car to meet it. But I certainly would like your special unlisted toll-free number, as it would give me great status in the newspaper world.

I am certain that Mr. Buckley was very embarrassed to see that the letter was addressed to me. He doesn't want anybody to know that he gets 30% off Hertz. The only other thing I could guess is that Hertz is trying to make trouble between me and Mr. Buckley. You can't do it! Yale men always stick together.

Cheers,
Art Buchwald

Upon receipt of Buchwald's note, the chagrined president of Hertz sent a letter apologizing for the mistake along with assurances that yes, indeed, Buchwald was welcome to join the Five Star Club. Moreover, because of the embarrassment caused by the error, a gift certificate for "MR. BUCHWALD" was happily enclosed for use on any future car rental. But something was still missing:

SEPTEMBER 26, 1979

Thank you so much for sending me the gift certificate. What I don't have is the International Five Star credit card, so I don't believe that the certificate would do me any good. You probably sent the card to Mr. Buckley and the certificate to me!

Sincerely,
Art Buchwald

Days later the head of Hertz wrote again, obviously concerned that the "MR. BUCKLEY" and "MR. BUCHWALD" mix-up was getting out of hand. In an October 4 letter, Art was assured that the management of Hertz is "usually a little more buttoned up around here than your experiences would indicate." Within days Buchwald had in hand his own Hertz International Five Star Credit Card, putting him, at least for now, on equal footing with Mr. Buckley.

But in the fall of 1982, Hertz was on the move again, prompting a challenge from Buchwald to Buckley:

SEPTEMBER 14, 1982

Dear Bill:

I just received this letter concerning the new Hertz Express Service which, apparently, puts our Hertz International Five Star card out of business.

What hurts (I won't resort to a pun) is that we Five Star cardholders used to get special treatment. Now, anyone with an Express Service pass will receive it. I am thinking of resigning but would prefer to do it with others of my ilk. The resignation of Buckley and Buchwald from the Five Star Card organization could have financial repercussions throughout the banking world. Are you willing to go along with me, or don't you care?

Cheers,
Art

Only silence from Mr. Buckley, but not from the people at Hertz. In November 1982, Art was informed that as an "International Five Star" member, he had been automatically enrolled in their brand-new Hertz Frequent Renter Program. An excited Buchwald couldn't resist contacting Buckley:

NOVEMBER 2, 1982

Dear Bill:

I don't know if you received a similar letter, but we can now earn points for renting Hertz cars. . . . I suggest that we each keep the other informed as to how many points we have, and then, on September 30,

1983 we can both take our families to a Marriott hotel in Flint, Michi-
gan.

I feel this Hertz Five Star membership is the thing that binds our
friendship, and if it weren't for them we would just be two columnists
working different sides of the political fence....

Sincerely,
Art

This time, Buckley was quick to respond:

NOVEMBER 8, 1982

Dear Art:

You ask how many bonus points I have been credited with by Hertz?
Art, who won the election in 1980, the Republicans or the Democrats?
If it is true that we are working different sides of the political fence, how
many points would you give, if you were Hertz, to the columnist who
delivered 44 states, as opposed to the columnist who could only limp in
with six states? [Buckley is referring to Republican nominee Ronald
Reagan's landslide win over incumbent Democratic president Jimmy
Carter in 1980. Reagan won forty-four states. Carter won six states and
the District of Columbia.]

I don't want to advertise, Art, that this is a tough world that appor-
tions perquisites with some consideration of merit, but if you—No, with
that aposiopesis I change the subject. Let us agree only that we will keep
each other informed on how many points we earn beginning at this junc-
ture.

My belief in full disclosure impels me to confess that, as I write, my
wife is going round and round on the Hawthorne Circle in a Hertz car
listening on the cassette player to tapes of your columns, and laughing
and laughing, oh my, how she is laughing.

Cordially,
Bill

"ONE MILLION FIVE A YEAR IS NOT MUCH TO LIVE ON"

For award-winning news anchor and acclaimed author Tom Brokaw, it all began in Yankton, South Dakota, when, at the age of fifteen, he decided to become a television newscaster like his idols Chet Huntley and David Brinkley, hosts of NBC's legendary prime-time news program *The Huntley-Brinkley Report*. After working as a part-time radio announcer in Yankton, Brokaw enrolled at the University of South Dakota, where he worked his way through college as a radio reporter. After graduation Brokaw did a stint as a local television reporter in Omaha, Nebraska, before moving on to Atlanta, where he covered civil rights stories for NBC News. In 1966, he took a position as a local television reporter in California, covering such nationally significant stories as the gubernatorial campaign of Ronald Reagan. Five years later, Brokaw's big break came when NBC offered him a position as their chief White House correspondent. He arrived in Washington just in time to cover Richard Nixon's resignation and the two-year presidency of his successor, Gerald R. Ford. In 1976, Brokaw was tapped to cohost NBC's *Today* show, and in July 1981 he signed a lucrative multiyear contract with the network pairing him with Roger Mudd as co-anchor of the network's nightly news program. Brokaw eventually became sole anchor in September 1983.

During Brokaw's years in Washington he and Buchwald became close, lifelong friends, sharing an affable manner, a sense of humor, and a fondness for practical jokes. In July 1981, immediately after Brokaw signed his multiyear deal with NBC, Buchwald felt compelled to send a note of sympathy to his friend:

JULY 12, 1981

Dear Tom,

Most people write to you when something good happens. I'm the other type of person. I write when a friend is in trouble. I read in the newspapers about the raw deal you got at NBC, and how you got screwed financially....

Well I want you to know Tom I think you showed a lot of class, by swallowing your pride and taking the anchorman's job and a reduction in pay to one million five hundred thousand a year....

I know one million five a year is not much to live on in these inflationary times, but I believe you and Meredith can do it. Of course it might mean the kids have to go to public school, and you can't eat steak every night, but I know a lot of people who are making do with a lot less. Fortunately Meredith still has the toy store, and there is no reason you can't moonlight at night driving a taxi to earn a few extra bucks. I remember when Ann and I were making one million five a year. She used to bake pies and wedding cakes so the kids would have shoes and jeans and we used to eat day old bread. But when we look back on it now it was the happiest days of our lives. If it wasn't for the $500 a month I got from the National Guard I might not have pulled through. But Tom we never took food stamps and we always had enough money to go to the movies once a month.

What you and Meredith have to do is sit down at the kitchen table and say to yourselves, "We've only got a million five a year and therefore we have to change our lifestyles. There are a lot of things we can do without and we won't even miss—because we have our love to keep us warm."

The thing to remember is being an anchorman on NBC won't last forever. Someday you may even have your own radio show again or become host of "Family Feud."

You have talent and you just need a break. The powers at NBC can't keep you in the closet forever.

I want you to know there are a lot of friends like myself who are pulling for you. I don't have a lot of money myself, but if you ever need a few dollars to get you through the month I hope you'll call on us.

You got a rotten deal through no fault of your own, but I've been there myself so I know how you feel.

Tell Meredith if she needs any clothes, Ann has a lot in her closet she never wears.

As for the kids—you're going to be amazed how easily they'll adjust to your new salary. So what I'm saying guy is keep your chin up. Do the lousy anchorman's job without complaining. They're waiting for you to quit in a huff—but show them they can't grind you into the ground. A lot of those NBC honchos won't be around in a year or two and then you'll be able to write your own ticket.

And for Christ's sakes stay off the bottle. It's no solution to your problem and isn't going to bring one more buck into the house.

I know it's tough for Meredith to be making more money than you are. But just because she's successful now and you're on the skids is no reason to figure you're worthless. You've been in broadcasting a long time, and someday they're going to realize experience in this business counts a lot more than who you know.

I hope this letter cheers you up. Someday when you're on the top again we'll all get together and have a good laugh about this period, and we'll blow a whole million five on a meal at Four Seasons.

Keep the faith buddy,
Your friend

Days later Brokaw wrote back with a thank-you note scribbled in pencil on a scrap of paper torn from a brown grocery bag—with a food stamp coupon attached for his friend:

Dear Mr. Buchwald—The missus and I shure appreciate your helpful advice on how to get along on my new wage. We ain't got much, but we want to share what we have.

Sincerely,
Tom

A SATIRIST WINS A PULITZER, BUT LOSES HIS HUMIDOR

(1982–88)

SO LONG, DOC

Doc Dalinsky's pharmacy had the look and feel of a cramped and cluttered small-town drugstore right out of Middle America, where townsfolk gathered each day for coffee, a snack, the morning news, and the latest gossip. But Doc's drugstore was not set in the rural Midwest. It was in the heart of Georgetown, and for nearly fifty years it was the gathering place for some of the most celebrated and powerful people in Washington and Hollywood, including Art Buchwald, Ben Bradlee, cartoonist Herblock, Supreme Court justice William Brennan, Lauren Bacall, Dustin Hoffman, and Robert Redford (who once stopped by while filming *All the President's Men*), and novelists Larry McMurtry (who had a bookstore nearby) and Herman Wouk (whose house was just around the corner on N Street).

Alger Hiss was a regular at Doc's, as was President Franklin D. Roosevelt, who every Sunday had his son Jimmy call in an order for a

carton of Chesterfield cigarettes and two pints of ice cream. Georgetown residents Senator John F. Kennedy and his wife, Jackie, were
also known to drop by before moving on to the White House. (Dalinsky loved to tell the story about the night of Kennedy's inauguration in
January 1961 when he received a call from the White House asking
him to send over a heating pad to soothe the new president's ailing
back. Doc immediately sent one over in a taxicab.)

Visitors to Doc's, located at the corner of O Street and Wisconsin
Avenue, entered through a set of double glass doors, where they were
greeted by a two-foot Ex-Lax thermometer, marking their arrival into
the colorful and haphazard world of Doc Dalinsky's narrow aisles with
jam-packed shelves and shop cases stocked with newspapers, maga-
zines, sparklers, "dog-eared and dusty" greeting cards, hairbrushes,
Noxzema, toothpaste, sunglasses, Big Ben clocks, and a vast assortment of pipes, cigarettes, and cigars. "Mysterious cartons piled atop
mysterious cartons," a reporter for *The New York Times* observed.

The store had an eight-stool soda fountain, and in the back, where
Dalinsky spent most of his day, a modest sales counter with a blue
neon PRESCRIPTIONS sign beaming overhead. The constant flow of
customers delighted Doc, especially when they came by with their
children. He once gave Caroline Kennedy a wind-up toy for her birthday. If a customer happened to stroll in with a dog, Dalinsky was quick
to offer a treat of ice cream from a Dixie Cup, knowing that the grateful canine would always drag his owner back into the store for more.
Doc's was lively and chaotic, and that was much of its charm. "The
whole place was right out of central casting," Art Buchwald said.

Harry Alexander "Doc" Dalinsky was born in Russia in 1910.
When he was two his parents immigrated to America and eventually
settled in Baltimore, where his father found work as a capmaker. As a
boy, Dalinsky had dreams of becoming a doctor, but when the Great
Depression hit he was forced to abandon all hope of medical school
and decided to become a pharmacist. In 1933, he left Baltimore to
take a job in Washington, D.C., and within three years had saved
enough money to buy the Georgetown Pharmacy for $2,000.

Small in stature, but hardworking and self-effacing, Dalinsky was always on the job, working ten to twelve hours a day, seven days a week. When not in the back filling prescriptions, Doc was often out front standing in the midst of the cluttered aisles chatting with customers, looking the part of a small-town druggist with his glasses propped up on his forehead, wearing an old sleeveless sweater that, as one patron noted, seemed "to have come with the mortgage."

Dalinsky always had time to share a story or joke—most of which "apparently came over on the *Mayflower*," one visitor surmised. He loved cigars and gossip and was never too busy to flirt with a female customer. He would even take a break to play a game of gin rummy with Buchwald (Doc usually won) or a game of pool with journalist David Brinkley. But Dalinsky was never starstruck by the many celebrities who visited his drugstore—especially Art. "Buchwald may be funny," Doc once said, "but he never pays his bills."

The one quality nearly everyone remembered about Dalinsky was his kindness. "A lovely man with marvelous primitive qualities that don't get muddled up by life," Ben Bradlee recalled. "For most of us, Doc was the unofficial mayor of Georgetown, dispensing wisdom, advice, cigars, jokes, psychiatric consultations, and newspapers to his friends. He's the kind of man people just grew to love."

But to Buchwald, Doc was more than just a friend. "Doc and Art became inseparable, and one day I figured out why," Ben Bradlee later remembered. "Art decided to visit his old man, who was living in Flushing [New York]. He wanted company and asked me to come along. We were sitting in some restaurant near the New York airport when this guy shuffles in, the spit and image of Doc. It was Art's dad."

Because they were both regular customers, Buchwald and Bradlee were always invited to Doc's weekly Sunday brunch. Befitting his unpretentious manner, the breakfast setting was a makeshift affair: a white tablecloth draped over the cigar and pipe counter located just across from the deodorants section. From ten A.M. to noon each Sunday, the typical Dalinsky menu featured Danish from the nearby Georgetown Inn, bagels and lox, grits, cooked sausages, and coffee served from a two-gallon jug bearing a handwritten note: *Private Party*. For two hours Doc's place was filled with chatter about football, baseball, politics, theater, and, of course, the latest Washington gossip.

But by the winter of 1982, age and the daily grind of maintaining the store were starting to take their toll, and Doc decided to call it quits. Art arranged a retirement party to celebrate the life of his beloved friend and the cherished Washington institution he had created. On January 20, 1982, Buchwald, designating himself as the "Georgetown Pharmacy Window Display Manager," sent out a notice to a select group of Doc's longtime friends:

JANUARY 20, 1982

THIS IS YOUR FINAL NOTICE

On May 1st of this year, a group of friends is going to celebrate a special event in Washington—the 45th (and 8 months) anniversary of the opening of the Georgetown Pharmacy, one of the country's great historical landmarks.

Whether he likes it or not, we are honoring our godfather, Doc Dalinsky, who has kept our bodies healthy and our minds sane through the turbulent years....

Please act now so we know if you're coming. The reason I'm writing to you is that I pumped Doc for a list of the people he likes very much, and you are one of the lucky ones. The only purpose of this dinner is to honor someone we all love, and to thank him for just being "Doc."

> *Sincerely,*
> *Art Buchwald,*
> *Window Display*
> *Manager*
> *Georgetown Pharmacy*

On the night of the dinner, more than two hundred of Dalinsky's friends were in attendance, including Edward Bennett Williams, David Brinkley, Jack Valenti, and Herman Wouk, who had flown in from Israel that day. In his remarks for the occasion, Buchwald paid a humorous tribute to his old friend:

> When Doc first came to Washington President Franklin Roosevelt came into the store, and he was so impressed how well Doc was organized, that he asked Doc to join his Kitchen Cabinet. Every president but Nixon has since sought Doc's advice.
>
> It would be too long to list all of Doc's contributions to the movers and shakers in this town, but let me just list a few. Doc thought up the New Deal, the Marshall Plan, NATO, the Peace Corps, the War on Poverty, and Supply Side economics....
>
> But we don't honor Doc tonight for what he's done for the high and the mighty. We do, and I'm being serious now, honor him for what he has done for the thousands of faceless people over the years, in being their confidant, their anchor with reality, and someone who has helped young people, troubled people and men and women in all walks of life.
>
> We hear about Doc and his celebrities who have come to his store. But the real contribution Doc has played in Georgetown is for all he has done for all the ordinary persons he has helped in the past 46 years. We go to Doc's because he is our friend and someone we can trust.
>
> He is a kind man and a good man. He is a religious man and a family man. He is truly a man for all seasons. Tonight's dinner is a small way of paying him back for all the things he's done for us. We love you, Doc.

Doc's health slowly deteriorated over the next ten years as Alzheimer's set in, and on April 9, 1992, at age eighty-two, he died. Buchwald perhaps said it best about Dalinsky and his beloved store: "He is one of the last of the race of people who care. Hell, that store of his isn't a pharmacy. It's a family."

A PULITZER

In the summer of 1975, Art Buchwald sarcastically grumbled that he had been slighted by the Pulitzer committee when they failed to award him a prize for his "journalistic coup" in landing an "exclusive interview with the Statue of Liberty."

Seven years later, however, his dream finally came true when on April 13, 1982, Art Buchwald received the Pulitzer Prize for Outstanding Commentary. Letters of congratulation poured in from friends and admirers everywhere, including a note from Katharine Graham of *The Washington Post*:

Dear Art,

For once, I can think of no smart-ass remark to make, except congratulations on the Pulitzer Prize. You deserve it, and should have had it long ago.

> *Much love,*
> *Kay*

And from Eppie Lederer:

APRIL 13, 1982

Dear Art:

About the Pulitzer—what in the hell took them so long? Where have they been? Don't they read? Wow, plus L[ove] and K[isses],

> *Eppie*

And a heartfelt note from Ethel Kennedy:

Dear Artie:

I never dreamed anyone winning the Pulitzer Prize would mean so much to me. I'm so thrilled for you and Ann and for Joel, Connie and Jenny.

All your friends are basking in your reflected glory.

But even the best prize of all couldn't be as rewarding as knowing the fun you give us all, the numbers you reach and the good you do.

Mother Teresa—eat your heart out.

Robert Browning was off the mark: It isn't because morning's at seven and the hillside's dew-pearled—it's because Artie won the Pulitzer!—That God's in His heaven and all's right with the world.

A MENACE TO AMERICA

In 1982, American novelist Kurt Vonnegut, Jr., a master of satire and black humor, turned sixty. Forever looking a bit "like an out-of-work philosophy professor," Vonnegut was the author of *Cat's Cradle*, *Breakfast of Champions*, *Player Piano*, and *Slaughterhouse Five*— novels that firmly established him as a true cult hero among college and high school students during the 1960s and '70s.

In celebration of Vonnegut's sixtieth birthday, his wife, author and photographer Jill Krementz, assembled a book of remembrances from friends and fellow writers, including tributes from John Irving, Garry Trudeau, Truman Capote, and Art Buchwald, who had a special message for the Vonnegut "festschrift":

MAY 17, 1982

I don't have time to write 250 words about Kurt Vonnegut, but I will say a few things if you wish to use this letter in the limited edition.

Kurt Vonnegut is a menace to the United States of America. His books are subversive and could do incalculable damage to the young minds of our children. They should be banned from every library and school in America. I have read Vonnegut, but I wouldn't want my sister to open one of his books.

I would like the names of everyone who is honoring him on his sixtieth birthday. We are not interested in the dupes, but the ones who are aware that Kurt Vonnegut is a secular humanist, and are still paying tribute to him.

Sincerely,
Art Buchwald

"A FACSIMILE OF ONE HALF OF A RULER"

The year 1983 began with a letter from William F. Buckley, Jr., announcing big news from Hertz:

JANUARY 4, 1983

Dear Art:

Have you heard from Hertz recently? Well, I have. And not just a letter, a package. A card was enclosed which read, "It is a pleasure to send you the enclosed gift as our way of thanking you for your continued support of the Hertz Corporation. Please accept it with our Best Wishes for a Joyous Holiday Season and a Happy and Prosperous New Year."...

The gift, Art, is a most beautiful heavy lucite paperweight, a facsimile of one half of a ruler, measuring exactly six inches. My question is, Did you receive a gift from Hertz? I doubt that you did, because Hertz has a very good sense of what in this world, and who, are, well, Number Two. But, perhaps, you received a three-inch ruler? I write to extend holiday greetings, and to tell you that if you ever need to borrow my six-inch ruler, I'll be glad to send it along. Or, you can send someone in a Hertz car to pick it up. And don't fret, Art. I hear nothing but the best about you.

Most cordially,
Bill

JANUARY 10, 1983

Dear Bill:

I can't believe you would be taken in by the Hertz six-inch ruler. [Hertz] has sent out about 2 million of them. What happened was, Hertz bought a heavy lucite company for $86 a share just when the recession started. The demand for lucite plummeted and they found themselves stuck with the rulers. Rather than admit they were involved in a disastrous takeover, they told the stockholders they bought the company to get a wholesale price on 6-inch rulers.

I have one on my desk right now. I have no idea what to do with a 6-inch ruler. My columns run 7½ inches, so it's useless for my work....

In answer to your question, I did receive the ruler. Now my question to you is, what the hell are you doing with it? If Hertz thinks I'm going to rent a car from them because they gave me a little paperweight, they're nuts.

"A BIRTHDAY SEUSS"

On March 2, 1984, Dr. Seuss lovers everywhere celebrated the eightieth birthday of one of the most widely read authors of children's books: Theodor Seuss Geisel. During his career Dr. Seuss wrote and illustrated more than forty books, including *The Cat in the Hat, How the Grinch Stole Christmas,* and *The Butter Battle Book.* By 1984, Geisel's books, translated into twenty languages, had sold an estimated one hundred million copies. On Seuss's eightieth birthday, Art Buchwald offered his own personal tribute to his friend:

> What does one do with a birthday Seuss?
> You can bake a Zook, or stuff a mousse.
> You can choose a wine that is Snick Berry fine
> But you can't drink Moody's and you can't drink mine.
> You can raise a glass and say something bright

If you can't think fast you can always sit tight.
A Toast—A Toast
Hail Master of Grinches and Star Bellied Sneetches
And Cats in Top Hats with all that it teaches
Praise Turtles and Yurtles and Knoxes in Boxes
And chicks who do tricks
With foxes in soxes.
But pray tell us Dear Doctor
Now that you're fed.
Which side does a Seuss
Smear his butter on bread?

Happy Birthday
Art Buchwald

"IF YOU COME ACROSS A MIRACLE OR TWO"

In the spring of 1984, news came that novelist Irwin Shaw was gravely ill. Art responded immediately with a letter of heartfelt love to one of his dearest friends:

APRIL 19, 1984

Dear Irwin,

Word reached Washington that you are severely ailing and all your pals here are disturbed. Don't know if I mentioned it but I really enjoyed your summing up in "Playboy" of how you took on the world, professionally and personally. It was a beautiful piece and I have saved it.

Once again I must reiterate what an important part you played in my life when I was a young man in Paris trying to make my way. You were a role model for any would be writer and the interest and kindness you showed in people like myself will never be forgotten. You inspired a whole generation of writers in Paris, and we all owe you a great debt. You are also a great human being and I have always considered you as one of the few friends I could count on if I ever got into serious trouble.

I didn't have to do it, but it was comforting to know that if I did you would be there.

One doesn't say this to another man when he meets him at a party or in a bar or even his home, but I love you Irwin for what you are and what you have meant to me.

Please get well for all of us. We don't want anything to happen to you because you are very important to all of us. Ann and I send our love and our prayers.

My next letter will inform as to what is going on in Washington. If I put it in this you would only get depressed.

God Bless,

Art

Less than two weeks later Shaw, now in declining health, sent this handwritten note to Buchwald:

MAY 1, 1984

Klosters, Switzerland

Dear Art,

Thank you very much for your letter. Ever since we first met so many years ago there has been a strong current between us and it flows both ways. I had the advantage. Being so much older and well established I could look upon you as a close younger brother and delight in your triumphs.

My triumphs have probably just come to an end. In the hospital, along with all the other ills, none of them charming for which they are treating me, I discovered that I had double vision. I can't type and you can see how I have to struggle to keep the pen moving and making sense. This has been going on for six weeks now and the doctors here, while they seem good and compassionate, don't seem optimistic about the whole business. We'll hang in for a couple of weeks then make our way to Southampton and a last shot at my doctors there in N.Y.

Curiously enough, I look better than I did before—by losing 15 kilos.

If you come across a miracle or two, flag it down. It will get first class treatment.

Love,
Irwin

Fifteen days later Irwin Shaw died in Davos, Switzerland, at age seventy-one.

"BETTER THAN THE OSCARS OR AIR FORCE ONE"

Actor Charlton Heston was often called a "colossus" of the silver screen. During his acclaimed Hollywood career, which spanned more than half a century, Heston starred in a fabled collection of some of the greatest films of all time: *The Ten Commandments* (1956), *The Greatest Story Ever Told* (1965), and *Ben-Hur* (1959). Heston was respected for the hard work and discipline he always brought to his roles. He memorized passages from the Old Testament to prepare for the role of Moses, read hundreds of Michelangelo's letters prior to his performance in *The Agony and the Ecstasy,* and trained to handle a chariot for his role in *Ben-Hur,* for which he won an Oscar as Best Actor in 1960.

Off-screen one of Heston's great passions was the game of tennis. He loved to play the game, and he loved to watch it. And he was "excited as well as honored" to frequently be invited to sit in the Royal Box at Wimbledon. During the summer of 1985, while Heston was in London to star in and direct a stage adaptation of Herman Wouk's *Caine Mutiny Court-Martial,* he was invited to sit in the Royal Box during the Wimbledon matches but declined because he was appalled by the on-court antics of American tennis star John McEnroe and his all-too-frequent temper tantrums on the court. Heston hoped and expected that any American playing at Wimbledon would act with dignity and respect, and with McEnroe playing in the matches that year Heston had no desire, he told the London *Daily Mail,* "to sit in that box at that wonderful place and risk the embarrassment . . . of seeing an American disgrace our country."

When Buchwald read Heston's comments in the paper, he knew he had his column for the week. On July 1, 1985, Art published a farcical piece titled "Wimbledon's Royal Pains" about an imaginary day he spent at Wimbledon with Queen Elizabeth, Prince Philip, Princess Diana, and Prince Charles. "We were laughing and joking...when John McEnroe came on the court. I stiffened measurably as McEnroe gave the drinking fountain a good kick," Buchwald wrote. "The queen turned to me and said, 'A fellow countryman?' I smiled weakly. 'Not really, Your Majesty. He's from Long Island.'" Soon, after three double faults and a series of temper tantrums, Buchwald's fictional match descends into chaos as tennis balls start whizzing through the air headed directly for the Royal Box, forcing everyone to scramble for cover. "Chuck, you can take it from somebody who has been there," Buchwald wrote. "Even if you now have a lousy seat at Wimbledon, you did the right thing."

Charlton Heston, a longtime Buchwald fan, loved the column and on July 5, 1985, wrote:

Dear Art:

I've done it! Better than the Oscars or Air Force One, better than creative approval or cut of the gross, better than "Lean is directing," or "Liked Your last film." Better, by God, than the Royal Box. I've made Buchwald.

Mom always said I could do it, she always had faith. So did my wife, who stood by me in the dark times, and the kids. And of course I'd like to thank the little people: my makeup man and the script girl, the receptionist who let me in to see the producer who gave me my first job. And of course, above all, to Art Buchwald himself.

Thanks!

Chuck

P.S. A spokesman for the Palace has asked me to point out that no member of the Royal Family, most certainly not Her Majesty, actually sought shelter on the occasion when you shared their Box.

GORBY, ZIGGY, AND NUKES IN CLEVELAND

On March 11, 1985, fifty-four-year-old Mikhail Gorbachev became the new leader of the Soviet Union after the death of Konstantin Chernenko. The young, dynamic, reform-minded Gorbachev quickly signaled a radical new approach and outlook for the Soviet government. His efforts to modernize the nation's economy and Russian society—known as "perestroika"—and his moves to display a more open approach to foreign policy—known as "glasnost"—went a long way toward reducing diplomatic tensions with the rest of the world.

On December 1, 1987, the NBC television network aired an exclusive hour-long interview of Gorbachev by Tom Brokaw. It was an extraordinary moment. *The Washington Post* said Brokaw's journalistic scoop had given "Americans their most intimate and penetrating look yet at the Soviet leader—indeed, probably the best TV close-up ever of any Soviet leader." During the interview, Gorbachev revealed to Brokaw that he had been heartened by having received in the past year more than eighty thousand letters from well-wishing Americans.

Pouncing on Gorbachev's remarks, Buchwald concocted a series of imaginary letters to the general secretary in a column titled "The Mail Mikhail Missed." One of the make-believe letters was signed "Ziggy from the Carryout," who queried Gorbachev about a nuclear arms reduction issue:

Dear Mr. Gorbachev:

I understand that the treaty you wrote with Ronald Reagan requires both countries to destroy all intermediate range nuclear missiles. I have a question to ask. Where are you going to bury the warheads? If you haven't decided yet, may I put in a good word for Cleveland?

Ziggy from the Carryout

Two days later the people of Cleveland, Ohio, had a crisp response for Buchwald:

As a syndicated columnist in Paris for the *New York Herald Tribune* in the 1950s, Art Buchwald was the man-to-see and the man-to-read. In no time he became a journalistic celebrity keeping company with the rich and famous, including Humphrey Bogart and Lauren Bacall. (Courtesy Joel and Tamara Buchwald)

While Buchwald was in Paris, his column was a must-read for visiting tourists or adventurous young Americans traveling abroad, including a young art student named Robert Redford, who was living in Paris in the late 1950s. Decades later, one day over lunch in Washington, Redford would tell Buchwald how much his column meant to him while living in France. "I was young and very lonely. I read your entertainment column . . . about restaurants and bars that tourists might want to go to. Believe it or not your . . . columns were a lifesaver to me." (Courtesy Michael Geissinger)

After arriving in Washington in the early 1960s, Buchwald became close friends with Robert and Ethel Kennedy. As a frequent guest to their Hickory Hill home in McLean, Virginia, Art was always the life of the party, most notably as presiding judge of the annual Kennedy family pet show charity event. Here, Art presents the Kennedys with one of their many pet show victory cups.
(Courtesy Joel and Tamara Buchwald)

One "ringmaster" meets another. Art's duties as judge of the annual Kennedy pet show sometimes required a second opinion. In this case heavyweight boxing champion Muhammad Ali was brought on board by Ethel Kennedy to help Art with the final selection of best pets.
(Courtesy Gordie Corbin and Judy Switt)

ADAM WEST

April 1, 1966

Mr. Art Buchwald
New York Herald Tribune
230 West 41st St.
New York, New York

Dear Mr. Buchwald:

I've finally emerged from the Batcave
long enough to write this note to you, and to tell you
how much I enjoyed the enclosed piece, which appeared
in the Los Angeles Times.

Reading your most apt columns in the
Times is one of my regular morning activities, and it
always amazes me that you can sustain your high tone of
humor behind your observations.

If President Johnson gets out his axe
after you, please rest assured that Robin and I will
superjet to your aid in our multi-multi-powered Batplane
and do our stuff in full Technicolor.

Should you be out this way at any time,
it would be a great pleasure to meet you.

Sincerely,

Adam West
"Batman"

AW:pm

In early 1966, as the war in Vietnam worsened, Art Buchwald proposed a new strategy for President Lyndon Johnson in Southeast Asia: send in America's celebrated caped crusader "Batman" and his sidekick, "Robin." After reading Buchwald's column, "Batman" (Adam West) sent a note to Art vowing to rush to his rescue if the president retaliated.

(Reprinted with permission of Marcelle West on behalf of Adam West Enterprises and the estate of Adam West)

One of Buchwald's closest lifelong friends was *Washington Post* managing editor Ben Bradlee. Their friendship began when the two were young journalists in Paris during the 1950s. "He was a straight shooter," Buchwald said of Bradlee. "He also had humor, and we took an instant liking to one another." Here, Buchwald and Bradlee enjoy a moment at the 1972 Republican National Convention in Miami, Florida.
(Photograph courtesy of Diana Walker)

Robert F. Kennedy, Jr., said his mother's "best friend through the years was the warm, rotund, and gentle humorist Art Buchwald," pictured here in the rabbit suit he wore each year to Ethel Kennedy's Easter egg hunt at Hickory Hill.
(Courtesy Joel and Tamara Buchwald)

The Washington Post

1150 15TH STREET, N. W.

WASHINGTON, D. C. 20071

(202) 223-6000

Nov. 8, 1977

Art

Deep Throat asked that I pass along
his deepest thanks. It was thoughtful
of you to have them airbrush out his
body and face. Though it looks like
you are having lunch just with a hand,
he thinks---in fact, is sure---no one
will recognize him. Of course, the
half empty glass of Ovaltine gives
away something.

Woodward

When Buchwald was caught on camera at the Sans Souci restaurant lunching with a mysterious guest whose right arm only was shown in the photograph, *Washington Post* investigative reporter Bob Woodward playfully wrote to Art expressing gratitude for protecting the secret identity of his fabled Watergate source "Deep Throat."
(Reprinted with permission of Bob Woodward)

December 10, 1987

Mr. Art Buchwald
c/o New York Newsday
780 Third Ave.
New York, NY 10017

Re: Your 12/8 column in New York Newsday

Dear Mr. Buchwald:

Fuck you.

Sincerely,

The City of Cleveland

In 1987, Buchwald's legendary "Buchshots" backfired when, in the midst of U.S.-Soviet arms reduction talks, Art offered a whimsical proposal as to where Mikhail Gorbachev could deposit abandoned Soviet nuclear warheads. The citizens of Cleveland were not amused.
(Art Buchwald Papers, LOC)

Dear Art —

Thank you for "I'll
Always Have Paris" and
the lovely inscription!
What's most important
is that we always
have Buchwald.

As ever
Herb

8-16-96

A letter of admiration from friend and renowned political cartoonist Herbert
Block ("Herblock") after the publication of Buchwald's 1996 memoir, *I'll
Always Have Paris*.

(Reprinted with permission of The Herb Block Foundation)

Edward M. Kennedy

June 28, 2000

Mr. Art Buchwald
C/O Mr. Joel Buchwald
4329 Hawthorne Street, NW
Washington, D.C. 20016

Dear Artie:

I was so sorry to hear that you are having a difficult time
right now and Vicki and I want you to know that you are very much
in our thoughts and in our prayers.

I am told that you are already making excellent progress and
that is great news. I have no doubt that with your ability to use
humor to meet adversity, and your fighting spirit you will conquer
this latest challenge. After all, anyone who can take on and beat
Paramount has got a terrific track record! When you are feeling
better I will try to fight my way through the crowd of friends at your
bedside to drop by and catch up.

In the meantime, concentrate on feeling better and know that
all of your friends are at your side and with you in spirit.

As Ever,

Edward M. Kennedy

We miss you + love you

After suffering a heart attack in the summer of 2000, Buchwald received a get-
well note from longtime friend Senator Edward Kennedy and his wife, Vicki.
(Reprinted with permission of Ms. Vicki Kennedy)

One of Buchwald's closest friends on Martha's Vineyard was Pulitzer Prize-winning novelist William Styron. Both struggled with what Styron called the "dreadful and raging disease" of depression. Dubbing themselves the "Blues Brothers," they went public about their own battles with depression to help others who suffered as they did. (Courtesy Joel and Tamara Buchwald)

Singer-songwriter Carly Simon (*left*) and Art Buchwald. Each summer Buchwald would emcee the "Possible Dreams" auction on Martha's Vineyard to raise funds for the island's community services programs. Simon was often on hand to help Art with the event and to sing for the crowd. In August 2006, when Buchwald was ill, Simon wrote a beautifully poignant song for him, "Too Soon to Say Goodbye." (Courtesy Joel and Tamara Buchwald)

DECEMBER 10, 1987

Dear Mr. Buchwald:
 Fuck you.

> *Sincerely,*
> *The City of Cleveland*

"IF YOU SAY THE WORD 'TRUMP' "

Nearly thirty years before becoming president, Donald Trump, real estate mogul and casino tycoon, launched the inaugural flight of his Trump Shuttle, which provided service from New York to Washington, D.C. A reporter on hand that day noted that Trump had "lived up to his reputation for hoopla" by offering his customers the finest in traveling comforts at both ends of the line.

Days after the shuttle got off the ground, Buchwald received a form letter from Trump inviting him to fly on his new airline, along with details about the benefits he would receive from logging miles on the new Trump Shuttle.

In response, Art wrote to Trump:

23 JUNE 1989

Dear Donald:
 Thank you so much for the warm and touching note you sent on 8 June. I am so glad to hear the news about the shuttle. I know that it's going to be a lot of fun, and I am looking forward to flying on it. Also, thanks for all the free mileage you are handing out. As I understand, if you say the word "Trump" in a gathering of over twenty people, you get forty-three miles of credit on your OnePass account. If you walk by the Trump Tower between the hours of five and seven in the evening, you get to fly to Bangkok with another person. If you lose more than $100 in a slot machine in Atlantic City, and you are over 79 years

old, Trump Airlines will allow you to be co-pilot on a round-trip from Washington.

Donald, it was great to hear from you. I just don't see how you get the time to write.

> Cheers,
> Art

THE BIG NONSMOKER IN THE SKY

At the beginning of 1988, Art Buchwald had some shocking news for his fans. "I know you weren't ready for this, dear reader, but I have given up cigars." The dedicated six-or-seven-cigars-a-day journalist was now calling it quits. From now on, he proudly proclaimed, he would be able to "walk into any crowded room without stinking up the joint."

It had not been easy. For over forty years a cigar had been a signature part of his persona and, like his typewriter, an essential part of his craft. Twenty-five years earlier, during his first serious bout with depression, a cigar had helped pull him out of his despair and put him back to work. But now, he told readers, word had come down from the "Big Nonsmoker in the sky" that it was time to quit. "PUT OUT THAT DAMNED CIGAR," a stern voice had commanded him from above. (Actually it had been pains in his chest and stern advice from his doctor that caused the conversion, not a majestic "thundering voice" from above.) But like any devoted six-or-seven-cigars-a-day puffer, Buchwald tried to negotiate down to only two or three a day. However, as he related in his column, the "Big Nonsmoker in the sky" would have none of it.

When Buchwald tried going cold turkey, his writing inevitably suffered from withdrawal symptoms: The song "Smoke Gets in Your Eyes" kept popping into his head, while visions of the Marlboro Man galloping across his computer screen were a constant distraction. Desperate for help, he received advice again from the heavens above: "TRY

CHEWING GUM" bellowed the voice from on high. It worked, and his conversion was complete. Relieved that he could still earn a living as a columnist without a cigar and secure in the knowledge that his "brain cells" would not be forced to "absorb soot from morning until night," Buchwald expressed unfettered joy to his readers that after forty years he was, at last, a "born-again nonsmoker."

The year had started on a high note. But things were about to turn sour.

TEARS OF THE CLOWN

* * * * * * *

A MATTER OF HONOR

Buchwald v. Hollywood—Act I (1982-88)

The humorist has a quick eye for the humbug.

—W. SOMERSET MAUGHAM

There was little funny business afoot during the Fourth of July weekend in 1988. Art Buchwald was in a sullen and bitter mood. Not even
the normally relaxed setting of Martha's Vineyard could help lighten
his spirits. He had just seen Eddie Murphy's new hit movie *Coming to
America* at the Capawock Theatre in Vineyard Haven, and as the
credits rolled by on the screen that evening he seethed with anger
when he saw no mention of his name on a film he truly believed was
inspired by an original idea that he and a producing partner, Alain
Bernheim, had optioned to Paramount studios five years earlier.

Buchwald's idea, set out in an eight-page film treatment, had been
inspired by an actual event he witnessed in the fall of 1977 as violent
protestors clashed in the streets of Washington during a state visit by
the shah of Iran to the Carter White House. As Buchwald watched the
skirmish between the pro- and anti-shah protestors that day, a curious
idea popped into his head. "I watched the scene and the premise for
a movie hit me," Art later wrote. "Suppose a ruling prince came to

Washington, D.C., on a state visit and was overthrown back home by his brother-in-law with the help of the CIA. All the prince's bank accounts are frozen, he is tossed out of the White House, and he winds up in the ghetto, where he sees life as it really is."

After shopping the treatment around Hollywood for nearly a year, Bernheim had finally negotiated an option on the project—titled *King for a Day*—with Paramount Studios in the spring of 1983. Not only was Buchwald thrilled, but to his great delight, there was even talk that one of the studio's brightest comic stars, Eddie Murphy, might be cast in the lead role.

For the next two years Bernheim and Buchwald remained hopeful that their dream would become a reality and make it to the big screen. But then the roof fell in. After a personnel shake-up at Paramount, the incoming studio executives announced they were dropping their option on the Buchwald-Bernheim project and that *King for a Day* was dead. "The only explanation we could elicit," Buchwald later said, "was that [Eddie] Murphy hated it." But under the terms of the contract, Bernheim and Buchwald had a year to make a new deal with another studio.

Things began to look promising when they negotiated a new option with Warner Bros. But then, in the fall of 1987, bad news struck again when executives at Warner Bros. learned that Paramount and Eddie Murphy already had a movie in the works about "a king going from Africa to America." Immediately, Warner Bros. announced that it was dropping its option on *King for a Day*, a move that put Buchwald and Bernheim "out of business" once more.

The news about the Paramount-Murphy film project left Buchwald and Bernheim flabbergasted and outraged. Believing that they might have a reasonable legal claim against Paramount, Bernheim immediately enlisted the assistance of several Los Angeles entertainment lawyers, who contacted the studio to see if an equitable settlement could be worked out. But in the midst of the negotiations, Paramount announced that the Eddie Murphy film project, now called *Coming to America*, was finished and scheduled to appear in theaters in early July.

With the film set for release, the studio's lawyers now took a decid-edly "hard line" in the settlement negotiations. When a demand was made to resolve the matter for $600,000, Paramount's lawyers re-fused, stating that they found the "quantum of similarity to be com-pletely insufficient to support legal claims." They were, however, willing to schedule a private screening of Coming to America for both Bernheim and Buchwald and then, "with all of the facts before all of the people," discuss some kind of a settlement.

With Art vacationing on Martha's Vineyard, Bernheim reluctantly accepted Paramount's invitation to attend the private screening, which was scheduled only days before the film's release. After viewing the movie, Bernheim left the studio "fuming" and immediately called Buchwald to urge him to see the film as soon as possible.

Three days later, during the Fourth of July weekend, Coming to America hit the theaters and was an immediate box office success. With a hit now on its hands, Paramount finally came forward with a counteroffer to Bernheim and Buchwald of $50,000, plus a 1 percent interest in "net profits" from the film's revenues, and the execution of a confidentiality agreement about the settlement. When Paramount's offer was conveyed to Bernheim and Buchwald, they both felt as if they were being treated "like two schleppers with no credentials and less credibility."

Annoyed, angry, and fed up with Paramount's behavior, Buchwald took Alain's advice and made his way to the Capawock Theatre that holiday weekend to see Coming to America for himself. By the time he left the theater, there was no doubt in his mind that the film was in-spired by the story he and Bernheim had sold to Paramount. It was a "blatant ripoff," he thought to himself. "Did Paramount really think that it could fool him?"

But as he strolled home that night, he was puzzled about what to do next. He had been warned about trying to take on Hollywood and about how costly and time-consuming a lawsuit might be. To make matters worse, his beloved friend Edward Bennett Williams, who had helped guide him through so many scrapes during their long friendship, was dying of cancer back in Washington and unable to be at his side to counsel and advise him.

Although Buchwald had never sued anybody or been sued by anyone (the closest he had ever come was in 1970 when Joe Alsop issued his veiled threat to file a lawsuit over *Sheep on the Runway*), he was certain of one thing: A long, drawn-out court case would be wearing and distracting for himself and his family. He was reassured, however, by his wife, Ann, who told Art to "do what he thought was right." He was also aware that such a high-profile case as this—with the names of Art Buchwald and Eddie Murphy attached—would inevitably attract worldwide attention from the media. Then there were the racial implications of such a lawsuit. Although Buchwald respected and admired Murphy, the press might turn it into a toxic struggle between a celebrated white writer and an African American megastar. But the more he thought about it that night, the more "pissed off" he was about what Paramount had done. It was a matter of honor to him. He despised being taken advantage of, a hatred that had been ingrained in him early in life. Although he was brilliantly funny and exceedingly kindhearted, he could also be tough, resourceful, and resolute when times required, especially when he felt he was in the right. He knew that if he went ahead with a lawsuit, it would take time, energy, and enormous financial resources. But he also knew that if he won, it would "teach the studios a lesson" and provide encouragement to many less famous scriptwriters who faced exploitation by the powerful Hollywood studio system. So, after "brooding" for two hours, Buchwald marched into his kitchen and grabbed the phone. "Alain? It's Art. I just saw *Coming to America*. Let's get a lawyer."

Pierce O'Donnell was a brilliant, fearless, and resourceful lawyer, much like his mentor, Edward Bennett Williams. A graduate of Georgetown University Law School in 1972 and a clerk for Supreme Court justice Byron White, he was now a partner in the prestigious law firm of Kaye, Scholer, Fierman, Hays and Handler in their Los Angeles office. O'Donnell's practice at the time consisted mostly of complex civil matters, along with an assortment of entertainment law cases. And he was a huge fan of Art Buchwald, whom he considered a "genuine American legend." O'Donnell had first read about the dispute between Buchwald and Paramount when he saw a small item in the *Los Angeles Times* on July 13, 1988. Although intrigued, he thought little more about it until he received a call from Alain Bernheim about the matter. After hearing a brief summary of the case, O'Donnell bluntly told Bernheim that they had no legal leg to stand on in a pure copyright suit against the studio. It was a "dead-bang loser," he told Alain. But after studying their contracts with Paramount, O'Donnell thought that if he could prove the studio had "used Art's treatment as the basis for *Coming to America*," they might—just might—prevail under a simple "breach of contract" action. It was a stretch, he conceded, but he was willing to look into it after he returned from a family vacation to New Orleans.

Days later, just after O'Donnell and his family arrived in Louisiana, he received a message from Art Buchwald. When he returned the call, Art told him that he had a commitment to cover the Republican National Convention the following week in New Orleans and he wondered if the two could meet face-to-face to discuss the Paramount matter. After O'Donnell agreed, they set up a time to meet at Art's hotel when he arrived for the convention two days later.

On late Sunday afternoon, August 14, 1988, as O'Donnell headed to meet Buchwald, he heard a report on the radio that Edward Bennett Williams had died. Although stunned by the news, a despondent O'Donnell still proceeded to the hotel for his meeting with Art, where his spirits were lifted by Buchwald, who greeted him at the door with a gentle and warm smile. "He had the rubbery face of a comedian," O'Donnell remembered, "but the manner of a perfect gentleman." At first, both avoided any mention of the news about their mutual friend's death. Instead they chatted briefly about their families and careers: O'Donnell talked about his clerkship at the Supreme Court, and Art spoke of his early years as a journalist in Paris. "Life was uncomplicated then," a wistful Buchwald said at one point.

Soon, however, the conversation turned to the death of Edward Bennett Williams. "Art's smile vanished," O'Donnell remembered, "his lips pursed and he slowly shook his head."

"Ed died peacefully last night," Buchwald said. "He was ready to go. . . . I guess the arrangements haven't been finalized yet, but he asked me a long time ago to be one of his pallbearers." O'Donnell then watched as Buchwald "planted his forehead in his hands . . . mourning in his own way."

"He was my best buddy," Buchwald told O'Donnell. "God, did we have a lot of fun." After a few silent moments, Buchwald snapped back into action. "All right. The case. We've got some business to take care of. Should Alain and I stick our necks out on this one or not?" O'Donnell outlined his proposed theory of suing Paramount for breach of contract rather than copyright infringement. Buchwald liked what he heard and said that although he wanted to get even with those "bastards" in Hollywood for "ripping me off," he wanted to clarify two points. First, if they did sue Paramount, would that mean *not* having to sue Eddie Murphy?

"That's right," O'Donnell assured him. "You signed a contract with Paramount, not Murphy."

Buchwald was relieved. "It might help defuse the race issue," he told O'Donnell.

"Race has nothing to do with this case," O'Donnell countered.

"Pierce, believe me, I know it. You know it. But race will lurk right below the surface if we go ahead. Just watch." O'Donnell concurred and agreed not to "speak ill" of Murphy if they proceeded.

Buchwald's second stipulation was that he would not sign a confidentiality agreement. "You need to know that going in," he explained. "I'm a newspaperman. That type of agreement goes against everything I believe in. . . . So, do I have your word? No confidentiality?" O'Donnell agreed. After shaking hands, the two rose and proposed a toast to their recently departed friend Eddie Williams.

Williams's funeral was held on Tuesday, August 16, 1988, at St. Matthew's Cathedral in Washington, D.C. Both Ben Bradlee and Art Buchwald were pallbearers. In keeping with his last wishes there were no eulogies, even by his closest friends. But Buchwald couldn't resist setting down in words a private remembrance of his friend, written in classic Buchwald style:

> Eddie was my friend—pure and simple. We had no business to transact, nor did either person ask more of the other than a meal, a sympathetic ear, or, most importantly, a good laugh. . . .
>
> Many friendships are based on traditions. One of our traditions was an annual Thanksgiving Day touch-football game between the Williams and Buchwald families. Our children were all little, and Williams, being the fierce competitor he was, played very hard.
>
> One year my family showed up at the Glen Echo High School field, and there in the backfield next to Eddie was Sonny Jurgensen [quarterback for the Washington Redskins]. Our family screamed that it was illegal, as Jurgensen was not a member of the Williams family. Eddie claimed that since Sonny was coming to his house for dinner he qualified as family.
>
> The happy ending to the story was that we beat the Williams family, mainly because Sonny threw his passes so hard and so accurately that no one on Eddie's team could catch them. . . .
>
> As I drive around Washington, scene after scene discloses a time and place I laughed with Eddie. He was one of those friends whom you miss more as time goes on.
>
> The world was a more exciting place because he was here.

After returning to Los Angeles, Pierce O'Donnell spent days finetuning his novel plan of attack against Paramount. Despite the fact that friends and colleagues were warning him that a suit against the studio was foolish, there were three things that appealed to him about the case. First, he liked and admired Buchwald for his willingness to take a stand against Hollywood. Second, O'Donnell always enjoyed a case with an "intellectual challenge." Basing a lawsuit against Paramount on breach of contract, rather than copyright law, was certainly the type of case that intrigued him. And third, as a lawyer, O'Donnell was always willing to fight the good fight for a case and a client he truly believed in. He knew it would be a long, messy, uphill struggle, but O'Donnell was ready. The partnership of Buchwald and O'Donnell was off and running.

One of Art Buchwald's closest friends in the entertainment business was Martin Davis, chairman and chief executive officer of the Gulf + Western corporation, then the parent company of Paramount. Davis, who presided over his powerful corporate empire from a New York office overlooking Central Park, was a tough, cunning, colorful, and wily man. He hated weak people and bad press, and had a legion of friends from all walks of life: Jack Valenti, head of the Motion Picture Association; Pete Rozelle, commissioner of the National Football League; and Donald Trump, to whom he had once given as a gift a copy of Hitler's *Mein Kampf*.

Early in 1988, after it had been announced that Paramount was going ahead with the Eddie Murphy project, Buchwald ran into Davis at an event and told him he was troubled about how he and Alain were being treated by his studio. At first Davis thought Art was joking, but Buchwald assured him he was dead serious. "Don't bother yourself, Marty," a clearly irritated Buchwald told Davis. "The lawyers will work it out." Months later, still believing that the Paramount matter was little more than a trifling nuisance between two old friends, Davis invited Art to deliver a speech at a charity affair he was hosting in January. And in a lighthearted gesture that Davis thought Buchwald would appreciate, the invitation came with a 1982 bottle of Dom Pérignon and an audiocassette recording of the song "Sue Me" from the Broadway musical *Guys and Dolls*. Buchwald was not amused and told Davis that by sending "such an expensive bottle of champagne," he was clearly admitting that Paramount was guilty.

After receiving the invitation from Davis, Art forwarded a copy to Pierce O'Donnell who called and asked, "What the hell's going on?" Buchwald told him about the exchange with Davis and asked whether he should attend the dinner or decline. O'Donnell, who was in the midst of preparing his final settlement offer to the studio, advised Art to accept because offending Davis might jeopardize any chance of settling the case.

On November 10, 1988, O'Donnell sent his final offer to the studio's general counsel stating that in consequence of the "shocking and callous disregard" for the contractual rights of his clients, they would be willing to settle for $5 million. After seeing a copy of the demand letter O'Donnell had sent, Buchwald wrote his lawyer:

NOVEMBER 17, 1988

Dear Pierce:

I read your letter and the accompanying exhibits and I have never been so angry at Paramount in my life. I didn't realize what varmints they really are until I studied your letter. Boy, they piss me off! How could a big movie company like that pick on two little Jewish boys. That's the way it is in America—the big guys always steal from the little guys. If it weren't for people like you, Alain and I would be sleeping in the streets right now. It makes me sick when I see what Paramount is really up to. . . .

Cheers,

Art

Several days later, while awaiting a response from Paramount's lawyers, O'Donnell received a surprise telephone call from *Wall Street*

Journal reporter Jill Abramson, who had obtained a leaked copy of his settlement offer to the studio and wanted a quote for a story she was working on. O'Donnell refused to comment, hung up, and "began to sweat." On November 21, Abramson's article appeared on the front page of the *Journal* with the headline ART BUCHWALD SAYS EDDIE MURPHY STOLE HIS IDEA FOR A MOVIE. Unbeknownst to O'Donnell, Buchwald had talked to Abramson and in his interview had tried to make clear what the dispute was all about. "I want to sue Paramount, a big conglomerate that eats up little people like me," he said. "I have nothing against Eddie Murphy." But it was the headline that made O'Donnell shudder. It was exactly what he had wanted to avoid—the media sensationalizing the dispute by pitting Buchwald against Murphy.

Days later O'Donnell received a response to his settlement offer. Not only did Paramount refuse his demand, but it accused him of an "outrageous breach" of conduct by leaking his letter to *The Wall Street Journal.* With settlement options now closed, O'Donnell filed a thirty-page complaint in Los Angeles County Superior Court alleging breach of contract and a litany of other claims against Paramount, which, the complaint argued, displayed a "calculated act of corporate cover-up of literary theft." The matter of *Buchwald v. Paramount*, docket number C-706083, was now under way. At first Art took it all in stride and with some measure of amusement. "I was in a post-election depression," he told *Newsweek* after George H. W. Bush won the presidency in November 1988. "Nothing to write about, everything was dull. Then this came along and it made me feel cheerful."

Nearly twenty years earlier, Buchwald had survived the Joe Mayflower feud, which had played itself out against the backdrop of Washington's theater of the absurd. But now, he, Bernheim, and O'Donnell were engaged in a legal battle to challenge the very foundations of Hollywood's corporate culture—a battle that would last an agonizing seven years. Art could hardly have known, or even imagined, that his fight with Hollywood would quickly turn from a simple matter of honor into an ugly struggle to save his reputation.

CHAPTER 12

DRAMA IN DEPARTMENT 52

Buchwald v. Hollywood—Act II (1989-95)

Paramount is trying to destroy my reputation!

—ART BUCHWALD

"Ladies and gentlemen of the jury!" Buchwald bellowed as he took the stage at Martin Davis's charity affair on the evening of January 28, 1989. After entertaining the audience with a few friendly jokes, Buchwald turned on his classic saucy charm. "I am suing Paramount Pictures . . . one of the companies that Martin owns," Buchwald joked. "So how, you may ask, did I get this dinner? Well, the lawsuit is nothing more than an honest disagreement between good friends. I say Paramount screwed me. And they say they didn't." Throughout Art's speech Davis appeared to take most of it in good cheer, although several of Buchwald's barbs clearly stung, bringing "strained" laughter from an increasingly uncomfortable Davis.

After the event, Davis sent a thank-you note to Art for appearing at his dinner. "No plaintiff has ever honored a defendant with such eloquence and wit—even in America!" he told Buchwald. Days later, Art told Davis that while he was pleased the event had been a success, he was sorry that he didn't have a chance to discuss another new film idea he had, which was safely tucked away "in a vault in the Bank of England and only my lawyer and myself have the combination."

It would be nearly a year before *Buchwald v. Paramount* went to trial, but during those hectic twelve months O'Donnell and his legal team sorted through mounds of business documents and memos in the Paramount archives, resisted motions by Paramount to dismiss the case, and took the depositions of potential witnesses, including Eddie Murphy.

In late April 1989, Paramount's lawyers questioned Buchwald during a three-day deposition in Washington. Although the interrogation was rigorous, O'Donnell was pleased and relieved at how well Art had held up. The one exception was at the end of the last day when a frustrated and fatigued Buchwald couldn't resist telling Paramount's lawyer exactly how he felt. "The idea which is mine—I consider mine," an irritated Buchwald blurted out. The studio had "lifted" his idea and then "spent a lot of money on it . . . and then they said they weren't going to make it. And then they made it. That is what I am saying."

As Art spoke, O'Donnell saw him "redden a bit, his eyes narrowing in anger behind his horn-rim glasses." For the first time he truly saw the passion Buchwald felt about the case, his words "eloquent, unwavering and straight from the gut."

In mid-November 1989, Paramount replaced its existing counsel with a new lawyer, Robert Draper, whom Pierce O'Donnell described as "bright, tough and tenacious." After reading the transcript of Art's first deposition, Draper asked to schedule another session with Buchwald. With O'Donnell's consent, Art sat for another round of questioning on December 5, but this time the interrogation got rough. When Draper hit Art with several questions about the requirement in his contract for his treatment to be "original," O'Donnell grew anxious, sensing that Draper was trying to set Art up. In his last question of the day, Draper asked Buchwald: "Is there a definition of plagiarism you feel comfortable with in terms of your own understanding?"

"I'll give you mine, and I don't have any dictionary basis for it," Buchwald shot back. "Somebody who takes and claims it as his own when it doesn't belong to him. Theft. I think plagiarism is theft." Draper then let the matter drop, but with only ten days before the trial was set to begin, O'Donnell had an "uneasy" feeling about where Paramount's lawyer had been heading.

The matter of *Buchwald v. Paramount* convened promptly at 9:45 A.M. on Friday, December 15, 1989, in Department 52 of the Los Angeles County Courthouse, the bailiwick of Judge Harvey Schneider, a brilliant yet modest, no-nonsense judge. Many lawyers found the taciturn Schneider to be inscrutable and enigmatic, but any lawyer who appeared in his courtroom quickly learned that he ran a tight judicial ship and was not to be trifled with. Lack of preparation or a lack of decorum in his courtroom would cause Schneider to "snarl like a Doberman pinscher and scowl like a substitute teacher on the first day of school," Pierce O'Donnell later recalled.

As soon as Judge Schneider pounded the gavel for the proceedings to begin, O'Donnell was ready. In his opening statement he asserted that Buchwald's treatment and *Coming to America* were "as close as any fraternal twins born of the same parents." The evidence would show, he argued, that Eddie Murphy had been "fully exposed" by the studio to Buchwald's original idea and, once that occurred, it was impossible to separate the two. "You simply cannot have an immaculate conception after you have been pregnant," he insisted.

Paramount's counsel, Robert Draper, refuted each of O'Donnell's contentions and then took the gloves off, taking direct aim at Buchwald's reputation, suggesting that he had actually violated his contract with Paramount by delivering a plagiarized idea to the studio. Referring to a *Herald Tribune* film review Art had written in Paris about the 1957 Charlie Chaplin movie, *A King in New York*, Draper hinted that Buchwald had "stolen" his idea from Chaplin. O'Donnell was outraged. "He was trying to turn the case into a plagiarism suit, regardless of the contract," he later said of Draper. "Art's worst nightmare had come true."

On Monday, December 18, the trial took on a circus-like atmosphere when Eddie Murphy's friend and co-star in *Coming to America*, Arsenio Hall, entered the courthouse. Pandemonium broke out in the hallway when a wild, shrieking mob of stargazers swarmed the actor as he made his way to the courtroom. Once Judge Schneider restored order, Hall took the stand and offered his account of the creation of *Coming to America*. He testified that he had never heard of the Art Buchwald project from Eddie Murphy and that Murphy's idea was to tell the story as a "black fairy tale" that provided a "positive image of royalty in Africa."

At the conclusion of his testimony, Hall stopped outside the courthouse to talk to reporters, telling them he was shocked that he and Murphy were being accused of stealing Buchwald's idea. "It's obviously our script [and] I'm offended because Eddie's a very bright man," Hall told the press. "I am a very bright and talented man . . . myself. Why do we have to seek a stolen concept? It's insulting. That's what bothers me most." Then in a jab at Buchwald he said, "It's very unfair what's going on. I'd rather loan Art Buchwald some money than go through this."

The next morning, December 19, Art took center stage. When Buchwald entered the courthouse he was mobbed by reporters as he made his way through lights, television cameras, photographers, and streams of cables. Due to a gag order imposed by Judge Schneider, Buchwald remained silent and brushed away all questions except one: When asked whether he was trying to stand up for Hollywood writers, he shouted back, "Damn right!" Once inside the courtroom, he took a seat next to an old friend, Billy Wilder, director of *Double Indemnity*, *Sunset Boulevard*, and *Some Like It Hot*. Wilder told reporters he was there as a show of support for Buchwald and the position he had taken against Hollywood. "I sympathize with him," he told the press.

When Art finally took the witness stand, O'Donnell noticed that he appeared "nervous," but once questioning got under way, Buchwald responded in a relaxed manner, sometimes with a humorous quip that made even the normally stone-faced Judge Schneider crack a smile. O'Donnell's questions to Buchwald, mostly about the history of the lawsuit, took up the remainder of the day. Day three had gone well, but tomorrow Art would be back on the stand to face Robert Draper.

Day four was filled with high drama and fireworks. When Pierce O'Donnell resumed his questioning that morning he got right to the point.

"Why did you file this lawsuit?" he asked his client.

"First, I'd like to say it's very hard for a so-called humorist to be taken seriously when he does something seriously," Art responded. "I consider this a very serious matter. I feel my property was stolen, invaded, raped—whatever you want to call it. I was very upset by it and I didn't know what to do about it." After that frank and pithy response, O'Donnell sat down. As he waited for Draper to strike, he was relieved to see that Buchwald appeared "rested and chipper" as Paramount's counsel approached the witness stand.

After a few preliminary questions, Draper moved in for the kill, asking Buchwald what his definition of the word "original" was.

" 'Original' is something that you wrote without help from anybody else, with your own little fingers," Buchwald answered.

Draper: "And did you write your treatment . . . all by yourself, without any help from anybody else?"

O'Donnell and Buchwald knew where Draper was headed; it was back to the plagiarism issue first hinted at in the deposition. When Draper pressed on, asking about the review Buchwald had written of Chaplin's film, O'Donnell jumped up and objected, calling Draper's insinuation an "offensive" attempt to "trot out the Big Lie in front of the court and the world press." In an effort to calm things, Judge Schneider interjected: "We are dealing here with adults who have thick skins. I suspect Mr. Buchwald has, I'm sure, taken criticism as

I'm sure all of the rest of us have. So I'm sure he will be able to bear up under it."

Although bothered by the accusation, Buchwald calmly responded to the question by explaining that his "ideas came from experience, not movie reviews" and reasserted the point that the idea for *Coming to America* was his and his alone. As Draper's questioning ended, O'Donnell felt good about how Art had held up under the stream of accusations and innuendos. As the morning session concluded, both sides continued to spar outside the courtroom. When asked by reporters about Draper's suggestion of plagiarism, Buchwald called it a "bunch of baloney" and O'Donnell called it a "damnable lie."

On December 21, Robert Wachs, Eddie Murphy's agent, took the stand. Under cross-examination, O'Donnell pressed him about the extent of his knowledge of Buchwald's original treatment, confronting him with a letter he had sent to novelist and screenwriter Jim Harrison on September 10, 1984. In the letter, Wachs had rejected a treatment Harrison had submitted for a possible Murphy film project, telling him his idea was "fairly close" to a Paramount-Murphy project already under way based on an "unpublished Art Buchwald story." (Harrison, who had contacted Buchwald through their mutual friend Rose Styron, had sent Art a copy of Wachs's letter on November 28, 1988. When he received Harrison's note Buchwald was ecstatic, telling him, "Thank you for sending me the 'smoking gun.' I am sure it will be very valuable, particularly since Bob Wachs pretends he has never heard of me." Buchwald immediately forwarded a copy of the letter to Pierce O'Donnell, telling him, "This is the first smoking gun ever sent by Federal Express." After reading the letter O'Donnell told Art, "This is dynamite . . . goddamn dynamite.")

In response to O'Donnell's questions about the letter to Harrison, Wachs conceded that he had, indeed, been aware of a Buchwald story, but that he used that knowledge only as a convenient way to brush off Harrison's treatment, which he considered "a poor piece of work and . . . so terribly written that I did not want to go on. I thought the fastest way was to say Paramount had something in development." O'Donnell also got Wachs to confirm that at a dinner with Eddie Murphy and a Paramount executive, Buchwald's treatment had, indeed, been mentioned but, according to Wachs, was raised only in "a two-sentence description" as part of a "menu listing about ten or twelve other projects."

At the end of the day, O'Donnell was overjoyed by Wachs's testimony. "Mission accomplished," he later wrote. "Wachs had admitted that he was keenly aware . . . Paramount had a Buchwald story in development *specifically for Eddie*, and [that he] clearly knew more about Buchwald's story than what could be told in a two-sentence pitch."

After a holiday recess, the trial resumed on December 26 when the two volumes of Eddie Murphy's October 1989 deposition were entered into the record.

During the two-day deposition, O'Donnell had asked Murphy if he had ever heard of Art Buchwald. "Yeah. He is—like a political satirist," Murphy replied. "I've seen his stuff sometimes."

O'Donnell: You like his work?
Murphy: Some of it, yeah.

While Murphy admitted to O'Donnell that he had once been told about the *King for a Day* idea by someone at Paramount, he said he "never read" Buchwald's treatment or any of the early script drafts based on it. "I know I never read [Buchwald's story]," the actor said. "It was like a very short—an idea from blah, blah, blah, something about an African guy whose government gets overthrown and he's in America, in D.C., and something like that."

O'Donnell then pressed Murphy about whether his hearing of Buchwald's treatment may have impacted or "subconsciously influenced" his thinking about *Coming to America*.

Murphy: Was my subconscious triggered by something I heard from *King for a Day*?

O'Donnell: Possible, yes. Do you know for a fact whether it was or not?

Murphy: I don't know what triggers my subconscious.

O'Donnell: That's my point. Okay. So you really can't tell, can you?

Murphy: No.

The following morning, as Pierce O'Donnell sat at home preparing for closing arguments, his phone rang and at the other end was an enraged Art Buchwald, who told him he had just received a call from a reporter who said Paramount was going to countersue him for breach of contract for stealing his idea from the Chaplin movie. "Paramount is trying to destroy my reputation!" Buchwald hollered through the phone. "They're making me pay for suing them! They don't care anymore whether they win or not. They're going to take me down with them. It's all over. If I win, I lose." Buchwald told O'Donnell he was unsure about whether it had all been worth it. Faced with the stark reality that his reputation and livelihood were on the line, he grumbled, "I knew it, Pierce. I knew it. Those bastards have stolen from me again. But this time, I'll never get it back. Never. I've worked for forty years as a writer. I have never, *ever*, never been accused of stealing someone else's work. I have always written my own material. God, why did I do this?"

O'Donnell sympathized with Art and regarded what Paramount's lawyer was alleging as the "most dastardly thing imaginable." He had never heard Art "so down" or so angry. "Art, you have every right to be pissed off," his lawyer told him. "Paramount's behavior is outrageous. But it's because they are desperate. They know you're going to whip their ass tomorrow. They're pulling out all the stops. You have 'em on the ropes, Art. One more day and it's all over."

But Buchwald could hardly contain his fury. "It's just beginning," he told O'Donnell. "I'm the one who'll have the plagiarist rap hung on him. You get to go on to another case. For the rest of my life, I'm the plagiarist."

O'Donnell then knew it was time for some tough talk. "Art, that's bullshit!" he shot back. "You're no plagiarist. You know it. I know it. And I'll bet my eyeteeth the judge knows it too." Buchwald then asked O'Donnell why he was so sure. "I think he'll see the whole Charlie Chaplin thing as a smear campaign," he replied. "I'm going to make you a promise. I'm taking off the gloves on this Chaplin crap. Don't worry any more about it. Just hold on for twenty-four more hours."

Buchwald hesitated, and O'Donnell hung on in silence. Then Art spoke: "Okay, Pierce. We've gone this far together. I'll trust your judgment. I hope you're right. God, do I hope you're right."

Thursday, December 28, 1989, was the eighth and final day of the trial. Department 52 was packed with an overflow crowd of press, onlookers, and Hollywood stargazers, all on hand to hear the closing arguments in *Buchwald v. Paramount*. Art was at home in Washington that day anxiously awaiting news of the final clash between his lawyer and the attorney for Paramount.

After settling the courtroom, Judge Schneider nodded to the plaintiff's counsel to begin. "Victor Hugo once said, 'Greater than the march of mighty armies is an idea whose time has come,'" O'Donnell declared. "What did Paramount buy under its agreement with Buchwald? I submit to you that it bought a great idea ... conceived by a great writer and humorist. It was original in every sense of the word. Far more than a creative spark, it ignited a fire that lasted for five years and raged in two studios." Under tough questioning from the judge, O'Donnell reaffirmed his contention that Buchwald's idea formed the basis for *Coming to America*, calling it a "catalyst," "starting point," and "springboard." "I do not hang my hat on the fact that there is a little snippet here, a little snippet there," he continued. "It was wholesale, it was in gross, and it was used in *Coming to America*."

When Judge Schneider pressed O'Donnell again on how similar

two works must be for one to be "based upon" the other, he pointed to thirty-five similarities between Buchwald's treatment, the two script drafts, and the final *Coming to America* screenplay. "There comes a point where too much is enough, and in this case, we have it," he concluded. When asked whether there would be "anything inconsistent about finding a great deal of creativity by [Eddie] Murphy and still finding 'based upon,'" O'Donnell conceded that it would not be "inconsistent at all."

As O'Donnell wound up his argument, he remembered his promise to Art and took direct aim at what he called Draper's "scurrilous" plagiarism allegation against his client. "I submit to your honor it's an intentional act by Paramount Pictures to hurt Art Buchwald. No fair-minded human being could see, could watch, could experience—even in a stupor—Charlie Chaplin's movie and conclude that there is any resemblance." Then, his voice rising, he continued to hammer away at the charge:

> It's a lie broadcast around the world now twice, your honor.... That is a desperate act of a desperate defendant! Your honor, that's not just dirty pool, that's scurrilous conduct by a defendant who should be sanctioned in this case. Art Buchwald does not have to have his well-deserved reputation tarnished in a California court by this defendant merely so it might be able to win a lawsuit. The fact remains that this is a damnable lie! Your honor, if you would do one thing in this case, for Art Buchwald and writers like him who have the guts to stand up to Paramount Pictures . . . I would ask that you proclaim that it is a damnable lie. And that there is not a shred of evidence in this record to support any finding, much less an argument by counsel, that Art Buchwald is a plagiarist. Art Buchwald is one of the great writers of our time and I submit to you whatever happens in this case, let's keep his good name intact.

After a fifteen-minute recess, Paramount's counsel came out swinging. "Now, of course, Eddie Murphy's black," he said, "and Eddie

Murphy's a megastar and Eddie Murphy makes a lot of money. But Eddie Murphy has some feelings too. And he's not a Pulitzer Prize winner like Mr. Buchwald and he's not white like Mr. Buchwald and he's not an attorney. Not an establishment person like Mr. Buchwald." And then in a backhanded swipe he continued, "But I don't really think that Mr. Buchwald is submitting this treatment that's in evidence for his next Pulitzer Prize. In fact, the meanest thing I could do to Mr. Buchwald is . . . to distribute it to the press." When Draper then returned to his assertion that Murphy was a "victim of racial prejudice," Judge Schneider jumped in and with a "stern voice" cut Draper off: "I don't perceive this to be a case about race, Mr. Draper."

During the remainder of his argument, Paramount's counsel sparred back and forth with the judge over the definition of "based upon," as applied to Buchwald's treatment, and then rested his case. Judge Schneider gathered his papers and said, "All right, gentlemen, the case will now stand submitted."

Knowing he would want to hear what had been said in his defense, O'Donnell overnighted an audiotape of his closing argument to Buchwald. After listening to the recording, Art called O'Donnell to thank him from "the bottom of his heart" for the "vigorous defense" he had offered of his reputation. Then Ann Buchwald got on the line to thank him for all he'd done and to say that their mutual friend "Ed Williams had to be smiling too."

On Monday, January 8, 1990, at eight-thirty A.M., Judge Schneider issued his opinion from the bench in the matter of *Buchwald v. Paramount*. In his decision he ordered Paramount to pay Buchwald and Bernheim $250,000 plus interest, along with 19 percent of net profits from the film. Buchwald, Alain Bernheim, and Pierce O'Donnell had won. David had beaten Goliath. When O'Donnell heard the news he was overjoyed, declaring to his legal team, "A year ago, everyone said we were crazy and would be annihilated. Well, we proved them wrong. The good guys beat a studio."

News of the judge's decision was flashed around the world. The *Los Angeles Times* proclaimed PAY BUCHWALD, STUDIO TOLD, and *The Washington Post* wrote ART BUCHWALD WINS SUIT AGAINST PARAMOUNT. Days later, Peter Jennings, on ABC's *World News Tonight*, anointed Buchwald as their "Person of the Week," by declaring he had "taken on the big guy—Paramount Pictures—and won."

That afternoon, Art told a reporter for *The Washington Post* that he was exhausted, having barely slept a wink during the weekend as he awaited the judge's decision. Speaking in a "somber" voice, he talked about the strain the case had placed on him and his family. "When you go through one of these things you feel very, very washed out at the end of it. All you want to do is get your reputation back." But Art was more upbeat with a reporter for *The New York Times*, saying he was "absolutely thrilled" by the decision. "We considered ourselves the little guys, and the big guys tried to get us, but we won." Winning money was never the point of his lawsuit, he told a reporter for the *Los Angeles Times*, but "he hoped to strike a blow for the creative people in Hollywood." In the end, he said, the victory was "probably the fourth or fifth happiest day" of his life, right up there with the day that he left the U.S. Marine Corps.

Although it was still to be determined how much in net profit damages the studio would have to pay, Judge Schneider in his thirty-four-page decision gave Art something much more valuable to him than a pure monetary award: He decreed that Buchwald's untarnished reputation was intact, dismissing entirely any suggestion that he had plagiarized his treatment. "There is not a scintilla of evidence that Buchwald's treatment was in any way based on [Chaplin's] A *King in New York*," the judge declared.

Also, despite the fact that Eddie Murphy was not a party to the suit, Judge Schneider made it clear that he found no fault with the actor. "It is clear to the Court that each of these men is a creative genius in his own field and each is a uniquely American institution," he wrote in his opinion. "This case is also not about whether Eddie Murphy made substantial contributions to the film.... The Court is convinced he did. Finally, this case is not about whether Eddie Murphy 'stole' Art Buchwald's concept. . . . Rather, this is primarily a breach of contract case between Buchwald and Paramount."

After Judge Schneider's ruling, Buchwald received calls and letters from fans and admirers everywhere, including tributes from two old friends, Russell Baker and William F. Buckley, Jr.:

JANUARY 11, 1990

Dear Art:

You have done a great thing for writers. You deserve a statue. It should stand at the entrance to Ma Maison [the famous Hollywood restaurant on Melrose Avenue], *as a warning to all thieves who enter there.*

Humbly and admiringly,
Russ

And from Buckley a letter congratulating him on the verdict along with a suggestion about what he might do with the money from Paramount:

JANUARY 10, 1990

Dear Art:

. . . Now that you own Hollywood, maybe you should think of sending Mr. Hertz a present at Christmas-time?

Warmest,
Bill

Although Buchwald, Bernheim, and O'Donnell had beaten Hollywood, they didn't own anything—yet. Astoundingly, it would take another five and a half years before the case of *Buchwald v. Paramount* was finally resolved.

At first Paramount's attorneys argued that there were no "net profits" available from *Coming to America* to pay Buchwald and Bernheim under their contract—despite the fact that it was one of the highest grossing films of 1988. In fact, the studio's lawyers contended, the film had actually *lost* money.

Astonished and outraged by Paramount's claim that such a successful film was, in fact, in the "red," O'Donnell mounted a new legal challenge against the legitimacy of the studio's contract. Although it took twelve more months of legal wrangling in and out of court, on December 21, 1990, Judge Schneider ruled in favor of Buchwald once again, declaring the studio's contract "overly harsh," "unfair," and "unconscionable," and, as a consequence, Paramount would be obligated to pay Buchwald and Bernheim a "fair and reasonable" compensation for their creative services.

O'Donnell was ecstatic when he received word of Schneider's second major ruling. "This is a fantastic victory," he told *Variety* magazine. Back home in Washington, Buchwald was equally ecstatic: "I can't tell you how happy I am," he told a reporter for *The New York Times*. "I think it's a great thing for Christmas—a good Christmas for the little people."

Buchwald, Bernheim, and O'Donnell were now two for two against Paramount, but they still needed one last victory: a final determination from Judge Schneider as to just how much of Hollywood they would "own."

On March 16, 1992, Judge Schneider rendered his final decision in the case, granting an award of $900,000 to both plaintiffs: $150,000 for Buchwald and $750,000 for Alain Bernheim as "fair and reasonable" compensation for their work. Initially, O'Donnell was upset over the size of the award, but quickly put a positive spin on it all. The judgment is "close to four times what Paramount wanted to pay," he told a *New York Times* reporter. "We won the case. We won the legal rulings. We still consider it a victory."

Buchwald was thrilled by the outcome. "I'm delighted. We beat Paramount," he told *The Washington Post.* "Sure, if I counted on making millions, I'd be disappointed. But I didn't count on that. . . . The important thing is not the money, but that we won the battle. We won every battle."

The next morning, March 17, Art had one more small victory to savor. When he arrived at his office, he took the bottle of Dom Pérignon which Martin Davis had mockingly sent to him nearly four years before, packaged it with care, and then returned it to the head of Paramount Communications with an enclosed note:

Marty—
I believe this belongs to you. You need a drink.
Art

A delighted and relieved Buchwald hoped that Judge Schneider's decision in his favor would finally bring an end to the long, drawn-out struggle with Martin Davis and Paramount. But to his great dismay, he soon learned otherwise. Paramount's lawyers were ordered to file an appeal. "Marty was . . . the King of Chutzpah," Buchwald said, and the whole matter had become a professional and personal challenge and embarrassment to Davis. *Buchwald v. Paramount* had become "the lawsuit that will not die," Art said in despair.

As he and O'Donnell prepared for one final round against the titans of Hollywood, Buchwald turned his attention back to his life, his family, and his friends in Washington: a welcome distraction from lawyers, corporate overlords, and studio executives.

THE CASE OF *MCDONALD'S V. CHEESEBURGER*

Despite Buchwald's fame as a celebrated columnist and Hollywood crusader, recurrent episodes of mistaken identity seem to have been an ongoing occupational hazard. As if the long-running Hertz Rental Car Company mix-up of Buckley and Buchwald wasn't enough, in the spring of 1991 he was faced with a new dilemma after he was mistaken for the legendary political cartoonist Herbert Lawrence Block—popularly known as Herblock.

MAY 28, 1991

Dear Herb:

I cannot live with this any longer, and I have got to get it off my chest.

Last Saturday at 12:25 p.m. I went into McDonald's at Mazza Gallerie and ordered a Big Mac, a diet cola and french fries. I was just about to pay when the manager rushed up and said, "Don't take this man's money. This man doesn't pay."

I looked at him and he explained, "I have been waiting for years for you to come into my place. I want to thank you for all the pleasure you have given me and—YOU DON'T PAY."

He turned to the cashier and said, "His money is no good." He then turned back to me and continued, "You are the greatest man I know, and in my place you can have anything you want."

I was feeling pretty good as he announced, with everyone watching, "Herblock, you are the greatest cartoonist of our time and you honor me by letting me buy you a hamburger."

So, here was the situation: Do I tell the guy the truth and ruin his day, or do I eat a free hamburger and live a lie for the rest of my life? I opted for the latter.

The only reason I am telling you this, Herb, is so that you don't go into the McDonald's at Mazza Gallerie and claim to be Herblock. They will accuse you of being an imposter and throw you out on your ass.

Cheers,

Art

Days later, a sympathetic Herblock responded:

JUNE 4, 1991

Dear Art:

Re: the McDonald's incident—your uncoerced confession is in hand. You are obviously familiar with McDonald v. Cheeseburger, *which you wrote about, and there are also the earlier decisions,* Sullivan v. Corbett, *and* Willard v. Dempsey. *I'm entitled to my hamburger and my attorneys or federal marshals may call on you with a warrant and a stomach pump—although I understand the statute of limitations on burgers is pretty short.*

On second thought, you may have suffered enough already. What were you doing eating burgers and french fries anyhow? Forget the attorneys—I'll talk to Annie about this.

> *Yr obdnt srvent, and*
> *Cnstnt fan,*
> *Herb*

A NEW BUCHWALD DISCIPLE

The presidential campaign of 1992 pitted incumbent president George H. W. Bush against former Arkansas governor Bill Clinton. As the two nominees made their final push for the White House, Buchwald was, as always, ready for another round of bipartisan humor. When both Bush and Clinton tried to embrace the legacy of Harry Truman after the publication of David McCullough's *Truman* biography, a reader asked Buchwald why Bush "would try to identify with Harry Truman." Buchwald had a ready response: "Because someone told Bush that Truman attended Yale." When Buchwald was asked about Clinton's ability to provide him with comic material if he was elected, Art responded that when he heard Clinton admit he had smoked marijuana but never inhaled, he was certain his column would be safe for at least four years. When questioned about his views on

Texas billionaire Ross Perot, who was running as an independent third-party candidate, Buchwald simply replied, "That's not the question. Come to think of it, it's not the answer either."

On Tuesday, November 3, 1992, William Jefferson Clinton was elected the forty-second president of the United States. Although most Democrats rejoiced in Clinton's victory over Bush, Buchwald noted that many of Georgetown's "Democratic cultural elite" seemed "uncomfortable and ill at ease" with the outcome. In an unusually serious column written shortly after Clinton was sworn in, Art wrote that after engaging in twelve years of partisan bashing of the Reagans and Bushes at dinners and cocktail parties, the Georgetown crowd weren't quite sure how to behave or entertain themselves with a *Democrat* now in the White House.

This bizarre cultural-political disorientation was on full display one evening in late January 1993 when Buchwald attended a party at the Georgetown home of his friend film producer and director George Stevens, Jr., founder of the American Film Institute and creator of the annual Kennedy Center Honors award program. Stevens casually suggested to Buchwald that with a Democratic president now in the White House he might consider tempering his columns about Clinton and "never discuss his flaws in public."

Buchwald was floored by Stevens's suggestion. "Are we allowed to criticize Clinton at all?" he asked.

"Sure," his host replied, "if he's going to do something wrong, which he is certainly not going to do."

An astonished Buchwald said he would not allow anyone to "muzzle" him. He had a reputation as a political satirist to uphold and a "living to make." While several other guests at the party sided with Buchwald, Stevens had the last word. "We've waited too long to have a person like you make light of the greatest leader in the free world. If you want to stoop to your juvenile media tricks, do it in someone else's home." With that, Art left the party "in a huff," dumbfounded as to what "one li'l old Democratic presidential victory will do to lifelong friendships."

Days later Buchwald received a sympathetic letter from Christopher Buckley, novelist, commentator, political satirist, and son of Buchwald's longtime Hertz Rental Car Company rival, William F. Buckley, Jr.:

JANUARY 29, 1993

Dear Art,

I've been a fan of yours for many, many years, but your column about that encounter at George Stevens' house made me into a Buchwald disciple. Though not a denizen of the Georgetown scene myself, I've experienced it, and I recognized it in your piece so well. Good for you for holding a mirror up to it, and bless you for storming out into the night. Ideologues of any stripe tend to lose the thing that matters most to people like us—if I may be so bold as to include myself in your company— their sense of humor.

I just wanted you to know that, as you afflict the comfortable, I'm up here in Cleveland Park cheering you on loudly.

> *Be well,*
> *Christopher Buckley*
> *Holder of the molybdenum card*

Days later, Buchwald sent a letter of thanks to Buckley for his support:

FEBRUARY 3, 1993

Dear Christopher:

Thank you so much for the kind letter. It was the only one I have received in 1993.

I don't know where the future will lead us, but I hope that I can afford a large Hertz car to take me there. . . .

> *Cheers,*
> *Art*

"BABY-BOOMERS LOVE A PRETTY FACE"

In February 1993, it was announced that Russell Baker, former *New York Times* columnist and charter member of the American Academy of Humor, would replace Alistair Cooke as the host of public television's *Masterpiece Theatre*. Buchwald was thrilled by the news:

24 FEBRUARY 1993

Dear Russ:

Congratulations on getting the job with Masterpiece Theater. I turned it down because I couldn't stand the sex and violence on the MacNeil/Lehrer News Hour—but I suggested you as a second choice.

Russ, I think you made the right decision. Writing for a living is old hat and nobody gives a damn anymore about the written word, but the baby-boomers love a pretty face, and, God knows, you have one.

I have had experience with television so I'd like to give you some tips: Always look into the camera even when you know that your fly is open. Pretend that you are talking to one person instead of the millions who have nothing better to do on Sunday nights. Don't worry if you get the title of the play wrong, because fifty percent of all PBS audiences go to the bathroom when the host is talking.

Your most important role as host of Masterpiece Theater comes at the end of the month during public television's fundraising drive. It is then that you are expected to be sincere and persuasive. Frankly, I think that's why they hired you anyway, because everyone says that you can squeeze money out of a turnip.

Russ, I want you to know that you do honor to the Academy. You can't get a Pulitzer Prize by introducing Thackeray on television, but there are thousands of Emmys out there waiting to be picked up. I hope that you become a household face. Remember your friends—those of us who chose to stay with the printed word, knowing that there was no money in it. Walking down the street won't be the same anymore. Little

old ladies will be stopping you on Madison Avenue for your autograph,
and asking whether you knew Jane Eyre personally.

Your friend,
Art

"WHERE'S COKIE?"

For decades, Buchwald's brand name had earned him a steady and lucrative income as a speaker and toastmaster at tribute dinners, college commencements, book fairs, and annual trade association meetings. At each stop along the way, Buchwald entertained overflow crowds with political one-liners and satirical commentary on the state of the world.

But as any celebrity speaker knows, the lecture circuit can be grueling work. "Lecturing, according to insurance statistics, is among the most hazardous professions in the United States," Buchwald once joked, "and only 7 out of every 10 speakers ever return from a tour."

Despite the perils of life on the road, Art was always happy to fill in for a friend in need. In mid-February 1993, Cokie Roberts, author, historian, and acclaimed ABC News and National Public Radio correspondent, was scheduled to be the keynote speaker at a business conference in Fresno, California. When a last-minute schedule glitch forced Roberts to cancel, Buchwald was happy to fill in. The day after his appearance he sent a full trip report to his friend:

18 FEBRUARY 1993

Dear Cokie:

You probably heard that I filled in for you in Fresno. I thought you might want to know how it went. I flew from Washington to Kansas City where I joined a mule train on its way to Salt Lake City. It started to snow so I rented a dog sled and made it to Tulsa where someone stole my dogs so I had to buy a horse and make my way to Colorado where I had to build a raft in six days to cross the Colorado River. I got to the other side but I was held up by bandits and they took all my money and my clothes so I worked in a copper mine for a month to be able to buy new ones.

Then I bought another horse and was almost killed by Indians in Arizona. I finally made it to the outskirts of Fresno when Mexican out-laws shot my horse out from under me. I crawled the last five miles on my hands and knees to the Chamber of Commerce where a large crowd had gathered. When I got within six feet of the building a hush fell. A man wearing a black hat and smoking a cigar looked down at me and said angrily, "Where's Cookie?"

So much for show business,

> *Cheers*
> *Art*

"A MILLION OUT OF THOSE HOLLYWOOD BASTARDS"

Finally, in the summer of 1995 Buchwald's long, drawn-out seven-year struggle against Hollywood in the landmark case of *Buchwald v. Paramount* came to an end. After Judge Harvey Schneider's last ruling in favor of Buchwald and Bernheim, Paramount had hired a new law-yer, Bertram Fields, a highly successful appellate attorney, to try to overturn the judgment. But as Fields prepared his appeal, a corporate shake-up at Paramount signaled the end of the matter when the studio was bought out by the entertainment conglomerate Viacom, headed by Sumner Redstone. Shortly after the takeover, Martin Davis was out the door.

Soon Redstone and his top assistants, who wanted to put an end to the bad publicity generated by the Buchwald case, made overtures to settle the case. "This new Paramount crowd just didn't want any part of [the suit]," a relieved Buchwald said. "They said, 'Get rid of it.'"

When it appeared likely that an agreement was near, Art wrote a heartfelt note to his lawyer: "I want to tell you something from the bottom of my heart," he told O'Donnell. "You and your colleagues have fought for us for seven years. You never quit, never despaired, no matter how tough things got. Right up to the end, you were our fearless champions."

Finally, in late June 1995 the case came to an end when O'Donnell reached an agreement with Paramount's lawyers to settle for $1,021,466, and, just as important to Art, there was no requirement to sign a confidentiality agreement. Years later, O'Donnell would reflect on what the titanic struggle against Paramount had meant. "Of all the lessons learned . . . the most valuable one is something that they do not teach you in law school: nothing worth anything comes without a struggle; and fighting for what we believe is right, no matter the sacrifice, is ennobling. . . . Art has become a dear friend whose unfailing decency and integrity, as well as his wit and charm, made him an implacable plaintiff and inspiration to us all."

In the fall of 1995, only months after the Paramount case was settled, Art wrote an admiring letter to Maureen Dowd of *The New York Times*, whose brilliant and incisive writings about American politics and culture would eventually earn her a Pulitzer Prize in 1999 for distinguished commentary. In his letter Buchwald wrote:

19 SEPTEMBER 1995

Dear Maureen:

I just wanted to tell you how much I have been enjoying your columns. It's very hard for one columnist to write a letter like this to another because it seems disloyal to oneself! But you are really wonderful. . . .

Sincerely,
Art

Days later, Dowd wrote back with thanks and a salute to Buchwald for taking on Hollywood:

Art—

I had dinner with [Ben] Bradlee the other night, and told him how happy I was that you had gotten a million out of those Hollywood bastards, and he said you didn't, after all the whittling.

Anyway, you deserve the best of everything. You're the gold standard.

I love your note. I'll keep it in my desk drawer for luck!

Maureen

BUCHWALD BLUES

Years of Laughter, Years of Sorrow (1991-95)

Humor is the other side of tragedy.

—JAMES THURBER

Art Buchwald's fellow columnist Erma Bombeck once said, "There is a thin line that separates laughter and pain, comedy and tragedy, humor and hurt." During the 1990s, Buchwald's life veered to and fro, back and forth across that thin line.

Early in his life he learned that humor—"the greatest defense in the world"—was a gift that helped him survive the difficulties and uncertainties of life. But even for an accomplished funny man like Buchwald, the 1990s truly tested his belief in the power of humor. During these years he would say goodbye to old friends; go public about his lifelong battle with depression; and, finally, struggle to carry on his fabled funny business in the midst of a personal life afflicted with upheaval and loss. But, in the end, he would carry on with the steady support of friends and a deep abiding faith in the power of humor to overcome difficulties and the tragedies of life. As Senator Edward Kennedy observed, Art had an "ability to use humor to meet adversity" and a "fighting spirit" equal to any challenge.

Back in the spring of 1963, Art had suffered his first serious attack of depression, a case so severe that he had been hospitalized for several weeks. At the time he was convinced he would never recover and that his career was over. But he fought back and recovered. When the incident occurred, Buchwald never disclosed the episode or discussed his battle with depression in public. He was too afraid and too embarrassed, but he also knew that his struggle was not yet over.

During the next several decades, the sadness that always lurked inside would occasionally surface, with one troubling episode occurring in the midst of the *Buchwald v. Paramount* lawsuit. But nothing matched the attack he experienced during the summer of 1985—an attack marked by severe, erratic, and unpredictable outbursts and behavior. "No one recognized my manic phase," he later said, "because people thought I was being funny." Those manic episodes were soon followed by a horrible emotional crash, plunging him, he later wrote, "into a terrible black inky lake" and sending him to the hospital once again for treatment in a psychiatric ward.

At one point he even considered suicide, but he later recalled an incident that convinced him he had to live. One day during a visit by his wife, Ann, she placed a photograph of their children next to his bed. "I knew I could never kill myself as long as those three children were there."

Finally, he was discharged, and by the end of the summer Art's condition had improved to a point where he and Ann could go to Martha's Vineyard, by way of Edward Bennett Williams's private jet, to enjoy several weeks of much-needed rest and recovery time. Although it had been a "sad summer," Ann told Williams in a letter of thanks in early September 1985, the time away from Washington had done them a world of good, providing a bit of "pleasure and peace of mind" on the island they both loved.

During those difficult summer months, many of Buchwald's friends had stayed close at hand, offering constant help and encouragement. "Thanks for being so kind to me throughout my illness. You are a true friend and I'm grateful," Art told Kay Graham when he returned to work that fall. And by November he was pleased to report to Jacqueline Kennedy Onassis that his time on Martha's Vineyard had done him a world of good. "Thanks for your note," he told Mrs. Onassis, "I'm feeling great and seem to be over the blues of the summer. I will give the Vineyard 90% credit for my coming back."

It would be six more years before Buchwald finally went public about his battle with depression, but when he did he was typically candid, philosophical, and bravely whimsical about it all. "People ask, 'Why would a funny man be depressed?'" he wrote. "My answer is, 'Why not?' Humorists (also people in show business, writers and artists) are funny to cover up the hurts they have suffered as children. When the humor fails to work for them, they have a depression."

Buchwald admitted that it was often difficult for him to reconcile his public persona with his inner agony. "Funny men like me were supposed to be immune to the serious blues. But it wasn't so," he once wrote. "The price I paid for success was that by building a wall around me, no one could penetrate my real feelings. The scars of childhood were always there, and I was a fool to think I could get away with humor forever."

Despite his periods of despair, Buchwald learned that by overcoming his demons he became a stronger person. "A funny thing can happen to you in a depression," he wrote late in life. "If you don't hurt yourself, you can gain tremendous insights and empathy, find inner strengths and hidden talents. It's a mysterious process, but if you can hold on, you become a wiser and better person."

The "empathy" Buchwald learned during his own battle with depression inspired him to help others who suffered as he did. One of his proudest moments was his ability to help two close friends, journalist Mike Wallace and novelist William Styron—the "Blues Brothers" as the trio dubbed themselves. In his bestselling book *Darkness Visible*, Styron vividly and movingly writes about his own painful and personal struggle with depression. In almost Shakespearean terms he characterizes the "dreadful and raging disease" of depression as being like a "storm—a veritable howling tempest in the brain."

In the fall of 1991, Art wrote a piece for *Vanity Fair* about his friend-ship with Styron and their mutual battle against depression:

When Bill Styron went into his depression, he called me. It wasn't that I was his best friend. It was just that I was coming out of a de-pression of my own and he wanted to talk with someone who had recently been down there. . . .

As a fellow victim, I knew that a telephone call from someone who is suffering from depression must be treated with respect. This is particularly true if that person calls to announce that he or she is contemplating bodily harm. Bill announced his intention to hurt himself not because he wanted to do it, but because he wanted someone to talk him out of it. I had used the same game plan time and time again during my depression.

When I received the call from Bill that day, he assured me there was no hope and he was going to take his life. I told him, in a drill sergeant's voice, "Bill, that is unacceptable." Apparently it was the right thing to say. To this day Bill remembers "unaccept-able" as the word that stopped him in his tracks.

The depressed person spends a good portion of his day crying out for help. As Bill's depression adviser I was able to pass on knowledge that other people had given me. For example, when things are bad you must offer the depressed person alternatives to his plans for self-destruction. One suggestion that seemed to work for Bill was that he take long walks with another person. . . . Walk-ing is an activity that produces different thoughts from the ones you get staring at the ceiling. I remember one night, when things were really cold and bleak, I ordered Bill to put on his coat, take his wife, Rose, and his dog, and get the hell out of the house. It gave him a diversion which is absolutely essential at that moment.

At some point, a person with a sick relative or friend thinks he or she is getting nowhere. It is no time for the helpmate to get dis-couraged. Communication is a most important link between light and darkness, and must be maintained. A strong case for living has to be made over and over again—death cannot even be discussed as an option.

Styron dealt with his depression in two ways: he was a victim and at the same time he was an observer. He read articles on it and pumped anyone who he heard was an expert. He told me that the only worthwhile contribution I made to his cure was when I assured him that anyone with a depression comes out of it—and comes out of it a better person. Bill didn't trust many people, but he was willing to accept a little of what I said about depression because I confessed to him that I still wasn't over mine. I spoke with authority even though I had none. But caring for Bill was very therapeutic for me, because the worse he got, the healthier I felt.

Bill has been able to describe the hell one goes through better than anyone I know. Because his account of the journey into (and out of) the black pit was recognizable to so many depressed people, he has become a role model for an entire legion of the damned. His articles and now his book, *Darkness Visible*, have made a wonderful contribution to those who are afflicted. He came not out of the closet but rather up through the cellar to tell people they were not alone.

One of the most important things a depressed person needs is a support system. My advice to those who wish to help their loved ones is to listen to them. Do not put them down when they are not making the type of sense you would like them to.

Refrain from telling anyone in a depression to straighten up and fly right. If he could, he wouldn't need you in the first place.

Repeat over and over again, no matter how tiresome it sounds, that everyone eventually recovers from a depression.

Above all, remind a depressed person that there are therapists who can treat the disease, and many drugs to alleviate the pain. . . .

Bill Styron and I often talk about our depression like two aging ex-Marines, which we are. One day, after we were both on the road to recovery, Bill claimed he had a much more severe depression than I did. He snarled, "It was a 9.5 on the Richter scale." I shot back that his depression was no more serious than a rainy day at Disneyland.

We had climbed one more step out of the pit. We both could laugh again.

Five years later, during a 1996 public radio program titled "Gray Matters: Depression and the Brain," two of the "Blues Brothers" talked candidly about their battles with depression and how their friendship with Art had helped them. Mike Wallace described how Buchwald was always there for him during his darkest moments. "He would stay with me on the telephone, night after night, after night, listening and listening, and giving me the benefit of his understanding of what happens when you are clinically depressed. And I'm certain that I would never have survived if it weren't for Buchwald. And I believe he did the same thing more or less with Styron." Echoing Wallace's sentiments, Styron described the help he received from Buchwald. "I have to give Art credit. He's basically a funny man and we all know that, but he is capable of depth":

> In effect, he was the Virgil to our Dante, because he'd been there before like Virgil. Unlike Dante, we had not been there. And he really charted the depths, and it was very, very useful to have Art on the phone. Because we needed it. Because this is a new experience for everyone, it's totally terrifying. And you need someone who has been there to give you parameters and an understanding of where you're going.

WE'LL ALWAYS HAVE PARIS

While the marriages of many of Buchwald's friends had fallen apart over the years, Art and Ann had held together. "All my buddies are split," Buchwald once told an interviewer. "I look around and I'm the only one still married. I guess it's because I never learned to pack."

Despite some occasional ups and downs, all in all, his life with Ann had been "a happy marriage, if you don't count the unhappiness," Buchwald once mused. But in the mid-1980s, things began to change and their marriage started to fall apart. A cloud of "unhappiness" and sadness started to overshadow their lives as a series of health issues and professional and personal differences took a tragic toll on their marriage. The first blow came in the early 1980s when Ann, a longtime smoker, suffered a severe heart attack, requiring bypass surgery at Georgetown University Hospital and months of recuperation time at home. Then, in the summer of 1985, Art was hit hard with his crippling bout of depression. It was a difficult time for them both, and over the next several years the stress of Art's job, health concerns, and tensions and disagreements over work and family matters continued to take a heavy toll on their thirty-year marriage. "They were like two ships drifting apart," their son, Joel, said.

Although Art often tried using humor to keep things upbeat and relaxed, by the fall of 1992 life at home had become so sad and difficult that Art decided "it was best for them both" if he moved out.

When Art left Hawthorne Street in October 1992, Ann was hurt, "shocked, and angry." And many of their close friends were furious at Art's decision to leave. Others, however, including their friend Erma Bombeck, were saddened but sympathetic to the separation:

NOVEMBER 13, 1992

Dear Art—

You doin' okay? I think about you a lot. Decisions like that are never easy.

I wrote a note to Ann. I love you both. My friends who have been through this say it gets easier after the initial shock.

If you need something to look forward to—I saw a fruitcake last week with your name on it. . . .

Love,
Erma

Two weeks later Buchwald responded with a touch of painful humor:

NOVEMBER 22, 1992

Dear Erma:

Thank you so much for your kind letter. I am getting along okay. Every woman I have met so far is after me—not for my body but they all want to be my decorator. They come sashaying up to me and start showing me swatches of upholstery fabric. You never told me that living alone was this fascinating.

I know that it's been tough on all our friends, particularly since they like both of us. But most people seem to be able to top the story that we have when it comes to their friends or themselves.

As you say, it does get easier as time goes on.

Love,

Art

But things didn't get easier. Tragically, only nine months later, Ann was hit with more devastating news. In August 1993, their physician, Dr. Michael Newman, informed her that she had lung cancer. Days later, Joel Buchwald, who had been traveling in Europe, arrived at home in Washington, where he learned the horrible news. Alone and still estranged from Art, Ann asked her son to stay on to help her cope with the shock of the news and her illness. Joel immediately agreed.

When Art heard the report about Ann, he, too, was devastated—and racked with guilt. Although they remained apart, over the next several months the two had a reconciliation of sorts, brought about by Art's work on a memoir about their life together in Europe titled *I'll Always Have Paris.* Nearly every day, Art would stop by the house to see Ann and to "read passages to her" from the manuscript. "I can't write about my life without including you as the star," he told her.

As Ann's health continued to deteriorate, Art spent more and more time with her at Hawthorne Street, sharing memories about their years together in Paris. Those sessions brought some joy to them both and helped soothe some of the bitterness from their separation. "Paris had been the scene of our happiest moments and, after a short while, I found that she looked forward to correcting my facts and adding details that I had forgotten. Those last days were very precious. Paris brought us together in the beginning and it brought us together at the end."

And the end came all too soon. On July 3, 1994, only eleven months after she was diagnosed with cancer, Ann passed away. "Art was shattered by Ann's death," Joseph Califano later recalled, and for years after he always felt a sense of remorse about how things had ended. "When a loved one dies, you carry around a lot of guilt," Buchwald later wrote. "I still do. And even now, I hurt when I think about her."

When preparations were being made for Ann's funeral, Joel Buchwald suggested a soloist sing "La Marseillaise," since Paris had played such a significant role in his mother's life. Art loved the idea, and as the soloist sang the French national anthem at the memorial service, he knew it was the "perfect tribute to Ann, and to Paris, which had given both of us so many glorious years."

Four days after Ann's death, Art received a letter of condolence from Arthur Schlesinger, Jr.:

7 JULY 1994

Dear Art:

Alexandra and I read the news of Ann's death with great sorrow. She was a charming, admirable and gallant woman, and I hope the end came without too much pain.

I know from my own experience how marriages can go sour and yet one retains respect and affection for people you can no longer live with. Your friends loved you both and well understood the dilemmas of life. Alexandra joins in sending all sympathy and affection at this sad time.

Yours ever,
Arthur

"MOST HONEST STUFF I'VE EVER DONE"

In January 1994, six months after Ann's death, Buchwald's poignant and, at times, painful memoir *Leaving Home*, about the difficult years of his childhood, was published. Reviewers across the country praised it, many expressing surprise at its candor. One critic called it a "searing account of his traumatic childhood." Another commended him for being so open about "the dark forces behind his comic vision."

His friend William Styron praised the book as "a compelling memoir, told with Art Buchwald's inimitable drollery, but deepened by moments of poignancy and wise reflection." Even Art's friend Eppie Lederer gave it a plug in her Ann Landers column: "Have I got a treat for you!" she told her readers. "Go out and buy the book. . . . If your bookstore doesn't have it, shame on them." Art also took great joy in sending a copy to William F. Buckley, Jr., telling him, "It's the story of a poor boy who could never afford a Hertz credit card."

For Buchwald, the experience of writing the memoir was "therapeutic." He told a reporter for the *Los Angeles Times* that it was "the most honest stuff I've ever done. Putting it down on paper . . . has freed me from all of those demons."

"A TWINKLE IN HER EYE"

Rose Fitzgerald Kennedy, the matriarch of one of America's most celebrated political families, had always been an admirer of Ann and Art Buchwald. On January 22, 1995, Rose Kennedy died after an extraordinary life of 104 years. Four days after her passing, Art Buchwald sent a letter of condolence to Eunice Kennedy Shriver:

26 JANUARY 1995

Dear Eunice:

The loss of a parent is one of the most grievous blows that someone can sustain. Your mother lived longer than anybody I have ever known personally.

I consider myself amongst the privileged who knew her. Perhaps because of my profession I was terribly impressed by her sense of humor. Many times when I was talking to her, and she was pretending to be serious, I would notice a twinkle in her eye. It was as if she was trying to get a reaction from me.

A particular memory I have is an occasion when she was in her 80's. Ann had written her a letter and as soon as she saw me she said, "I want to talk to you. I just received a letter from Ann and she is a much better writer than you are, and I think that she should be doing your column instead of you." I laughed and forgot about it.

Six months later I saw her again on the Cape. She said, "Did you tell Ann what I told you about the column?" I consider this a golden moment.

Eunice, I am going to use this letter to get personal. You are a true friend. With all that you have to do with Special Olympics and your other business affairs, you have always made time to be close to your friends. I will never forget what you did for Ann. I cherish what you do for me.

I love you very much.

I mean it,
Art

"THERE'S LIFE IN THE BOY YET"

Buchwald Is Back! (1997-2000)

If laughter is such good medicine, why won't Medicaid and Medicare pay for it?

—ART BUCHWALD

In January 1998, the nation was stunned to learn that President Bill Clinton had engaged in an affair with a young White House intern, Monica Lewinsky. When Buchwald first heard the news he was shocked. "If [Clinton] did it . . . it would be the dumbest thing I've ever heard of." But as the truth slowly emerged, Buchwald offered his "irresistibly irreverent" views on the latest sex scandal to rock Washington. "I consider myself the only clean person in Washington, D.C.," he told one reporter. "They can't touch me. And I'm willing to go before a grand jury and tell them that Monica Lewinsky has never been to my office."

Shock waves from the scandal rippled through Washington and the White House, putting a strain on the Clintons' marriage. In the summer of 1998, only months after the affair was exposed, Buchwald was a guest at a party on Martha's Vineyard attended by Hillary Clinton and Mike Wallace. In the midst of the conversation, Buchwald mentioned that he had just returned from Boston after having a "stress test." Wallace then turned to Hillary Clinton and asked, "Have you ever had a stress test?" Mrs. Clinton reportedly replied, "What do you think I've been doing for the last six months?"

"EVERY GIFT BUT LENGTH OF YEARS"

For anyone who was alive on November 22, 1963, one of the most enduring scenes from that tragic weekend was the image of three-year-old John F. Kennedy, Jr., saluting his father's casket as the funeral cortege made its way to Arlington National Cemetery.

After John had grown into manhood, his dashing good looks and winning smile gave him the aura of a Hollywood star. Despite the pressures of celebrity, his amiable charm, grace, and self-effacing humor helped him cope with the demands of his name and family legacy. Like many members of his family, he donated considerable time and energy to an assortment of charitable causes. In September 1995, he struck out on his own professionally, launching a monthly magazine, *George*, a publication designed for a younger generation of readers with glitzy stories about politics, culture, and fashion.

During his summers on Martha's Vineyard, Buchwald would occasionally run into Kennedy while they were both vacationing on the island. Knowing his affection for bicycles and attachment to charitable causes, in the spring of 1996 Art asked him if he would be willing to participate in that summer's annual fundraising auction:

5 MAY 1996

Dear John:

This is sort of a plea. Your mother loved the Vineyard very much. As you know every August I am the auctioneer for the Possible Dreams auction to benefit the Martha's Vineyard Community Services organization. . . . We don't auction off anything that can be bought at a store. We offer such items as a tour of "60 Minutes" with Mike Wallace, lunch

with Katharine Graham at the Washington Post, a sail on Walter
Cronkite's yacht, a private reading with Bill and Rose Styron, tea with
Carly Simon in her gazebo....

I know that you are driven crazy by all kinds of requests but you are
part of the island.... Last summer I noticed that you seemed to enjoy
riding your bike around the island. Would you be willing to take some-
one on a bike ride?

I don't want you to think that I am begging—well maybe I am.

Sincerely,

Art

Kennedy agreed and offered to put up for bid a personally guided
eight-mile bicycle trip around Gay Head on Martha's Vineyard. "Everyone is very excited about the item and we anticipate that it will gen-
erate some spirited bidding," Buchwald gratefully told Kennedy on
May 29. "Looking forward to seeing you this summer and thanks again
for helping—it is really appreciated." On the day of the auction, the
bidding was, as Buchwald predicted, spirited, as Carly Simon sang her
hit song "Nobody Does It Better" to spark higher and higher bids.
When Buchwald's gavel finally struck, JFK Jr. and his bicycle had
been auctioned off at a hefty $12,500.

Three years later, in early July 1999, Buchwald telephoned Kennedy and asked if he would be willing to participate in the Martha's
Vineyard auction for a second time, perhaps this time offering up a
lunch with him at the editorial offices of *George.* Kennedy paused and
then told Art, "I'll be honest with you. I hate to be auctioned off. I feel
part of a slave market." Kennedy suggested that Art contact actor Tom
Hanks, who was vacationing on the island, to see if he had something
to offer. "He loves Martha's Vineyard," John said. They both laughed
and Buchwald hung up. (Buchwald did, indeed, contact Tom Hanks,
who kindly agreed to autograph videos of his HBO series *From the
Earth to the Moon,* which, as Hanks joked in a note to Art, "may attract a dollar or two," and two tickets to the premiere of his film *The
Green Mile.* In a letter of thanks, Buchwald was pleased to hear that

Hanks had enjoyed his stay on the island. "I'm glad you liked the Vineyard. We are a simple people foraging for food on a simple spit of land, resorting to intermarriage to keep the bloodlines pure.")

Two weeks later, on the night of July 16, 1999, Kennedy, along with his wife, Carolyn Bessette-Kennedy, and sister-in-law Lauren Bessette, set out from New Jersey in a single-engine airplane to attend the wedding of Kennedy's cousin Rory in Hyannis Port. An hour after takeoff, the plane disappeared into the dark of night. After two days of searching, the bodies of all three were recovered from the wrecked fuselage of the plane located in the Atlantic Ocean just off the coast of Martha's Vineyard. On July 23, John's uncle, Senator Ted Kennedy, delivered a eulogy at a memorial service in New York City. "He was a boy who grew up into a man with a zest for life and a love of adventure," Kennedy said. "We dared to think . . . that this John Kennedy would live to comb gray hair, with his beloved Carolyn by his side. But like his father, he had every gift but length of years."

Four days earlier, Art Buchwald, who had memorialized President Kennedy in the poem "We Weep," wrote a remembrance for his young son. "John Kennedy, Jr., was not an astronaut, a war hero, a Nobel Prize–winning scientist," Buchwald wrote, "yet somehow we were connected. As with all the Kennedys, he was family. Not only was [he] very much part of our history, but he represented the type of person we wanted our sons to be." Several weeks later Buchwald disclosed that two days after JFK Jr. had disappeared, "a large donation" to the Martha's Vineyard auction fund had arrived in the mail. The check, Buchwald sadly reported, had been sent out by Kennedy two days before he took off on his flight.

"A GOLDEN AGE LONG SINCE GONE"

I'll Always Have Paris, the memoir Art had been working on during the months of Ann's declining health, was published in the fall of 1996. Art was pleased by the response the book received and thrilled that critics were starting to take him seriously as a writer. "People don't take humorists seriously," he told one interviewer during his book tour. "They don't even call them writers. . . . Now I'm being reviewed seriously. . . . That gives me great pleasure because I want to be known as a writer, not a humorist. It's one step up, and that's the direction I want to be headed in at this stage of my life."

In fact the book made such an impression on one critic from the Minneapolis *Star Tribune*—a critic who had never been an admirer of his work—that he became a true believer overnight. "I've never been a big fan," he wrote. "He's always seemed to me like a smartass and not much more. . . . Well, now I'm a convert. . . . His new book is as easy as a hot knife through butter." And just as encouraging to the seventy-year-old columnist was a review in *The Philadelphia Inquirer*. "I trust [*I'll Always Have Paris*] won't be Buchwald's swan song. From the present indications, there's life in the boy yet."

Along with notices from critics came letters from friends. On August 16, 1996, editorial cartoonist Herblock wrote:

Dear Art—
   Thank you for "I'll Always Have Paris" and the lovely inscription! What's more important is that we always have Buchwald.
                                        As ever,
                                        Herb

And this note from his old friend Russell Baker:

JULY 19, 1996

Dear Art,
   After reading your book I am seething with envy. Even with the rotten childhood, you have led the best of all possible lives. Mimi has also read the book and wants to know how somebody who's had such a terrific life can possibly need psychiatry. It's deprived, stunted people like me who need psychiatric help, and we can't afford it.

Okay, this is a terrific book—your best ever. It's about a golden age long since gone, and you capture the feel of it all, mostly through the richest lode of anecdotes I've ever encountered in a two-night read. Dropping all those famous names works for you, too, because they're names associated with an era that's gone, and it evokes a nostalgia, like all those books of our youth about Paris and of the Twenties.

The passages on Ann and the children make the reader feel your love for them, and also evoke a feeling of poignancy, which is what you feel when you're afraid you might start tearing up if somebody doesn't tell you a joke soon. I was moved by these passages. I was also impressed by how well you now understand yourself, as revealed on page 93. All this is beautifully told without fussy prose or showing off. It's easy reading, yet rich. I feel you enjoyed writing this one because it was sweet to find yourself reliving Paris days.

Parenthetically, I was struck by how incidentally it reflected the style of so many men of that age, a style that may have been pioneered by the Trib *crowd. It was a gentlemanly tough-guy style. Snappy retorts were cherished. Practical jokes were common. People sent funny telegrams. ("Streets full of water stop Please advise," Robert Benchley wired his pals on arrival in Venice.) The style was pronouncedly macho. Tough-guy manners were approved. So many* Trib *guys I knew had the easy-come easy-go polish, but so do Ben and a lot of others who passed their salad days. ("Please pass the salad days, Ma'am") in the New York-Paris atmosphere. It was probably the last period in history in which men had a thoroughly good time.*

If I write anymore I'll have to charge you for this. Congratulations. From now on you can call me Russ.

> *As ever,*
> *Russ*

In January 1997, Katharine Graham released her acclaimed memoir *Personal History* about her celebrated yet turbulent career. Reviewers praised Graham for the "fascinating and extremely candid" story she told of her personal life and the firm and resolute way she guided *The Washington Post* through the perils of the Pentagon Papers case and the Watergate scandal. After its publication, Art wrote a letter of congratulations:

FEBRUARY 11, 1997

Dear Kay:

Your wonderful book arrived. Amidst great excitement I opened it— to the index. I was so happy to see that I was mentioned three times, but I was even more grateful that you kept my name out of the Watergate investigation, and that you didn't mention my role in the Pentagon Papers. This kind of information could have been very detrimental to my career at this time. Kay, I expressed my love in a fax to you. I write this letter in admiration—not in fear.

Love,
Art

A year later, after Katharine Graham won the 1998 Pulitzer Prize for her memoir, Buchwald wrote again:

APRIL 15, 1998

Dear Kay:

Everyone on Martha's Vineyard is thrilled that you have won the Pulitzer Prize. There is very little that we have to be proud of on this island, and the fact that you are one of us gives us all hope in our own careers.

It's amazing that you started off being the most powerful woman in America, and through hard work and perseverance, became the most powerful Pulitzer Prize winner in America. I don't know anyone who doesn't think you deserve it. Kay Graham—Pulitzer Prize winner. It has such a lovely ring to it.

Love,
Art

"WE MADE EACH OTHER LAUGH"

On April 22, 1996, Buchwald's friend and fellow member of the American Academy of Humor Erma Bombeck passed away at the age of sixty-nine. Four years earlier she had undergone surgery for breast cancer and then a short time later was diagnosed with a serious kidney disease that required dialysis treatments.

In March 2000, nearly four years after Bombeck's death, the University of Dayton honored her with the four-day Erma Bombeck Conference on Popular American Humor, with Art as the keynote speaker. Buchwald opened his talk with a reminder to the audience that his friend would not want the gathering to be "a sad occasion," but a celebration of laughter. His forty-five-minute speech, titled "Things I Cannot Tell You," was a classic Buchwald stand-up routine filled with comic "setups and knock-down punch lines"—all delivered with great amusement to a crowd of three hundred friends, family, and admirers of Bombeck. He ended with a tribute to Erma, but in many respects a tribute to so many of the friends he had known throughout his long career. "We made each other laugh," he said. "If you have a friend that makes you laugh, don't let them go."

Two months later, Buchwald accepted an invitation to speak at the commencement ceremonies of Lakeland University in Sheboygan, Wisconsin, where he was awarded an honorary doctorate of humane letters for a "commitment to honesty" in his profession and the "remarkable life [he had] lived by the pen."

Buchwald began his address by complimenting the university for its decision to invite him. "To be chosen as your speaker over Leonardo DiCaprio shows the Class of 2000 has extremely good taste." After entertaining the assembled graduates, families, and faculty with "perhaps the shortest commencement in the history of the world" (it was fifteen minutes long), he left the audience with a fond memory for the future. "Most of you will forget this graduation speech in twenty minutes," he told them. "But you have something to tell your grandkids when they asked what you did on graduation day. You can say, 'I laughed.'"

Six weeks later, on June 16, 2000, seventy-four-year-old Art Buchwald was rushed to Georgetown University Medical Center after suffering a severe stroke. After spending nearly two weeks in intensive care, he improved to the point where his condition was listed as "serious, but stable." While in recovery, Buchwald received an affectionate letter from his friend Ted Kennedy:

Edward M. Kennedy

JUNE 28, 2000

Dear Artie:

I was so sorry to hear that you are having a difficult time right now and Vicki and I want you to know that you are very much in our thoughts and in our prayers.

I am told that you are already making excellent progress and that is great news. I have no doubt that with your ability to use humor to meet adversity, and your fighting spirit you will conquer this latest challenge. After all, anyone who can take on and beat Paramount has got a terrific track record! When you are feeling better I will try to fight my way through the crowd of friends at your bedside to drop by and catch up.

In the meantime, concentrate on feeling better and know that all of your friends are at your side and with you in spirit.

As ever,
Ted

[P.S.] We miss you and love you

By mid-September, Buchwald was on the mend. His son, Joel, was able to announce that not only was his father in fine condition, but in some ways would "be better than he was before the stroke." He was also pleased to report that Art would soon be back on the job. "He's got his humor back, he's walking and he's on the phone with his old friends," Joel told reporters. On September 26, 2000, Russell Baker wrote a supportive yet wistful letter to Buchwald expressing surprise that he was so anxious to get back to work:

Dear Art,

... Why you are eager to go back to column writing is beyond me. You'd have a better time writing for yourself. I haven't missed column-writing one single day since hanging it up at the end of 1998. I haven't even been back in the Times *building and doubt I ever will. Not that I don't love the memories, but there was nobody left that I knew. The place was filled with 23-years-old fresh out of the Ivy League. Walking through the newsroom I could hear them whispering, "Who's the old geezer? Why [do] they let people like that in here!"*

I'd worn out humor long before that. You probably noticed I rarely tried any humor pieces those last few years, and those weren't so hot. I've discovered the pleasures of writing 5,000-word pieces for the New York Review of Books. *I can be long-winded, dull, solemn and don't have to worry that nobody will read it. Nobody is expected to read anything in the* NYRB.

After you get re-settled and want to see people, let me know and I'll come by.... Have I mentioned that it's so good to have you back, Dolly. It is indeed. Blessings.

All best,
Russ

"I JUST DON'T WANT TO DIE THE SAME DAY AS CASTRO"

The Last Glorious Bit of Laughter (2000–2007)

I laugh at Life: its antics make for me a giddy game....
But best of all the laughing game—is laughing at myself.

— ROBERT SERVICE

"This is what I did on my vacation. I had a stroke," Buchwald reported to readers when he went back to work in early December 2000. He admitted that the time he spent in recovery and rehabilitation was all a bit foggy. "I was in a world of my own, even more secret than the FBI Witness Protection Program," he joked. What he did recall vividly, however, was news from his doctor that the legendary Buchwald diet would have to change forever. "Food has always been good to me, and I have always been good to food," he wrote. "At one time a chocolate éclair was the Viagra in my life. Now eating an extra handful of grits is a venial sin. I go to restaurants and watch with awe as people cut into their juicy steaks and French fries, and I ask why them and not me."

But in the end, Buchwald knew it was time for a change and that he had to accept the inevitable, just as he had in 1988 when he gave up his beloved cigars. But, as always, he wasn't above some good-natured grumbling. "I'm not complaining about a diet," Buchwald told readers, "but the closer it comes to dinner time the closer I get to wanting to eat the pizza off the television screen."

SOME FAREWELLS

When Katharine Graham celebrated her seventieth birthday in 1987, Buchwald was on hand to add his own words of admiration for the woman who had guided the *Post* through so many difficult times. "There's one word that brings us all together here tonight," Art told a packed gathering of some of the most powerful members of the Washington establishment. "And that word is fear." The audience "erupted in laughter," and no one enjoyed the joke more than Mrs. Graham.

On July 17, 2001, Katharine Graham died. In remembrance Buchwald wrote a column praising her as a powerful and "gutsy publisher" who was always loyal to those who worked for her. "When the going got tough, she stood by her people," Art wrote of the turbulent years of the Nixon administration. "Somebody like Kay Graham comes along once in a lifetime. I'm glad I knew her."

Two months later, on the morning of September 11, 2001, a stunned world witnessed on live television a horrific sequence of terrorist attacks on the United States, a ghastly tragedy seared into the memories of the American people. As the tragedy unfolded, Art Buchwald sat transfixed before his television set. "I saw on the screen rubble and flames and smoke and death," he later recalled. As he watched in horror, the event brought back to mind a story from the day John F. Kennedy was assassinated, when the grieving Washington columnist Mary McGrory told Daniel Patrick Moynihan, "We'll never laugh again," and in response a heartbroken Moynihan replied, "Mary, we'll laugh again, but we'll never be young again."

"I watched the same pictures over and over again," Buchwald wrote of the 9/11 attack. "The buildings on fire, and tumbling down, the soot on the faces of the rescued and the rescuers, and I know I'm entering a new world and things will never be the same. . . . The only thing I can be sure of—'We'll laugh again, but we'll never be young again.'"

One of the great regrets of Art Buchwald's life was that he never knew his mother, Helen Kleinberger Buchwald, who had been taken away from him and confined to an asylum shortly after he was born. Although his sisters visited her often while she was still alive, Art never took the opportunity to meet her, out of fear that she wouldn't recognize him or that meeting her might destroy the "fantasy" he had created of her in his mind.

When she died in April 1958, while he and Ann were living in Paris, Buchwald did not attend the funeral because he wasn't notified of her death until three days after she had been interred. It would be more than four decades before he finally had a chance to say goodbye.

On a pleasant spring day in March 2003, Buchwald and his son, Joel, traveled to the Mount Moriah Cemetery in Fairview, New Jersey, where they met Art's sister, Alice, for a long-overdue farewell to his mother. When Buchwald finally saw his mother's dark gray headstone in the cemetery, he stood before it in silence and, with tears in his eyes, gazed at the words chiseled on her grave: BELOVED WIFE AND DE-VOTED MOTHER.

Saying goodbye that day was "the end of a long journey," Buchwald later wrote, and although it had been a sad and difficult farewell, he felt a sense of comfort. At long last "the circle had now been closed."

A few weeks later, in April 2003, Buchwald announced to his readers that the *Herald Tribune*, the paper that had been part of his life for nearly fifty-three years, would no longer run his column. It was a sharp blow at a difficult time.

Unbeknownst to Buchwald, the editors of the *Tribune* had, for several months, grown increasingly concerned about the quality of his columns. As early as August 2002, while the paper was still jointly owned by *The New York Times* and *The Washington Post*, Katherine Knorr, features editor of the *Tribune*, had confided to David Ignatius, the executive editor, that Buchwald's columns "were getting stale." While Ignatius agreed with Knorr's assessment, he decided not to formally cancel Buchwald's column, but instead told her to "exercise [her own] judgment" and publish Art's columns based "on merit" only. (Neither the concern about the quality of Buchwald's columns nor the decision to publish "on merit" was ever communicated to Art at the time.) The end result was that the only Buchwald column the *Tribune* ran from August 23 until the end of 2002 was his famous Thanksgiving Day piece, "Le Jour de Merci Donnant."

Then, in late February 2003, after *The New York Times* became sole owner of the *International Herald Tribune* when the *Post* sold its interest in the paper to the *Times*, Art was finally delivered the devastating news that the paper "was no longer running his column." When Buchwald learned the news he was shocked, hurt, and angry. But in the days and weeks that followed, the pain he felt was exacerbated by the confusion as to how it had all happened.

Walter Wells, who had replaced David Ignatius as managing editor of the *Herald Tribune*, insisted to Buchwald in an email of February 20, 2003, that it had, in fact, been "Ignatius's decision" to no longer carry his column, and that the failure to tell Art "was surely an oversight." Eight days later, in an angry email, Buchwald confronted Ignatius with what Wells had told him:

Dear David:

As you can imagine, I am trying to pin down what went on with my column in Europe. It turns out Wells says that you were the one who canceled it in August. He did not pick up on the cancellation, but he has not been running the column. His last letter to me indicated that he wasn't planning on it.

The genesis of all this seems to be that for some reason you moved me to the op-ed page from the back page, where I was anchored all those years. The second thing is I still cannot get a definite word from Wells that I'm out of the paper.

I am bitter about everyone involved with this cancellation—you, for not informing me and those at the Tribune *who let me fall through the cracks. I don't care if someone tells me he is sorry. That fact is, I still want to be in the* Tribune, *but if they are very adamant about it, so be it. . . .*

Yours sincerely,
Art Buchwald

On March 1, Ignatius responded to Art with his own explanation of what had happened: "I am sorry about the bad feelings. I did move the column from the back page to inside the paper—not to the op-ed page. . . . I did not cancel it at the time I was editor, so Walter is misinformed about that, but it is true that we ran it less frequently than before." As to whether the decision to cancel his column was irrevocable, Ignatius told Art, "As to the current cast at IHT [*International Herald Tribune*], I have less influence on them than my dog Bo. Because I admire you and your work, I am trying to be as straightforward as I can about this. You helped build the IHT, a paper I loved, and the IHT and its people (including me) owe you an immense debt. What they want to do about your column is their decision now. With my apologies for any confusion or bad feelings I do not intend."

With the fate of his column now in the hands of *The New York Times* and its new management at the *Herald Tribune*, Buchwald reached out to Walter Wells in hopes of persuading him to continue running his column:

Dear Walter:

. . . I have been at the IHT for 53 years. I have always maintained it was my mother paper.

I am the only person that is connected with both the present and the past. I have had a love affair with the paper and its readers—American

*and foreign. They identify me with the IHT. I won't discuss our friend-
ship over the years. I always thought it was warm and mutual.*

*But to get to the practical side—in Europe my column sells newspa-
pers. I have always been identified as the "American Abroad." My letters over the years have indicated people considered me their lifeline to
the U.S.*

*For a long time I alternated with Russ Baker and we are great friends.
The two of us jazzed the paper up. Because the IHT was circulated all
over the world—leaders read it. The column was picked up in Western
Europe and even more so in the Communist countries.*

*I guess I could go on about it—but I'm hurting. . . . I hope you use the
column again—not as a favor—but because it is worth printing.*

Cheers,
Art

In response, on March 7, Wells told Art that although he could
see why he was "bitter" about what had transpired, there was nothing
he could "say or do [that] will change that." Offering no hope that
the *Tribune* would continue to run his column, Wells urged Buchwald to look to the future and to focus on the happy memories of his
"exceptional run" with the *Tribune*. After reading Wells's letter,
Buchwald was furious, responding with one of the angriest letters he
ever wrote:

MARCH 16, 2003

*One of the advantages of writing a column for 53 years is that I know
bullshit when I see it. Your letter was bullshit.*

*It's sad to have friends stab you in the back. . . . I don't know if your
letter was a letter of cancellation or not. . . . You mentioned in your first
paragraph that I am bitter. You are right on that score. I'm right when I
say your letter was bullshit.*

Art Buchwald

Despite Buchwald's protests and angry letters, by the end of March 2003, his fifty-three-year love affair with the paper was over. In the end, the management at the *Herald Tribune* and the *Times* made the final decision that they would no longer run his column. "It was the only paper I really loved," he said, and the cancellation of his column left him heartbroken. "Dad was terribly hurt by it all," his son, Joel, would later say. "He would have paid the *Tribune* to continue running his column."

Art would never get over the disappointment he felt about how the whole matter had been handled, later writing that the only two grudges he "carried throughout [his] lifetime" were against Paramount for "lifting" his idea for *Coming to America* and the "big one: After fifty years *The New York Times* dropped my column."

Although sad and hurt, in his farewell column to readers on April 4, 2003, Buchwald focused only on the fond and happy memories of his days in Paris at his beloved *Herald Tribune*. "It was a golden age for American tourists in Europe and most of us had a very good time," Art wrote. "The boulevards, the side-walk cafes, the croissants and coffee, the Seine in the morning and the Seine at night, the Champs Elysees, Montmartre and the Louvre—will all remain as important parts of my days on the *Trib. A bientot.*"

"MAGIC CIRCLE OF FRIENDSHIP"

Despite his bitterness over the cancellation of his column, Buchwald quickly gathered himself and got back to work. "I'm happy to be doing what I'm doing," he told a reporter in June 2003. "I get up each morning and say, 'Hey, I'm alive today' and that's enough for me." When not at work on his weekly column—still syndicated in nearly one hundred newspapers—or sorting through selections for his new book, *Beating Around the Bush*, an assortment of his best columns from the George W. Bush years, he devoted time to a number of worthy causes, including a fundraiser celebrating the life of George Plimpton and the fiftieth anniversary of *The Paris Review,* and pitching in, once again, for the twenty-fifth consecutive year, as celebrity host of the Martha's Vineyard "Possible Dreams" auction.

And he still maintained an active speaking schedule, spending several days a month out on the road discussing his lifelong battle with depression, at times accompanied by William Styron and journalist Mike Wallace, or onstage alone entertaining audiences with his patented political one-liners. "You can't make up anything anymore," he told one audience. "The world is a satire. All you're doing is recording it."

But in the fall of 2005, the laughter faded.

Shortly after his eightieth birthday on October 20, 2005, Buchwald was rushed to Georgetown University Hospital after he felt a "sudden onset of terrible pain" in his right foot. After conducting an examination, his physician, Dr. Michael Newman, determined that a vascular condition and a series of blood clots were cutting off circulation to the lower part of his right leg and that amputation was required or he would die. To make matters even worse, he suffered simultaneous kidney failure, which required dialysis treatment before the amputation itself could take place. A despondent Buchwald—initially angered at the "double whammy" that jolted his system—finally agreed to both dialysis and surgery.

In December 2005, his lower right leg was amputated and an artificial leg set in place. After the surgery Buchwald was told that because of the condition of his kidneys, he would have to continue dialysis. But after twelve treatments, Art decided he had had enough, and despite pleas from his physician and his family he decided to stop. "To hell with it," he declared. "I don't see a future in this and I don't want to do it anymore!"

On February 7, Buchwald was admitted to a Washington, D.C., hospice care facility, where it was assumed he would die within a matter of weeks. Newspapers provided periodic updates on his condition, telling readers that although he was "in the final stretch of what has been an amazing life," he was facing his imminent death bravely. "We knew he was a funny guy who liked to deliver his insights into the human condition with a punch line," one editorial in upstate New York noted. "But we didn't know about the courage." And, as always, he received letters of encouragement from friends. In late March, Arthur Schlesinger, Jr., wrote:

MARCH 27, 2006

Beloved Artie:

Alexandra and I are terribly impressed by the gallant way that you have confronted the ultimate decision. It all reminds me of Ben Franklin, the Art Buchwald of his day, who, dying, was queried by the president of Yale, a clergyman, about his religious views. Ben Franklin replied a few days before his death.

As to Christ, "I have some doubts as to his divinity, though it is a question I do not dogmatize upon, having never studied it, and think it needless to busy myself with it now, when I expect soon an opportunity of knowing the truth with less trouble." Your position is identical with Ben Franklin's—you stand on the threshold of the final mystery, and you make a joke.

In the meantime, you have brought across the weary years boundless pleasure and joy to boundless millions. And to your personal friends, you have given comfort, sympathy, love—and your friends compete in loving you. Alexandra and I deem ourselves in the magic circle of friendship. And you remind us all of human courage in the face of death.

We love you, beloved Artie.

Arthur

And fearing that Art's days were numbered, Pierce O'Donnell, Buchwald's friend and counsel in the seven-year legal struggle with Hollywood, came by for a visit. While sitting in the hospice visiting room with Art's son, Joel; daughter-in-law, Tamara; and his two grandchildren, Buchwald and O'Donnell shared memories and war stories from the past. It was an "extraordinary hour reminiscing, jousting, and laughing with an octogenarian who had not lost a beat," O'Donnell later recalled of the visit. "Art's legendary satirical talent . . . was in rare form." He was in "high-spirits" and displayed a wonderful sense of "dignity," never once showing the slightest hint of "self-pity," O'Donnell remembered. At one point, in an effort to keep things light, Buchwald asked, "Did you have any problem parking?"

"In fact, I did," O'Donnell responded.

"Dying is easy," Buchwald quipped. "Parking is impossible."

As their visit ended and with tears in his eyes, O'Donnell approached Buchwald to say farewell. He "gave him a long bear hug and kissed him on the top of his head."

With little to do but wait, Buchwald spent time soliciting pre-funeral "eulogies" from friends and family. "Instead of being memorialized after my death," Buchwald reasoned, "I get to read what they were going to say now." Tom Brokaw, Mike Wallace, Ben Bradlee, and Joel Buchwald were among those who contributed tributes for his pre-death review. Although many were written in a humorous vein, the offering by George Stevens, Jr., whose friendship with Art had been patched up after their brief rift during the early Clinton years, captured best what many felt:

> So Artie, in the sad times and in the glad times, you were the very best of friends. You brightened our lives and eased our burdens at the same time you were using your unmatched skills as a political humorist to make life miserable for the scoundrels. It is easy to say this—Artie, you are the very best.

Then in late February, to the astonishment of many, Buchwald agreed to do a live radio interview from the hospice facility with talk show host Diane Rehm. "I figure, what the heck," Buchwald said. "I had nothing else to do. I went on and talked about hospice, about not taking dialysis, and about what it was like to die." The courage and frankness he displayed during the interview prompted a series of follow-up interviews with network television outlets and national newspapers. The burst of media attention gave a much-needed lift to his spirits. "It gave me something to do besides watch *Wheel of Fortune,*" he said.

Then a miracle happened. "Against the odds," he said with glee, "my kidneys started working again and could function without dialysis." By April, Art was well enough to write his column again, to start work on a new memoir, and to begin receiving visitors at what soon became known as the Buchwald hospice "salon." Well-wishers came from all aspects of his life: friends from his childhood days at the Hebrew Orphan Asylum and from his days in Paris, and a steady stream of colleagues and friends from over forty years in Washington: Russell Baker, Senator John Glenn, Eunice and Maria Shriver, Joseph Califano, George Stevens, Jr., Tom Brokaw, Walter Cronkite, and Mike Wallace. Ben Bradlee, his companion for almost a half century, visited nearly every day, as did Ethel Kennedy.

Over the next several weeks, Buchwald received more than three thousand letters from well-wishers and calls from friends and admirers everywhere. Even Judge Harvey Schneider, who had presided over the *Buchwald v. Paramount* case, telephoned one day to say hello. In typical Buchwald fashion, Art asked Schneider whether there was still a chance of getting a bit more payout from the Paramount lawsuit. "I'm so glad to hear from you," Art said. "Is there any more money there?" The judge chuckled and said, "I'll reread the transcript."

By late June, Art's condition had improved to such an extent that preparations were made for his release from hospice care so he could spend the summer on Martha's Vineyard with his family. The laughter was back, and he was in good spirits. Once more Buchwald had defeated the odds. "I never realized dying could be so much fun," he declared with wicked delight.

VINEYARD HUES ONCE MORE

On July 1, 2006, Buchwald headed to Martha's Vineyard with his son, Joel; daughter-in-law, Tamara; and their two young children, Corbin and Tate; and his longtime assistant, Cathy Crary. "I didn't expect to be here," he told a reporter shortly after he arrived on the island. "My plan was to leave the earth. And then I thought, to hell with it, I'll go to the Vineyard."

For Buchwald, life on the island was familiar and comfortable, filled with vivid summer memories of the thirty-five years he had spent vacationing there: gatherings on the lawn with the Kennedys; tennis matches at the Yacht Club with Mike Wallace, William and Rose Styron, and Walter Cronkite; his wife Ann's morning exercise classes in the backyard; lunches and dinners with Kay Graham and Lillian Hellman; and the joy he felt each August as emcee of the "Possible Dreams" fundraising auction.

But there were bittersweet memories as well. It was the place where he had struggled with rewrites for *Sheep on the Runway* during that hectic summer of 1969, and where he first saw *Coming to America*, prompting the fateful decision to take on Hollywood. It was also where he had battled depression with his friends Mike Wallace and William Styron, and it was the final resting place of Ann, buried in the Vineyard cemetery.

Within days of his arrival on the island, his home was transformed into a new Buchwald salon, with friends telephoning or dropping in to say hello. "He's indomitable," Walter Cronkite said after stopping by one day. "At first we thought he would be lost to us, then, by golly, not only did he fool the medical world, he has fooled everybody else . . . and he's doing it with his usual humor." Rose Styron thought Art looked "absolutely remarkable" after paying a visit, and singer Carly Simon took time to write a song for him that summer. "When everyone thought I was bound for heaven, Carly said she would sing a song at my memorial service," Buchwald said. "Then, when it turned out I didn't die, she wrote a song to celebrate my still being there":

> For Art Buchwald
> Love From Carly
> August 10, 2006
>
> Too soon to say goodbye, my dear
> Too soon to let you go
> Too soon to say "Auf Wiedersehen"
> "Au revoir," no no
>
> Too soon to say goodbye, my dear
> Too soon to rest my case
> Too soon to start another journey
> When we've just won the race
>
> Not while the lanterns and chandeliers
> Sway in the pale moonlight
> Not while the shimmer of far and near
> Holds us both so tight
>
> Too soon to say goodbye, my dear
> Too soon the tide will rise
> But not 'til it reaches another shore
> Will I ever say goodbye
>
> Not while the music and fireworks
> Sing down the hill to the sound
> Not while the girls in their summer gowns
> Are dancing round and round
>
> Too soon to see the world beyond
> I'm willing to be late

Let's stay right here beneath the stars
Let the voyage wait

For it's too soon,
Too soon, to say goodbye
Too soon
To say . . . goodbye.

When Simon sent a recording of the song to Buchwald, he asked his daughter-in-law, Tamara, to play it over and over again, each time bringing tears to his eyes.

In addition to friends and colleagues, there was a steady stream of reporters who wrote profiles on the man who wouldn't die. "I was sort of forgotten," he told a reporter for *The Baltimore Sun* in late July. "Then all of a sudden based on this experience I'm going through, I have a whole new life." And he was thrilled by the attention. "I had a bunch of love that I didn't know was there," he told an interviewer. "I really tasted all of it, and by the way, I enjoyed it." There was only one drawback to the constant flow of well-wishers to his home. "You've got to feed them all," he said in typical Buchwald fashion.

On any given day, Art could be seen sitting in a hospital chair on the back porch, his legs propped up on an ottoman—or left leg only if his prosthetic limb was removed for the sake of comfort. Most times he dressed casually—wearing a white Vineyard T-shirt—but other times he sported a striped summer polo shirt, especially if he was posing for a news photographer.

When he wasn't working on a column or his new book, *Too Soon to Say Goodbye*, he spent time relaxing with his family. He would usually take a nap in the afternoon and then in the evening after dinner enjoy watching a classic black-and-white movie such as *The Third Man* or *On the Waterfront*, or catching up with episodes of the hit television series *The Sopranos*.

As summer came to a close, preparations were made to head back to Washington to put the finishing touches on his book. The time spent on the Vineyard had been just what he needed, and to the surprise of many, he seemed to be in good health. "He seems to be getting better and better," Cathy Crary said. "It's so bizarre." Now rested, in high spirits, and with his sense of humor once again in top form, Buchwald headed back to Washington with a new plan for the future. When he died, he told a reporter for *The New York Times*, he wanted his ashes "to be spilled over every Trump building in New York."

On October 20, 2006, Buchwald celebrated his eighty-first birthday with family and friends. Ben Bradlee and his wife, Sally Quinn, and Eunice Kennedy Shriver came by to sing "Happy Birthday."

Less than two weeks later, on November 1, 2006, Buchwald received news that his longtime friend William Styron had died. "Every once in a while your world stands still," he wrote in a remembrance. "This happened the other day when my good friend Bill Styron passed away. There are certain friendships that are so important they leave a mark on you long after the person is gone. So it is with Bill Styron, my friend for 40 years."

That same month, Art's longtime editor, Phyllis Grann, hosted a book party in his honor at her Fifth Avenue apartment in Manhattan. In attendance were a host of old friends from Buchwald's past, including Lauren Bacall, Joseph Califano, and Arthur Schlesinger, Jr. When he arrived at the celebration, Art was in a wheelchair manned by his son, Joel, and although he was fatigued by the journey from Washington to New York, he graciously signed books and chatted with old friends. One invitee who was unable to attend that evening was William F. Buckley, Jr., who had spent years with Art navigating the complex maze of Hertz Rental Car Company solicitations. On December 14, 2006, Buckley sent his regrets to Art for not being able to attend: "I had so hoped to go to your party, and even fished out references to you in my upcoming book—a collection of material from my Notes and Asides column. They don't make complete sense isolated, but then you never made complete sense, isolated or not. Bless you, my friend. As ever, Bill."

Shortly after the New York City book event, Buchwald's health began to deteriorate rapidly. He was then under the constant care of Joel and Tamara Buchwald at their home in Washington, D.C. On Friday, January 12, his friend Tom Brokaw paid a visit. "It was not easy," Brokaw later recalled. "He was anxious and slightly disoriented." After a brief stay, Brokaw kissed Art on the forehead, told him he loved him, and said goodbye. Four days later, Ethel Kennedy stopped by to see him for a short visit, something she had done each day since he had returned from the Vineyard.

The next evening, on January 17, 2007, the man who couldn't seem to die quietly passed away at home surrounded by his family.

"THE MARK TWAIN OF OUR TIME"

Buchwald once joked to Ben Bradlee, "I just don't want to die the same day Castro dies." His fear, he said, was that the simultaneous death of the Cuban dictator would bump his own obituary off the front pages of *The Washington Post* and *The New York Times*. In the end Buchwald's wish came true. The strongman of Cuba would live on for another nine years, but the master of political satire was no more. And just as he had hoped, the day after he died, his obituary appeared on the front page of the *Times* and the *Post*, paying tribute to his long and colorful career. "His life was a rich tale of gumption, heartbreak and humor, with chapters in Paris, Washington and points around the globe," the *Times* wrote. "He delighted in stirring the pot—never maliciously, always vigorously. The world was mad (or at least a little nutty), he said, and all he was doing was recording it." Friends everywhere mourned his death. The day after his passing, Senator Ted Kennedy offered a eulogy on the floor of the U.S. Senate:

Madam President:

It is with a heavy heart that I rise to pay tribute to Art Buchwald. Art finally said good-bye to all of us last night. It was far too soon. . . .

Art was an incredible friend to my wife Vicki and me and to the entire Kennedy family. We all enjoyed Art's company and columns, and President Kennedy was known to read Art's column regularly while he was in the White House.

We enjoyed so many delightful times together. Whether here in Washington or on Martha's Vineyard Art brought tons of laughter into our lives. We'll continue to remember him and his wife, Ann McGarry Buchwald, as they will now be laid to rest together on Martha's Vineyard.

Art was the Mark Twain of our time. He will forever live in our hearts and minds for his brilliant wit and observations. For decades there was no better way to start the day than to open the morning paper to Art's column, laugh out loud and learn all over again to take the issues seriously in the world of politics, but not to take yourself too seriously.

As Art said: "Whether it's the best of times or the worst of times, it's the only time we've got." The special art of Art Buchwald was to make even the worst of times better. We are fortunate to have had him for so long, and I will miss him very much. . . .

When we lost President Kennedy, Art honored him with his column "We Weep . . ."

Today, Art, the world weeps for you.

Several weeks later, on March 5, 2007, a memorial service was held in Buchwald's honor at the Kennedy Center for the Performing Arts in Washington, D.C. An overflow crowd of more than a thousand people was on hand that day to hear members of his family and old friends pay tribute to his life and career. Displayed onstage was an enlarged photo of Buchwald standing in front of the Eiffel Tower, appearing to all onlookers as if he were part of a 1950s Gene Kelly musical routine. There he was doing a playful dance, flashing his celebrated smile, all decked out in an overcoat and black bowler hat, a cigar jutting out of his mouth as he twirled his umbrella and joyously kicked his leg into the air. Ethel Kennedy, George Stevens, Jr., Mike Wallace, Tom Brokaw, Ben Bradlee, Dr. Michael Newman, and fellow columnist Dave Barry all delivered humorous and touching goodbyes, as did his daughter Jennifer; son, Joel; and daughter-in-law, Tamara.

Ethel Kennedy recalled fond memories of times spent with Art at Hickory Hill, rafting down the rapids of the Colorado River, and playing tennis at Hyannis Port. "May Jack and Bobby take care of you—who took such wonderful care of the children and me," she ended in her heartfelt farewell. "Goodbye, old friend."

Dave Barry praised Buchwald's singular sense of humor and view of life. Art was "funny without being mean-spirited, without being vicious, without being hateful," Barry said. "He was just funny. He talked funny, he wrote funny, he lived funny and, damned, if he didn't find a way to *die* funny."

Ben Bradlee told stories of good times with Art in Paris and Washington—lovely and humorous tales of a friendship lasting over half a century. "Life was good, life is good," Bradlee said of Art. "But it will never be the same without you."

One of the most moving farewells was from Tamara Buchwald, who spoke about Art's final months when she and her children, Corbin and Tate, would take cookies and milk to his bedroom each night and say, "Good night, sweet man, we love you."

Years after his death, the mention of Art Buchwald's name could still bring smiles to the faces of friends and colleagues who remembered his charm, chutzpah, love of life, loyalty to friends, and unique brand of humor. When former senator Gary Hart was asked about Buchwald's legacy, he responded, "My dear friend Artie Buchwald, who, alas, is not here when we need him most. He was a dear man in a more decent and humane time. His like may or may not ever be seen again."

In an appreciation written in *The Washington Post* shortly after Art's death, David Von Drehle wrote, "We've lost a great American Dreamer, the sort of self-invented, self-made success this country holds the patent on. Buchwald's adult life was an endless improvisation on American themes in both major and minor ways—resourceful Ben Franklin on one shoulder, desperate Jay Gatsby on the other, fizzy with glamour today and dark with depression tomorrow."

Art Buchwald's life was, indeed, the stuff of dreams: a sad foster child who learned to cope with the difficulties of life through a keen sense of humor; a high school dropout and World War II veteran; a young and ambitious adventurer who sailed to Paris and talked his way into a job on one of the greatest newspapers in the world and then, through good fortune, hard work, and a keen instinct for satire, turned himself into one of the most celebrated political humorists of all time.

When he died in January 2007, it was almost fifty-eight years to the day that Art Buchwald first sat down to a typewriter in the cold, crowded, noisy bureau of the *Herald Tribune* to write the first of thousands of columns that would entertain the world for over half a century. Shortly before his death he wrote one last column for his readers, expressing the gratitude he felt for the many opportunities he had been given in life:

> There comes a time when you start adding up all the pluses and minuses of your life. . . . I can't cover all the subjects I want to in one final column, but I would just like to say what a great pleasure it has been knowing all of you and being a part of your lives. Each of you has, in your own way, contributed to my life. . . .
>
> I think of a song lyric, "What's it all about, Alfie?" I don't know how well I've done while I was here, but I'd like to think some of my printed works will persevere. . . .
>
> I know it's very egocentric to believe that someone is put on earth for a reason. In my case, I like to think I was.

ACKNOWLEDGMENTS

Author Dorothy Parker once wrote, "The writer's way is rough and lonely, and who would choose it while there are vacancies in more gracious professions, such as, say, cleaning out ferryboats." Although there is some truth in Parker's witty observation, in reality no writer works alone. Debts of gratitude are always collected along the way, and I have been fortunate to have had the help of so many people without whom *Funny Business* would never have been possible.

First and foremost, I am enormously grateful to Joel and Tamara Buchwald for their support, confidence, thoughtfulness, and innumerable courtesies as I tried to capture in my book the humor and legendary life of someone they knew so well. Thankfully they took extraordinary care to preserve the rich collection of Art Buchwald's papers, which are now on deposit at the Library of Congress in Washington, D.C. Both Joel and Tamara were also extremely generous in offering their personal recollections and memories of Art. It is hard to imagine writing this book without their kind assistance throughout.

I am grateful to a number of people at the Library of Congress, including historian and curator Barbara Bair, who first introduced me to the Buchwalds, and to the outstanding archivists who processed and organized the Buchwald Papers: Colleen Benoit Kim, Tracey Barton, Thomas Bigley, Rebecca Gourevitch, Margaret McAleer, Kathleen O'Neill, Laney Stevenson, and Tammi Taylor.

I owe an extraordinary debt of gratitude to my longtime friend, author, and presidential historian Jon Meacham, who made this book a reality. When I first suggested the idea to Jon for a book about Art Buchwald, he immediately saw the rich possibilities in such a story and within weeks helped secure a book contract with Random House. I shall always be grateful for his support, guidance, and assistance.

I wish to express my deepest appreciation to Christopher Buckley. As a longtime admirer of his brilliant satire and humor, I am truly honored to have his foreword kick off the festivities to *Funny Business*.

From the very beginning I had the good fortune to work with so many brilliant and talented people at Random House. The legendary Kate Medina is one of the best editors of all time. Her vision, advice, encouragement, and editorial guidance were indispensable to me in so many ways. Noa Shapiro, Kate's editorial assistant, was a true delight to work with from start to finish. Her keen editorial eye, invaluable advice, patience, good cheer, and marvelous sense of humor were invaluable at every step of the way. I also want to express my sincere gratitude to a number of other extraordinary people at Random House for their support, encouragement, and hard work: Andy Ward, publisher of Random House; Avideh Bashirrad, deputy publisher of Random House; Benjamin Dreyer, vice president and copy chief; Richard Elman, senior production editor; Rebecca Berlant, managing editor; Luke Epplin, production editor; Jo Anne Metsch, senior book designer; Susan Corcoran and Maria Braeckel of the publicity department; Barbara Fillon and Michael Hoak of the marketing division; and, finally, Deborah Foley, director of copyright, who was unfailingly patient in providing much-needed advice and guidance on permission and other copyright issues.

I want to thank my literary agent, Rafe Sagalyn, who helped me navigate the complexities of a writer's contract and offered essential editorial advice and guidance throughout.

I am also indebted to a number of people who shared their personal recollections and memories about the life and career of Art Buchwald: Joseph Califano (and his assistant, JoAnn McCauley), Rose Styron, Cathy Crary, Tom Brokaw (and his assistant, Mary Casalino), former senator Gary Hart, and Art Buchwald's attorney in the landmark *Buchwald v. Paramount* case, Pierce O'Donnell, who patiently and thoughtfully helped me navigate the legal complexities and intricacies of the lawsuit.

Patrick Kerwin, Edie Sandler, and my longtime friend and archivist extraordinaire Jeff Flannery helped track down critical loose ends from the Buchwald Papers at the Library of Congress, and Hanna Soltys and Barbara Natanson of the prints and photographs division kindly helped with photos for the book. My thanks also to Andrea Meckley, Angie Kemp, and James Pape at the University of Mary Washington for their technical assistance with the manuscript and digital images for the book.

I also had the good fortune to have the assistance of my old friend Keith Wamsky, who offered invaluable advice and important editorial suggestions on the manuscript. This is the third book I've worked on with Keith and his help is always indispensable to the final product. I am also grateful to my brother, Thomas Hill, who with a keen eye for historical detail offered helpful editorial advice on the book. I also want to thank Richard Moe, Nathaniel Philbrick, and Jack Bales, who read early versions of the introduction and provided welcome advice and suggestions.

In a book such as this in which the letters of friends and colleagues of Art Buchwald form an essential part of the narrative, I am thankful for the courtesies of so many people and a host of family representatives or literary executors who helped with copyright and permission issues: Joel and Tamara Buchwald, Kathleen Kennedy Townsend, Vicki Kennedy, Christopher G. Kennedy, Christopher Buckley, Bob

Woodward, Maureen Dowd, Donald Graham, Tom Brokaw, Evan Thomas, Adam Shaw, Andrew Schlesinger, Tony Williams, Marcelle West and James Tooley on behalf of Adam West Enterprises, former senator Gary Hart, David Glenn and Lyn Glenn, Fraser Heston and Holly Heston Rochell, Mike Baker, Amanda Warren and Michael R. Whalen of the Hugh M. Hefner Foundation, David Ignatius, Sarah Alex and Jean Rickard of the Herb Block Foundation, Margo Howard, Matt Bombeck, Alexander Newley and Tara Newley, Hilary Wallcox, Jeffrey C. Briggs, Regina Robinson-Easter, Evan Rosenblum, Safae El-Ouahabi of the RCW Literary Agency, and Zoe Bodzas of McIntosh & Otis. I also want to thank the following for permission to publish several of the photos in the book: Michael Beissinger, Judy Switt, David Corbin, and Diana Walker.

Special thanks to my wife, Rebecca Purdy, for her love, support, editorial advice, and wise counsel at every step of the way. I also want to thank my father and mother, Clarence and Mary Hill, who early on instilled in me a love of history and books. And finally I wish to express my deep gratitude to my dear friend and mentor, David McCullough, who taught me how to tell a good story and to enjoy a good hearty laugh.

NOTES

Abbreviations

AB Papers, LOC: Art Buchwald Papers, Manuscript Division, Library of Congress, Washington, D.C.
NYT: *The New York Times*
WP: *The Washington Post*
WSJ: *The Wall Street Journal*

Introduction

xvii **"Will Rogers with chutzpah"**: Richard Severo, "Art Buchwald, Whose Humor Poked the Powerful, Dies at 81," *NYT*, January 19, 2007.

xvii **"greatest satirist in the English language"**: Dust jacket of Art Buchwald, *Down the Seine and Up the Potomac with Art Buchwald* (New York: G. P. Putnam's Sons, 1977); *WP*, March 4, 2006.

xvii **Columnist Arthur Krock**: *Newsweek*, June 7, 1965.

xvii **"one of the sharpest wits"**: James Michener, *The World Is My Home: A Memoir* (New York: Random House, 1992), 168.

xvii **"gold standard"**: Maureen Dowd to Art Buchwald, [no date], AB Papers, LOC.

xviii **"Gruppenfuhrer"**: Garry Trudeau to Art Buchwald, November 30, 1984, AB Papers, LOC.

xviii **The great British humorist**: P. G. Wodehouse to Mr. Bessie, April 14, 1959, AB Papers, LOC.

xviii **Even one of America's most celebrated**: Adam West to Art Buchwald, April 1, 1966, AB Papers, LOC.

xviii "almost fell out of his seat": Eppie Lederer to Art Buchwald, September 23, 1970, AB Papers, LOC.

xviii Creative genius Lincoln Kirstein: See letter from John Hay Whitney to Art Buchwald, [no date], quoting extract from letter of Lincoln Kirstein to Whitney, January 25, 1965, AB Papers, LOC.

xviii Supreme Court justice William O. Douglas: Justice Douglas cited Buchwald's column in an appendix to *U.S. v. Pabst Brewing Co.*, 384 U.S. 546 (1966).

xviii Silent film star Clara Bow: Art Buchwald to Clara Bow, December 23, 1963, AB Papers, LOC.

xviii "You are one of those people": Barry Goldwater to Art Buchwald, May 19, 1992, AB Papers, LOC. After receiving a complimentary letter from Senator Goldwater in July 1981, Buchwald responded, "I have blushed several times since reading your letter, and my chest swells with pride when somebody like you says something nice about somebody like me. I really appreciated everything you said, and I shall cherish the letter. I will put it in a safe place in case the Justice Department subpoenas my mail. I thank you and I hope to see you soon. All my friends to whom I have shown your letter claim that I have sold out—so what." Art Buchwald to Senator Barry Goldwater, September 9, 1981, AB Papers, LOC.

xix "everybody's trigger finger": *The Boston Globe*, March 16, 1976; *South Bend* (Ind.) *Tribune*, April 13, 1976.

xix "exchange of ideas": *The Miami News*, October 3, 1968.

xix "purpose [was] to keep speakers": Art Buchwald, *Have I Ever Lied to You?* (Greenwich, Conn.: Fawcett, 1969), 21–22.

xix "Letter to Santa": *The Sacramento Bee*, December 19, 1976.

xx "shy, introspective": Buchwald, *Have I Ever Lied to You?*, iv.

xx "social climbing": Art Buchwald, *The Brave Coward* (New York: Harper, 1957), 75.

xx "a violent disagreement": Dust jacket of Art Buchwald, *Lighten Up, George* (New York: G. P. Putnam's Sons, 1991).

xx "so outspoken that the last time": Back cover of Art Buchwald, *And Then I Told the President* (Greenwich, Conn.: Fawcett, 1965).

xx "Little Throat": Back cover of Buchwald, *Lighten Up, George*.

xx "A laundry hamper": Art Buchwald, *You Can Fool All of the People All the Time* (New York: G. P. Putnam's Sons, 1985), 82–83.

xxi "Buchshots": *Newsweek*, June 7, 1965.

xxi "The Supreme Court ruling on abortion": Buchwald, *Lighten Up, George*, 62.

xxi "Rewriting History": Art Buchwald, *I Think I Don't Remember* (New York: G. P. Putnam's Sons, 1987), 80–82.

xxi "How many people take you seriously?": Art Buchwald oral history, March 12, 1969, John F. Kennedy Presidential Library, Boston 53.

xxi "J. Edgar Hoover Just Doesn't Exist": Art Buchwald, "The FBI in Peace and War," WP, December 8, 1964; *The Boston Globe*, December 8, 1964.

xxi At the height of the Vietnam War: John Cassady, "When the NSA Spied on Art Buchwald," *The New Yorker*, September 26, 2013; Matthew M. Aid and

William Burr, NSA Archives online posting, September 25, 2013; Richard Leiby, "Declassified Documents Show NSA Listened In on MLK, Muhammad Ali and Art Buchwald," WP, September 25, 2013.

xxii "My function—if I have one": Art Buchwald interview with Larry Wilde, August 18, 1969, 17. A copy of the interview transcript is on deposit in the AB Papers, LOC.

xxii "What people don't understand about Buchwald": Ronald G. Shafer, "Buchwald Draws Blood with Satiric Thrusts at Capital Officialdom," WSJ, November 24, 1969.

xxii In the 1950s, at the height: Art Buchwald, I'll Always Have Paris (New York: G. P. Putnam's Sons, 1996), 80–81; Richard Kluger, The Paper: The Life and Death of the "New York Herald Tribune" (New York: Vintage Books, 1989), 487.

xxii Undeterred, and perhaps spurred on: Kluger, Paper, 487.

xxii "My style is different": Buchwald interview with Wilde, August 18, 1969, 14.

xxii "the gentleness of your satire": Garry Trudeau to Art Buchwald, November 30, 1984, AB Papers, LOC.

xxiii "inner strengths and hidden talents": Art Buchwald, Leaving Home: A Memoir (New York: G. P. Putnam's Sons, 1993), 101.

xxv "What are you going to leave behind?": Severo, "Art Buchwald."

Chapter 1: "Plastered in Paris"

3 "It is a strange force": S. J. Perelman, The Most of S. J. Perelman (New York: Simon and Schuster, 1980), xi.

3 "I'm having a ball": Art Buchwald to his sisters, Alice, Doris, and Edith, in Buchwald, Leaving Home, 202–3.

4 Art lived with thirteen other students: Ibid., 204.

4 "When asked what I intend": Ibid., 211.

4 "Foreign languages": Ibid., 206.

4 In one of his writing classes: Art Buchwald, "A Short Report on Satire," student paper, English 175b, Dr. Baxter, March 2, 1948, AB Papers, LOC.

4 "USC was my training ground": Buchwald, Leaving Home, 205.

4 He even tried his hand: Art Buchwald, Counting Sheep: The Log and Complete Play of "Sheep on the Runway" (New York: G. P. Putnam's Sons, 1970), 16–17.

4 "streets are lined": Shafer, "Buchwald Draws Blood."

5 "I wanted to stuff myself": Buchwald, Leaving Home, 234.

5 "I started adding up": Ibid., 239.

5 "My life had been a series": Author's note in Buchwald, I'll Always Have Paris; Buchwald, Leaving Home, 239.

5 "I didn't belong to anybody": Buchwald interview with Wilde, August 18, 1969, 7.

5 "bold and street wise": Ibid., 97.

5 "Later when I became a fan": Ibid., 95.

6 "I was the class clown": Ibid.

6 "This stinks!": Buchwald, Leaving Home, 61.

6   "Cigars [were] a very important part": Ibid., 146–47.

6   After Cherry Point: Ibid., 165.

6   "throw in the towel": Ibid., 168.

6   setting his sights: Ibid., 197.

7   Now, here he was: Ibid., 239.

7   "I am in Paris": Buchwald, *I'll Always Have Paris*, 5–6.

7   "like a stage setting": Ibid., 4.

8   "Franglais": Ibid., 5; Lance Morrow, "Franglais Spoken Here," *Time*, September 30, 1996.

8   "Just a short note": Art Buchwald to Johnny and Norma, September 5, 1948, AB Papers, LOC.

8   During his first few months: Buchwald, *Leaving Home*, 241–42.

8   At first, his Parisian neighbors: Buchwald, *I'll Always Have Paris*, 15.

9   Soon he moved to another hotel: Buchwald, *Leaving Home*, 246–47.

9   Although his stint: Ann Buchwald and Art Buchwald, *Seems Like Yesterday* (New York: G. P. Putnam's Sons, 1980), 20.

9   "I had dined for three years": Art Buchwald, *Whose Rose Garden Is It Anyway?* (New York: G. P. Putnam's Sons, 1989), 87.

9   "Every young journalist's dream": Buchwald, *I'll Always Have Paris*, 37–39.

9   "apex of [its] power": Kluger, *Paper*, 10.

10 In "quality of content": Ibid., 8.

10 Hawkins had been with: See obituaries of Eric Hawkins in *NYT*, August 19, 1969; and *WP*, August 19, 1969.

10 In June 1940, as German troops: *NYT*, August 19, 1969.

11 "tubby little fellow": Kluger, *Paper*, 482.

11 "The paper isn't interested": Buchwald, *I'll Always Have Paris*, 42.

11 "Some people might have considered": Speech of Art Buchwald in Paris, France, September 23, 1996. Courtesy of Joel and Tamara Buchwald.

11 The *Trib*'s new column: Ann and Art Buchwald, *Seems Like Yesterday*, 20–21; Buchwald, *I'll Always Have Paris*, 42.

11 "I was on the staff": Buchwald, *I'll Always Have Paris*, 42.

11 "He wasn't exactly a whirlwind": Ibid., 49.

12 Sensing he was in serious trouble: Ibid.

12 "His naivete served him": Ibid.

12 "Boy, when I made the decision": Art Buchwald to Walt and Bettie, December 3, 1951, AB Papers, LOC.

12 One of the notables: *St. Louis Post-Dispatch*, August 17, 1953; Morrow, "Franglais Spoken Here."

13 "Been working steadily": *St. Louis Post-Dispatch*, August 17, 1953.

13 "If the books didn't sell": Ibid.

13 "a smart-assed son of a bitch": Morrow, "Franglais Spoken Here"; Buchwald, *I'll Always Have Paris*, 21.

13 "Le Jour de Merci Donnant": Buchwald, *I'll Always Have Paris*, 10; Buchwald, *Down the Seine and Up the Potomac with Art Buchwald*, 64–65; *Washingtonian*, February 1990.

14 One of those visiting Americans: Art Buchwald, "The Redford Files," *WP*,

December 8, 2005; Michael Feeney Callan, *Robert Redford: The Biography* (New York: Knopf, 2011), 46–47.

Chapter 2: Raising the Stature of Ink

15 "It sure beat the hell": Dust jacket of Ann and Art Buchwald, *Seems Like Yesterday.*

15 "Hey there, McGarry!": Ann and Art Buchwald, *Seems Like Yesterday,* 19.

15 "He wore a sporty brown hat": Ibid.

15 Although she had no job: Ibid., 11.

16 She began her career: Ibid., 13–14.

16 "the biggest, loudest": Ibid., 16.

16 "I found her extremely attractive": Buchwald, *I'll Always Have Paris,* 86.

16 Over the next two years: Ann and Art Buchwald, *Seems Like Yesterday,* 78.

16 "He vacillated between wanting": Ibid.

16 "I'm so lonely": Art Buchwald to Ann Buchwald, October 1950, AB Papers, LOC.

16 "never find anyone": Ann and Art Buchwald, *Seems Like Yesterday,* 83.

17 "Bogey and I have watched": Ibid., 81.

17 In early October 1952: Ibid., 106.

17 "Listen, buster": Ibid., 82.

17 "I was the problem": Ibid., 132.

17 "So in no time": Ibid., 125–26.

17 "I'd been ready for motherhood": Ibid., 163–64.

18 "the scene of our happiest moments": Buchwald, *I'll Always Have Paris,* dedication page.

18 Ingrid Bergman: In January 1951, Ingrid Bergman helped Buchwald score a major journalistic coup after she stunned the world with her headline-grabbing love affair with director Roberto Rossellini, a romance that ended her marriage and produced a son by Rossellini. After the scandal broke, Bergman was vilified around the world, receiving thousands of hate letters condemning her and her lover. "At the time more was made of this than the U.S. dropping the atomic bomb on Hiroshima," Buchwald later said. Art, who had become a friend of Bergman's during the time they spent together in Rome and Paris, was shocked by the vile attacks she was subjected to and thought if some of the letters were made public they might produce a wave of sympathy for her. When Buchwald asked Bergman if she would allow him access to the letters for an article he hoped to write about the affair, much to his "surprise and delight" she agreed.

For days, Buchwald pored over bundles of correspondence packed away in Bergman's Rome apartment, transcribing excerpts from many of the letters, which were published in his article for *Look* magazine on February 27, 1951. The letters "included threats on her life, prayers for her salvation, poems of praise, anti-Catholic and anti-Italian obscenities, penciled notes of sympathy and printed and unsigned scrawls of disgust," Buchwald later wrote. Soon, the "scandal of the century" subsided as Bergman's fans and the Hollywood community forgave her. As Buchwald wrote years later, "Like many motion picture stars' scandals of the heart, Ingrid's trespasses were eventually forgiven, and she continued to be one of the finest and most sought-after actresses of our time." Buchwald, *I'll Always Have Paris*, 214-15; Art Buchwald, "Dear Ingrid Bergman," *Look*, February 27, 1951, 13. Buchwald's transcripts of the letters to Bergman are in the possession of Joel and Tamara Buchwald.

18   **Mike Todd:** Film producer Mike Todd (1909–58) is perhaps best known for *Around the World in 80 Days*, which won the 1957 Oscar for Best Picture. That year the forty-seven-year-old Todd married the more widely known twenty-four-year-old actress Elizabeth Taylor. After his marriage Todd jokingly referred to himself in telegrams to Buchwald as "Mr. Elizabeth Taylor, Jr." When Todd was killed in a plane crash in 1958, Ann said Art was "crushed" by the news of his death. A collection of telegrams from Todd to Buchwald are on deposit in the AB Papers, LOC.

18   **"He was a dimwitted man":** Ann and Art Buchwald, *Seems Like Yesterday*, 178.

18   **"a very sharp lady":** Ibid.

18   **"It's better now":** Morrow, "Franglais Spoken Here."

18   **"one of the most anti-American":** Buchwald, *I'll Always Have Paris*, 172.

18   **"I once asked her what American":** Ibid.

19   **"one of my favorite British people":** Ibid., 173.

19   **In 1946, while still a student:** Buchwald, *Leaving Home*, 211-13.

19   **"Have been wanting to tell you for a long time":** John Steinbeck to Art Buchwald, July 27, 1953, AB Papers, LOC.

20   **"scruffy" appearance:** Morrow, "Franglais Spoken Here."

20   **"The floors sagged":** Buchwald, *I'll Always Have Paris*, 45-46; Art Buchwald, *The Buchwald Stops Here* (New York: G. P. Putnam's Sons, 1978), 294.

20   **"wonderfully ratty":** Ben Bradlee, *A Good Life: Newspapering and Other Adventures* (New York: Simon and Schuster, 1995), 153-54.

20   **Buchwald's typewriter:** *Newsweek*, December 4, 1961; Buchwald, *I'll Always Have Paris*, 46.

20   **to help put out each edition:** Buchwald, *The Buchwald Stops Here*, 294.

20   *To Catch a Thief:* See opening scene of Alfred Hitchcock's 1955 film classic.

21   **"raised the stature of ink":** Dust jacket of Art Buchwald, *Art Buchwald's Paris* (Boston: Little, Brown, 1954).

21   **"treat light subjects seriously":** Talking Points of Art Buchwald for Paris Speech, ca. 1957, AB Papers, LOC.

21   **"Three Musketeers":** Bradlee, *Good Life*, 172.

21   **"There's no more room, Artie!":** Buchwald, *I'll Always Have Paris*, 159.

22   **"pulled a rabbit out of his hat":** Bradlee, *Good Life*, 173.

22   **"The reason for the feud":** Buchwald, *Down the Seine and Up the Potomac with Art Buchwald*, 55-57.

22   **"No Grimaldis!":** Ibid., 56.

22   **The next morning, shortly after:** A copy of Buchwald's invitation to the wedding is on deposit in the AB Papers, LOC.

23   **In mid-December 1957:** *NYT*, December 18, 1957.

23   **"very sophisticated control":** David Halberstam, *The Powers That Be* (New York: Knopf, 1979), 244.

23   "glut of informational": Ibid., 243.

23   "Jim, whose idea": Buchwald, *I'll Always Have Paris*, 177–78.

23   "laughed out loud": *WP*, December 18, 1957.

23   "simmer down": Buchwald, *I'll Always Have Paris*, 178.

24   "unadulterated rot": Ibid.

24   When asked for a comment: Ibid.

24   "was a glorious, unexpected": Ibid.

24   "occasionally amusing": Letter to the Editor, *New York Herald Tribune*, June 30, 1955, AB Papers, LOC.

24   "Why, oh why did you do it?": Letter to the Editor, *New York Herald Tribune*, January 26, 1955, AB Papers, LOC.

25   "The trick of the column": Ann and Art Buchwald, *Seems Like Yesterday*, 125.

25   "Coward in the Congo": Buchwald, *I'll Always Have Paris*, 200; Buchwald, *Down the Seine and Up the Potomac with Art Buchwald*, 49.

25   And in the spring of 1958: Buchwald, *I'll Always Have Paris*, 193.

25   "My plan was to travel": Ibid.

25   "loaded down with food": Buchwald, *Down the Seine and Up the Potomac with Art Buchwald*, 71.

26   "People gathered around the car": Buchwald, *I'll Always Have Paris*, 193.

26   "We found out why Napoleon": Buchwald, *Down the Seine and Up the Potomac with Art Buchwald*, 80.

26   "all the cooks left": Ibid., 84.

26   Their greatest coup: Buchwald, *I'll Always Have Paris*, 196–97.

26   "But we couldn't very well": Buchwald, *Down the Seine and Up the Potomac with Art Buchwald*, 87.

26   "Before his departure": Buchwald, *I'll Always Have Paris*, 198.

27   "All of us became very cozy": Ibid., 193.

27   A fun person was a "gasser": *The Boston Globe*, July 6, 1958; Art Buchwald, *More Caviar* (New York: Harper, 1959), 153–55.

27   And in 1959 he had an exclusive: *Los Angeles Times*, June 26, 1959.

28   "Thanks so much for the Buchwald book": P. G. Wodehouse to Mr. Bessie, April 14, 1959, AB Papers, LOC.

29   "Let me take this opportunity": Art Buchwald to Pierre Salinger, November 18, 1960, Pierre Salinger Papers, John F. Kennedy Presidential Library, Boston, Mass.

29   In the early 1950s: Shafer, "Buchwald Draws Blood."

29   He was making a salary: *Newsweek*, December 4, 1961.

29   "luncheon companions": Ibid.

30   "I had literally exhausted": Ann and Art Buchwald, *Seems Like Yesterday*, 214.

Chapter 3: "Salinger's Folly" and "Bounties of the Banned"

35   "Basically I deal": *Public Opinion* (Chambersburg, Pa.), February 2, 1968.

35   "of poetry and power": Theodore Sorensen, *Kennedy* (New York: Harper and Row, 1965), 244.

35 "the breath of the old poet": Arthur Schlesinger, Jr., A *Thousand Days: John F. Kennedy in the White House* (Boston: Houghton Mifflin, 1965), 2.

35 "fine spirits": Art Buchwald, "Frost on Sandburg," *WP*, March 25, 1961.

36 "I feel sorry for them": Ibid.

36 "To Mrs. Buchwald": A copy of the card autographed by Frost to Ann Buchwald on March 10, 1961, is on deposit in the AB Papers, LOC.

36 "We've got a lot of work": Sally Bedell Smith, *Grace and Power: The Private World of the Kennedy White House* (New York: Random House, 2004), 89–90.

36 broadcast live on CBS: Ibid., 255.

36 The program was a huge hit: Ibid., 256; Ben Bradlee, *Conversations with Kennedy* (New York: Norton, 1975), 54.

36 During the tongue-in-cheek visit: Art Buchwald, "Everybody's Giving White House Tours," *WP*, February 22, 1962; Art Buchwald, *Is It Safe to Drink the Water?* (Greenwich, Conn.: Fawcett, 1963), 198.

37 "never would have forgotten": Jacqueline Kennedy to Art Buchwald, November 12, 1985, AB Papers, LOC.

37 It was a "glitzy affair": Buchwald, *I'll Always Have Paris*, 225.

37 Both Buchwalds were charmed: Ibid.

37 After a "week of political stargazing": Ibid., 226.

37 "It seemed in those days": Ann and Art Buchwald, *Seems Like Yesterday*, 214.

38 "Everyone around the world": Buchwald, *I'll Always Have Paris*, 226.

38 "I think it's time": Ibid.

38 "You own Paris": Ibid.

38 "it's perfectly all right": Art Buchwald, *I Chose Capitol Punishment* (Greenwich, Conn.: Fawcett, 1964), 10.

38 "You'll get massacred": Ann and Art Buchwald, *Seems Like Yesterday*, 217.

38 "I knew we'd all be in": Ibid., 216.

38 "leave everything in Paris": Ibid., 214.

38 "Announce you're only going back": Ibid., 215.

39 "Art and I tried to be cheerful": Ibid., 217.

39 "as hard to find": M. J. Arlen, "Footnotes for Fun," *NYT Book Review*, November 4, 1962.

39 "The fifties had constituted": Schlesinger, *Thousand Days*, 606.

40 "For Kennedy wit": Ibid.

40 "He invited me to his office once": *The Boston Globe*, July 10, 1974.

40 "We read enough shit": Bradlee, *Conversations with Kennedy*, 103.

40 Finally, in a fit of temper: Ibid., 102–3.

40 "oblivious to the criticism": Ibid.

40 "It's a hard life, all right": James Reston, "Who Says a Good Paper Has to Be Silly?," *NYT*, June 1, 1962.

41 "Other newspapermen bought us drinks": Art Buchwald, "A *Trib* Man's Lament," *WP*, August 20, 1963.

41 "without a cigar, a thirst": Pierre Salinger, *With Kennedy* (Garden City, N.Y.: Doubleday, 1966), 240.

41 "contests of strength": Ibid.

42   "To many of us who weigh": Art Buchwald, "Calories Don't Vote," WP, February 12, 1963.

42   "The President's Council on Physical Fitness": Press Release, Office of the White House Press Secretary, February 12, 1963, AB Papers, LOC.

43   "exceedingly dull": Art Buchwald to John Huston, August 22, 1963, Academy of Motion Picture Arts and Sciences, Margaret Herrick Library, Beverly Hills, Calif.

43   "crept up": Art Buchwald, Too Soon to Say Goodbye (New York: Random House, 2006), 38.

43   "on a crying jag": Buchwald, Leaving Home, 15; Buchwald, Too Soon to Say Goodbye, 38.

43   "When you have depression": "Gray Matters: Depression and the Brain," a radio program produced in association with the Dana Alliance for Brain Initiatives, Public Radio International, 1996.

44   "I didn't ask God": Buchwald, Too Soon to Say Goodbye, 39.

44   "I was certain I would never": Buchwald, Leaving Home, 147.

44   "listless and sad": Ibid.

44   "The normal things": "Gray Matters: Depression and the Brain."

44   "I found myself sitting": Buchwald, Leaving Home, 147.

44   "Then I pulled open": Ibid.

44   "scars of childhood": Buchwald, Too Soon to Say Goodbye, 38.

45   "It wasn't easy to admit": Buchwald, Leaving Home, 101.

45   "You are ashamed": Buchwald, Too Soon to Say Goodbye, 39.

45   On May 4, he attended: Art Buchwald, "Mint Juleps and the Derby," The Lexington (Ky.) Herald, May 7, 1963.

45   "I love my work": The Capital Times (Madison, Wis.), November 27, 1962.

45   "taxes, expense accounts": Bridgeport Post (Bridgeport, Conn.), December 1, 1963.

45   "thoughtful interest in seeing": Evelyn Lincoln to Art Buchwald, October 28, 1963, John F. Kennedy Presidential Library, Boston, Massachusetts.

45   "magic to set you laughing": The Gazette (Montreal, Quebec), November 30, 1963.

45   "from cover to cover": Art Buchwald, "Obscure Author Receives Rave Review from Unknown Critic," WP, October 29, 1963.

46   A Harris Poll: WP, August 16, 1963, and November 10, 1963.

46   Buchwald and Bradlee: Buchwald, Too Soon to Say Goodbye, 79; Graham R. Hodges, "Dark Day in November: 100 Americans' Memories of the Day President Kennedy Was Assassinated" (unpublished manuscript, ca. 1999). A copy is on deposit in the AB Papers, LOC.

47   "We Weep": Art Buchwald, "We Weep," New York Herald Tribune, November 22, 1963.

47   "Mr. Sorensen was very kind": Art Buchwald to William Manchester, September 14, 1964, William Manchester Papers, Box 208, Wesleyan University Special Collections, Olin Library, Middletown, Conn.; William Manchester, The Death of a President: November 1963 (New York: Harper and Row, 1988), 464.

47   "magnificent sense of humor": Art Buchwald, "A Man with Humor," *WP*, November 26, 1963.

47   "One of the late President's lines": Ibid.

47   "It did not make any sense": Hodges, "Dark Day in November."

Chapter 4: Brumus, Batman, and Buchwald "Buchshots"

48   "Think of the trouble the world": E. B. White and Katharine S. White, eds., *A Subtreasury of American Humor* (New York: Coward-McCann, 1941), xix.

48   "J. Edgar Hoover Just Doesn't Exist": Art Buchwald, "FBI in Peace and War," *WP*, December 8, 1964.

49   One young girl in Springfield, Missouri: *Springfield* (Mo.) *Leader and Press*, December 15, 1964.

49   senator William Proxmire: William Proxmire to Art Buchwald, January 4, 1965, with enclosure from constituent in Waunakee, Wisconsin, dated December 15, 1964, AB Papers, LOC.

49   One infuriated reader told the editor: *The Emporia* (Kan.) *Gazette*, January 25, 1965; *Springfield* (Mo.) *Leader and Press*, December 15, 1964.

49   Other papers took a different approach: *Arizona Republic*, December 11, 1964.

49   Although the FBI director never spoke publicly: Anthony Summers, *Official and Confidential: The Secret Life of J. Edgar Hoover* (New York: G. P. Putnam's Sons, 1993), 101.

49   Perhaps the most perplexing response: *The Cincinnati Enquirer*, January 31, 1965.

50   "The satirist has his job laid out": Buchwald, "Short Report on Satire."

50   In one Vietnam-era piece: Art Buchwald, *The Establishment Is Alive and Well in Washington* (New York: G. P. Putnam's Sons, 1969), 111–13.

51   By the spring of 1966: *NYT*, May 3, 1966.

51   On March 3, *The New York Times* reported: *NYT*, March 3, 1966.

52   During the week of its debut: *NYT*, January 15, 1966.

52   "Lights up—we see a phone": Art Buchwald, "Batman Day at the White House," *WP*, March 13, 1966.

52   "I've finally emerged from the Batcave": Adam West to Art Buchwald, April 1, 1966, AB Papers, LOC.

53   In a column called "Price Per Head": Buchwald, *Have I Ever Lied to You?*, 34.

54   In September 2013: John Cassady, "When the NSA Spied on Art Buchwald," *The New Yorker*, September 26, 2013; National Security Archive online posting written by Matthew M. Aid and William Burr, September 25, 2013; Leiby, "Declassified Documents."

54   During the years 1964: William Manchester, *The Glory and the Dream: A Narrative History of America, 1932–1972* (New York: Bantam, 1974), 1058.

54   Estimates were that some three million: Ibid., 1059.

54   On March 7, 1965: Ibid.

55   "to eliminate illegal barriers": Speech of President Lyndon B. Johnson to a Joint Session of Congress, March 15, 1965.

55   "Bull Whip, Alabama": Art Buchwald, *Son of the Great Society* (Greenwich, Conn.: Fawcett, 1966), 72; Buchwald, *Down the Seine and Up the Potomac with Art Buchwald*, 252–53.

56   Decades later: Kluger, *Paper*, 671.

56   "pretty wild affair": Art Buchwald oral history, March 12, 1969, John F. Kennedy Presidential Library, 1.

56   Muhammad Ali: Associated Press, "Ali Highlights Pet Show," *Press and Sun-Bulletin* (Binghamton, N.Y.), May 15, 1977.

57   The "most unusual pet": "Pets Gambol at Kennedys'," WP, May 20, 1968.

57   One year, when a skunk: Ibid.

57   "I remember during the judging": Jean Stein, *American Journey: The Times of Robert Kennedy*, ed. George Plimpton (New York: Harcourt, Brace, and Jovanovich, 1970), 161.

57   1967 raft trip: Art Buchwald oral history, March 12, 1969, John F. Kennedy Presidential Library, 29–32; Buchwald, *Down the Seine and Up the Potomac with Art Buchwald*, 289–91.

57   "It's all right for Kennedy": Buchwald, *Down the Seine and Up the Potomac with Art Buchwald*, 289.

57   "I was an orphan": Art Buchwald oral history, March 12, 1969, John F. Kennedy Presidential Library, 9.

57   "He was sort of a Hamlet figure": Ibid., 12.

58   "I refused to become part": Ibid., 51.

58   "They had a good enough": Ibid., 39.

58   "I really cut him up": Stein, *American Journey*, 317.

58   "'I didn't invite you'": Art Buchwald oral history, March 12, 1969, John F. Kennedy Presidential Library, 21.

58   "fantastic" father: Ibid., 10.

58   "Brumus is a legend": Art Buchwald, "Brumus the Great: Bobby Kennedy's Huge Dog Is a Legend in His Own Time," WP, May 29, 1966; Art Buchwald oral history, March 12, 1969, John F. Kennedy Presidential Library, 4.

58   "He [was] known to attack mailmen": Buchwald, "Brumus the Great."

58   Brumus even provoked the ire: Evan Thomas, *Robert Kennedy: His Life* (New York: Simon and Schuster, 2000), 117.

59   "abandonment anxiety": Robert F. Kennedy, Jr., *American Values: Lessons I Learned from My Family* (New York: Harper, 2018), 185.

59   "legal justification": Thomas, *Robert Kennedy*, 117.

59   "Bobby and I were sitting": Art Buchwald oral history, March 12, 1969, John F. Kennedy Presidential Library, 2.

59   "These two women wandered": Stein, *American Journey*, 160.

59   "'How long do you have to be here'": Art Buchwald oral history, March 12, 1969, John F. Kennedy Presidential Library, 3.

60   "I have been retained by Mr. Art Buchwald": Edward Bennett Williams to Senator Robert F. Kennedy, August 7, 1967, AB Papers, LOC; Arthur

Schlesinger, Jr., *Robert F. Kennedy and His Times* (Boston: Houghton Mifflin, 1978), 810.

61 Hefner, the founder and publisher of *Playboy*: *Current Biography Yearbook: 1968* (New York: H. W. Wilson, 1968), 180–82.

61 In 1953, Hefner: Ibid.; David Halberstam, *The Fifties* (New York: Fawcett Columbine, 1993), 570–71.

61 some called it "genius": Halberstam, *Fifties*, 573.

61 "Hefner was fighting that part": Ibid., 575–76.

61 Expecting to catch: Art Buchwald, "Gin Rummy Is Name of Game at Hugh Hefner Chicago Pad," *WP*, November 9, 1967.

62 "Thanks for your nice note": Hugh Hefner to Art Buchwald, November 22, 1967, AB Papers, LOC.

63 "The whole thing . . . seems a little like": Campaign Journal of John Bartlow Martin, John Bartlow Martin Papers, LOC.

63 "He was fighting a battle": Art Buchwald oral history, March 12, 1969, John F. Kennedy Presidential Library, 49.

63 "I thought Johnson": Ibid., 50.

64 Kennedy's casket: See Schlesinger, *Robert F. Kennedy and His Times*, 915.

64 Along the way thousands: Ibid.; Thomas, *Robert Kennedy*, 393–94.

64 "I didn't know what to do": Stein, *American Journey*, 127.

65 "I dreaded the removal": Ibid., 344.

65 After Kennedy's coffin: Thomas, *Robert Kennedy*, 394.

65 Two days later, a grieving Buchwald: Art Buchwald, "When a Friend Dies," *The Boston Globe*, June 11, 1968.

66 "One of the stories": John H. Glenn to Art Buchwald, July 5, 1968, AB Papers, LOC.

66 "I think that the tragedy of Bobby Kennedy": Art Buchwald oral history, March 12, 1969, John F. Kennedy Presidential Library, 84–85.

67 Humphrey couldn't "look sad": *Public Opinion* (Chambersburg, Pa.), February 2, 1968.

67 "Without Rockefeller": *Akron* (Ohio) *Beacon Journal*, October 4, 1968.

67 "Boredom lay on the convention": Manchester, *Glory and the Dream*, 1142.

67 "armed camp": Ibid.

68 "The whole world is watching!": Ibid., 1144.

68 "The Democrats are finished": Ibid., 1145.

68 "Everybody over reacted": *The Daily Oklahoman* (Oklahoma City, Okla.), September 13, 1968.

68 One of his more comically: Art Buchwald, "The Heroes of Chicago," *Des Moines* (Iowa) *Tribune*, August 31, 1968.

68 "The convention was a gas": Irwin Shaw to Art Buchwald, August 16, 1968, AB Papers, LOC.

69 During their years in France: Buchwald, *I'll Always Have Paris*, 89–90.

69 Shaw was born: See obituaries of Irwin Shaw, *NYT*, May 17, 1984; and *WP*, May 17, 1984.

69 "one of the heroes": Art Buchwald, *I'll Always Have Paris*, 89–90.

69 "He was a big bear": Ibid.
69 "one of the most generous": Willie Morris, "Irwin Shaw's Quiet Craft," *WP*, May 18, 1984.
70 "The summer's been quiet": Irwin Shaw to Art Buchwald, August 16, 1968, AB Papers, LOC.
70 "I wanted to finish my book": Ibid., October 19, 1968.
71 "'I'm hacking away'": Ibid., November 2, 1969.
71 "humor conglomerate": Shafer, "Buchwald Draws Blood."
71 In 1962: *Time*, June 2, 1962; Buchwald interview with Wilde, August 18, 1969, 14; Shafer, "Buchwald Draws Blood."
71 "I think you're going": Russell Baker to Art Buchwald, February 10, 1966, AB Papers, LOC.
71 "one of the best satirists": Ward Just and Richard Pollack, "The Capital Wit of Art Buchwald," *Newsweek*, June 7, 1965.
72 *60 Minutes*: *The Pittsburgh Press*, August 5, 1968.

Chapter 5: Buchwald at Large

73 "Art Buchwald is a small": Alistair Cooke, "Letter from America," September 18, 1971.
73 "The column's a snap": Buchwald interview with Wilde, August 18, 1969, 18.
73 "I read your columns": Irwin Shaw to Art Buchwald, December 23, 1979, AB Papers, LOC.
73 "My typewriter practically stops": Buchwald interview with Wilde, August 18, 1969, 12.
73 "It's a beautiful business": Ibid., 27.
74 Nearly every year: Shafer, "Buchwald Draws Blood."
74 "The CIA for Fun and Profit": *Greenville* (S.C.) *News*, February 2, 1969.
74 "In a city awash": Just and Pollack, "Capital Wit of Art Buchwald."
74 "Buchwald is incomparable": Thomas Meehan, "Cruise Director on the *Titanic*," *New York Times Magazine*, January 2, 1972.
74 "A writer should concern himself": *The Writers' Chapbook: A Compendium of Fact, Opinion, Wit, and Advice from "The Paris Review" Interviews* (New York: Paris Review Editions, 2018), 41.
74 He often joked: Shafer, "Buchwald Draws Blood."
74 "We have a golden rule": *The Boston Globe*, July 10, 1974.
74 If fortunate enough: Shafer, "Buchwald Draws Blood"; Just and Pollack, "Capital Wit of Art Buchwald."
75 Once downstairs: Just and Pollack, "Capital Wit of Art Buchwald."
75 It was estimated: Ibid.
75 When the cab arrived: Shafer, "Buchwald Draws Blood"; Just and Pollack, "Capital Wit of Art Buchwald."
75 After arriving at nine-thirty: Meehan, "Cruise Director on the *Titanic*."
75 "That," one reporter for *The New York Times*: Ibid.
75 Then, after leisurely sorting: Ibid.
75 "I don't stew over it": Shafer, "Buchwald Draws Blood."
75 He was never "preachy": Ibid.

76 "I don't come into the office": *The Boston Globe,* July 10, 1974.

76 While still at the University of Southern California: Buchwald, "Short Report on Satire."

76 "I've always been against": Art Buchwald interview with Patricia Marx, January 6, 1964, WNYC radio.

77 "The extreme Left": Buchwald interview with Wilde, August 18, 1969, 16.

77 "A lot of times": Ibid., 11.

77 "He would give it to me": Author interview with Cathy Crary.

78 composer Richard Rodgers: Richard Rodgers to Art Buchwald, July 6, 1967, AB Papers, LOC.

78 comedian Phyllis Diller: Phyllis Diller to Art Buchwald, June 7, 1995; Art Buchwald to Phyllis Diller, November 28, 1995, AB Papers, LOC.

78 actress Joan Crawford: Joan Crawford to Art Buchwald, May 12, 1964, AB Papers, LOC.

78 "I burn incense": Frank Capra to Art Buchwald, November 11, 1977, AB Papers, LOC.

78 that made him "chuckle": Dwight Eisenhower to Art Buchwald, May 1, 1965, AB Papers, LOC.

78 columnist Anthony Lewis: Anthony Lewis to Art Buchwald, September 8, 1966, AB Papers, LOC.

78 "I didn't want to tell you this": Art Buchwald to Ben Bradlee, June 14, 1965, AB Papers, LOC.

78 "Thanks a lot for the football": Christopher Kennedy to Art Buchwald, August 31, 1978, AB Papers, LOC.

79 "Hundreds of prep schools": Art Buchwald to Mrs. Thurlby, Dana Hall School, August 12, 1971, AB Papers, LOC.

79 "My mother's best friend": Kennedy, *American Values,* 169.

80 "Who make everyday": Ethel Kennedy to Ann and Art Buchwald, Handwritten notation on the card says, "Christmas, 1975—Given at Sans Souci Lunch, 1/7/76." AB Papers, LOC.

80 "Science played no part": Art Buchwald to Phyllis Marcuccio, April 15, 1988, AB Papers, LOC.

80 "I have a hard time thinking": Art Buchwald to Thom Parker, March 10, 1988, AB Papers, LOC.

81 On his office wall: *Asbury Park* (N.J.) *Press,* October 14, 1977.

81 "You should be ashamed": Shafer, "Buchwald Draws Blood."

81 "cheap, cross, crude": Rev. Jones to Art Buchwald, February 7, 1973, AB Papers, LOC.

81 "I guess you are going": Art Buchwald to Rev. Jones, February 1973, AB Papers, LOC.

81 "remember" him on "Judgment Day": Letter to Art Buchwald, February 7, 1966, AB Papers, LOC.

81 "Hello Schnook!": Letter to Art Buchwald from Chicago, September 16, no year, AB Papers, LOC.

81 "Pink Kike" Socialist: Letter to Art Buchwald, January 12, 1984, AB Papers, LOC.

81   "BULLSHIT": See notation on letter to Art Buchwald dated June 9, 1982, AB Papers, LOC.

81   begin "prowling": Just and Pollack, "Capital Wit of Art Buchwald."

82   up to six to eight cigars: Shafer, "Buchwald Draws Blood."

82   Sans Souci restaurant: See Rob Brunner, "The Real Story of the Sans Souci: The Super-Exclusive DC Restaurant Where Even Mick Jagger Couldn't Get a Table," *Washingtonian*, July 21, 2019. The building where the Sans Souci was located is now a McDonald's. When the restaurant closed its doors in 1983, Le Maison Blanche, located at 1725 F Street, NW, became Buchwald's new favorite restaurant.

82   It was so difficult: Ibid.

82   A "savvy Frenchman": Ibid.

82   At noon each day: Ibid.

82   "Before Sans Souci": Ibid.

82   "No important decision": Art Buchwald, "The Sans Souci at High Noon," *The Buchwald Stops Here*, 25–27. On the dust jacket of the hardcover edition of the book is a photo of Buchwald sitting at his favorite table, number 12.

83   "Buchwald never drank": Brunner, "Real Story of the Sans Souci."

83   "Memorandum to Kay Graham": Memo dated December 15, 1966, Ben Bradlee Papers, Harry Ransom Center, University of Texas.

84   "Lunch at Sans Souci was": Eppie Lederer to Art Buchwald, February 13, 1969, AB Papers, LOC.

84   After lunch: Shafer, "Buchwald Draws Blood."

84   "Portrait of a Man Reading": John Greenya, "Portrait of a Man Reading," *The Washington Post Book World*, October 5, 1969.

84   "Please congratulate Joseph Heller": Tracey Daugherty, *Just One Catch: A Biography of Joseph Heller* (New York: St. Martin's Press, 2011), 225.

85   "Possibly. Take pornography": Greenya, "Portrait of a Man Reading."

85   "He was obsessed with watches": Author interview with Cathy Crary.

85   After several more hours: Author interview with Joel Buchwald.

85   "Everyone thinks I have": Just and Pollack, "Capital Wit of Art Buchwald."

Chapter 6: The Great Joe Mayflower Feud

89   "We're in show biz!": Buchwald, *Counting Sheep*, 16.

90   The financial backing: Ibid., 47–48.

90   "I found out from a friend": Ibid., 40.

90   "All I know is that Yale": Mel Gussow, "Buchwald Agonizes as Play Rehearses," *NYT*, January 22, 1970.

90   Soon Saks and Whitehead: Buchwald, *Counting Sheep*, 50.

91   His role was "too straight": Ibid.

91   "One gets the feeling that the Gods": Ibid., 54.

91   In background and pedigree: See sketches of the Alsop brothers in *Current Biography Yearbook: 1952*, 15–18.

92   "libelous spoof": See, for instance, the dialogue in act 1, scene 1, in Buchwald, *Counting Sheep*, 101, 118.

92   "anyone who went to the opening": Ibid., 59.

92 Alsop's brother Stewart: Sally Quinn, "Friends Flock to Buchwald's 'Sheep,'" WP, February 2, 1970; Shafer, "Buchwald Draws Blood."

92 "Alsop has not been": Maxine Cheshire, "'Sheep Feud,'" WP, January 15, 1970.

92 "Joe Alsop was sticking pins": Gussow, "Buchwald Agonizes as Play Rehearses," NYT, January 22, 1970.

93 "I haven't been home": WP, January 17, 1970.

93 During a preview performance: Buchwald, Counting Sheep, 60.

94 "because he understood": Ibid., 61.

94 He immediately contacted: Ibid.; author interview with Joseph Califano.

94 "Alsop might save": Buchwald, Counting Sheep, 61.

94 "No chance": Ibid., 62; author interview with Joseph Califano.

94 Bothered by the continuous: Buchwald, Counting Sheep, 62.

94 But now, Bradlee told her: Ibid., 63.

95 In the meeting at Williams's law office: Ibid., 63–64.

95 "You've got to talk Artie": Ibid., 64.

95 "Benjy, if Artie": Ibid.

95 It was Katharine Graham: Ibid.

95 On January 16: Ibid., 69.

96 "Light up your cigar": Christopher Kennedy to Art Buchwald, January 25, 1970, AB Papers, LOC.

96 "I want the play": Buchwald, Counting Sheep, 75.

96 "Please, Clive": Ibid., 77.

96 On opening night: Quinn, "Friends Flock to Buchwald's 'Sheep.'"

96 "The interesting part": Ibid.

97 It was reported that one prominent: Ibid.

97 Feud or no feud: Ibid.

97 "I never saw my father": Buchwald, Leaving Home, 46.

97 Only an hour before the show: Quinn, "Friends Flock to Buchwald's 'Sheep.'"

97 During the first act: Buchwald, Counting Sheep, 82.

97 "was spent ticking off": Quinn, "Friends Flock to Buchwald's 'Sheep.'"

97 When the curtain rose: Buchwald, Counting Sheep, 82.

97 As the final curtain came down: Ibid., 82–83.

98 "My God": Quinn, "Friends Flock to Buchwald's 'Sheep.'"

98 "I thought it was great": Ibid.

98 Shortly after eleven P.M.: Ibid.

98 "No matter what the critics say": Buchwald, Counting Sheep, 87.

98 "Art Buchwald's 'Sheep'": Clive Barnes, "Theater: Art Buchwald's 'Sheep on the Runway,'" NYT, February 2, 1970.

98 "Good old Clive Barnes": Buchwald, Counting Sheep, 88.

99 "The only people who couldn't": Ibid., 88–90.

99 The play had a sad and somber opening: Myra MacPherson, "'Happy Has-Beens' Attend Opening—Democrats Gather," WP, May 5, 1970.

99 "I told Art": Ibid.

99 "When I look back on it": Buchwald, Counting Sheep, 94.

100 **In his letter:** Robert Kintner to Joseph Alsop, February 2, 1970, Papers of Joseph and Stewart Alsop, LOC; Robert W. Merry, *Taking On the World: Joseph and Stewart Alsop—Guardians of the American Century* (New York: Viking, 1996), 485–86.

100 **"That was an exceedingly":** Joseph Alsop to Robert Kintner, February 4, 1970, Papers of Joseph and Stewart Alsop, LOC.

100 **"one of Washington's most publicized":** Maxine Cheshire, "No Hard Feelings," *WP*, November 7, 1972.

Chapter 7: "Cruise Director on the *Titanic*"

101 **"Watergate is the glue":** Art Buchwald, "Watergate Is Pure Entertainment," *WP*, February 24, 1974.

101 **"No, no I don't think he is funny":** Deposition of Richard M. Nixon in *A. Ernest Fitzgerald v. Alexander Butterfield*, October 2–3, 1979, 151–52. Copies of the pages from the deposition are on deposit in the AB Papers, LOC.

101 **"As a humor columnist":** *The Daily Item* (Sunbury, Pa.), August 14, 1974.

102 **"Nixon [looks] like someone":** *Greenville* (S.C.) *News*, February 2, 1969.

102 **Disregarding the age-old tradition:** Art Buchwald, "Nixon's First Four and a Half Days," *Democrat and Chronicle* (Rochester, N.Y.), January 25, 1969.

102 **"I have come to the conclusion":** Letter to Art Buchwald, May 11, 1973, AB Papers, LOC.

102 **"I wouldn't think of wasting":** "A Disgusted Reader" to Art Buchwald, June 16, 1973, AB Papers, LOC.

103 **"Now this could mean":** *The Capital Times* (Madison, Wis.), December 28, 1968.

103 **"Nixon is going to Red China":** NYT, January 2, 1972.

103 **"like going to Las Vegas":** *The Daily Item* (Sunbury, Pa.), August 14, 1974.

103 **"On the 27th of June":** "Brumus" the dog to Art Buchwald, June 30, 1971, AB Papers, LOC.

104 **"The Bite of B & B":** *Time*, November 6, 1972.

104 **Baker, like Buchwald:** See obituaries of Russell Baker in *NYT*, January 24, 2019; and *Canadian Press*, January 23, 2019.

104 **"She would make me":** *Canadian Press*, January 23, 2019.

104 **"His column in the *Times*":** Buchwald, *Too Soon to Say Goodbye*, 72.

104 **They often lunched together:** Ibid.

105 **"You may, if you like":** Russell Baker to Robert Pittman, February 24, 1970, AB Papers, LOC.

105 **"I think he suspects":** Stearns Morse to Russell Baker, March 31, 1975, AB Papers, LOC.

106 **"I am sending your letter":** Russell Baker to Stearns Morse, April 23, 1975, AB Papers, LOC.

106 **"Thank you so much":** Art Buchwald to Stearns Morse, April 29, 1975, AB Papers, LOC.

106 **"Up until a few months ago":** Letter to Russell Baker, June 17, 1976, AB Papers, LOC.

107 **"I am getting sick and tired"**: Russell Baker to Art Buchwald, June 29, 1976, AB Papers, LOC.

107 **"No supplicant"**: Buchwald, *Counting Sheep*, 42–43.

108 **"in the great American tradition"**: *The Daily Oklahoman* (Oklahoma City, Okla.), June 9, 1970.

108 **"Now they've got me"**: *The Des Moines* (Iowa) *Register*, June 11, 1970.

108 **"It was the wisest thing"**: *Chicago Tribune*, June 9, 1970.

108 **"Hell no!"**: *Connecticut Post* (Bridgeport, Conn.), June 9, 1970.

108 **"We were sitting in the Sans Souci restaurant"**: Art Buchwald, "An Absolutely Sure Fired Way to Lose Weight," *The Saturday Evening Post*, January 1974; Art Buchwald to Edward Bennett Williams, July 19, 1972, AB Papers, LOC.

109 **Williams "tipped the scales"**: Buchwald, "An Absolutely Sure Fired Way to Lose Weight."

111 **"It has comedy"**: Buchwald, "Watergate Is Pure Entertainment."

112 **"I consider myself the cruise director"**: *Journal-News* (Hamilton, Ohio), June 10, 1974.

112 **"Let me make this perfectly clear"**: Ibid.

112 **"stay out of Washington"**: *Los Angeles Times*, July 14, 1974.

112 **"For the life of me"**: *The Pantagraph* (Bloomington, Ill.), March 19, 1974.

112 **"If he ever wants"**: Ibid.

112 **"I think if Art Buchwald"**: *The Lexington* (Ky.) *Herald*, April 13, 1974.

113 **"a sense of outrage"**: *The Boston Globe*, July 10, 1974.

113 **"What impressed me more"**: Art Buchwald Commencement Address at Vassar College, June 8, 1975.

114 **"We're going after him"**: Stephen Ambrose, *Nixon: Triumph of a Politician* (New York: Simon and Schuster, 1989), 2:610.

114 **At the dinner honoring Williams**: Speech of Art Buchwald, October 16, 1974, AB Papers, LOC.

116 **"Deep Throat asked that I"**: Bob Woodward to Art Buchwald, [no date], AB Papers, LOC. In 2005 it was publicly disclosed that W. Mark Felt (1913–2008), associate director of the FBI from 1972 to 1973, was Woodward and Bernstein's Watergate source known as "Deep Throat." The details were fully recounted in Woodward's 2005 book, *The Secret Man*, and Felt's own 2006 book, *A G-Man's Life*.

Chapter 8: Say Amen, Art Buchwald, Say Amen

117 **"Sometimes I really believe"**: *Asbury Park* (N.J.) *Press*, October 14, 1977.

117 **"the other Buchwald"**: Marian Christy, "The Other Buchwald," *The Sacramento Bee*, October 22, 1980.

117 **"Buchwald saga"**: Ibid.

117 **People were particularly drawn**: *The Miami News*, May 27, 1966; *Los Angeles Times*, August 18, 1980, and October 21, 1980.

118 **"blithe spirit"**: Lady Bird Johnson to Art Buchwald, July 7, 1994, AB Papers, LOC.

118 **"wonderful listener"**: Marylouise Oates, "Buchwald's Back: USC's Got Him," *Los Angeles Times*, October 21, 1980.

118 **"whole jazz of housekeeping"**: Joan Nielsen McHale, "Ann On the Humor-Go-Round," *The Miami News*, May 27, 1966.

118 **"I don't think there is"**: Oates, "Buchwald's Back: USC's Got Him."

118 **"Thank you very much"**: Rose Fitzgerald Kennedy to Ann Buchwald, January 29, 1976, AB Papers, LOC.

119 **In the early part of the 1970s:** *The Sacramento Bee*, January 1, 1979.

119 **Without missing a beat:** Ibid.

119 **"hilarious account"**: *The Times and Democrat* (Orangeburg, S.C.), October 5, 1980.

119 **" 'Tell me, Mrs. Buchwald' "**: Julianna Hastings, " 'Torrid' Buchwald Memories," *The Press Democrat* (Santa Rosa, Calif.), November 30, 1980.

120 **"Marriage is work"**: Susan Watters, "Ann Buchwald: Agent for Some of the Capital's Sharpest Book Deals," *The Sacramento Bee*, January 1, 1979.

120 **"having first donned"**: Kandy Stroud, "The Art of Humor," *The Boston Globe*, July 10, 1974.

120 **"Many of [Ann's] friends"**: Ann and Art Buchwald, *Seems Like Yesterday*, 219.

121 **"Just a short note"**: Art Buchwald to Irwin Shaw, February 13, 1976, AB Papers, LOC.

122 **"*Rich Man, Poor Man* has become"**: Irwin Shaw to Art Buchwald, February 24, 1976, AB Papers, LOC.

122 **"Its own sort of heaven"**: Molly Sinclair, "Sojourn in the Vineyard," WP, April 24, 1983; author interview with Rose Styron.

123 **He started going to the island:** Sinclair, "Sojourn in the Vineyard."

123 **At first he rented:** NYT, July 27, 2006; Sinclair, "Sojourn in the Vineyard."

123 **"What a loss"**: Art Buchwald to Barbara Hersey, May 5, 1993. Courtesy of Joel and Tamara Buchwald. Journalist John Hersey (1914–93) was the author of *A Bell for Adano* (1944), for which he won a Pulitzer Prize, *Hiroshima* (1946), and *The Wall* (1950).

123 **"Possible Dreams" auction:** WP, August 10, 1981.

124 **"When questioned as to whether"**: "Latest Gallup Poll," *Vineyard Gazette*, August 23, 1966.

124 **"utmost confidence"**: Dr. George Schreiner to Ethel Kennedy, June 1978, AB Papers, LOC.

125 **"Dear Doc"**: Ethel Kennedy to Dr. George Schreiner, July 14, 1978, AB Papers, LOC.

126 **"the perfect Renaissance man"**: Buchwald, *I'll Always Have Paris*, 159–60.

126 **"Everyone knows about Ben Bradlee"**: Text of Art Buchwald's remarks, July 29, 1975, AB Papers, LOC.

128 **"The tendency in this country"**: Art Buchwald Commencement Address at Vassar College, June 8, 1975.

130 **In New York Harbor:** NYT, July 5, 1976.

130 **"day of mammoth presentations"**: Ibid.

130 **"Dear Pop":** Art Buchwald, "You Kept Telling Me There Was No Better Place to Live," *WP*, July 4, 1976; Buchwald, *Down the Seine and Up the Potomac with Art Buchwald*, 499–500.

131 **"It's very hard":** Art Buchwald to John Norbutt, February 6, 1979, AB Papers, LOC.

132 **"He said at the beginning":** *Intelligencer Journal* (Lancaster, Pa.), January 17, 1977.

132 **"When President Carter decided":** Buchwald, *The Buchwald Stops Here*, 15–16.

132 **"People are actually arguing":** Ibid., 182–83.

133 **"He's a gutsy Evel Knievel":** Ibid., 31.

134 **Years later Joseph Califano:** Author interview with Joseph Califano.

134 **Not "enough prestige":** Buchwald, *Too Soon to Say Goodbye*, 22.

134 **"Why not Erma Bombeck?":** Ibid.

134 **For nearly two decades:** See obituary of Erma Bombeck in the *Catholic Standard*, April 21, 1996.

135 **"I read the TIME magazine piece":** Art Buchwald to Erma Bombeck, May 23, 1978, AB Papers, LOC; R. Z. Sheppard, "She-Wits and Funny Persons," *Time*, May 29, 1978.

135 **Another Buchwald soulmate:** See obituary of Eppie Lederer, *The Boston Globe*, June 23, 2002.

136 **"There are a lot more disappointed parents":** *WP*, October 4, 1978.

136 **"Thanks for the plug":** Art Buchwald to Eppie Lederer, October 6, 1978, AB Papers, LOC.

136 **"Advice to the Gas Worn":** *WP*, June 24, 1979.

137 **"Very funny":** Eppie Lederer to Art Buchwald, [no date], AB Papers, LOC.

138 **"You were so funny":** Anthony Newley to Art Buchwald, November 16, 1979, AB Papers, LOC.

138 **"Thank you so much":** Art Buchwald to Anthony Newley, December 4, 1979, AB Papers, LOC.

138 **It's estimated:** *NYT*, January 2, 1972.

139 **"I love it":** *The Derrick* (Oil City, Pa.), April 8, 1976.

139 **"The world is getting crazier":** *Asbury Park* (N.J.) *Press*, October 14, 1977.

Chapter 9: Joining the Hertz Five Star Credit Card Club

140 **"I don't know if this made":** Art Buchwald to Irwin Shaw, February 5, 1980, AB Papers, LOC.

140 **"Brother, Can You Spare a John?":** *Newsweek*, February 14, 1980.

141 **"ART BUCHWALD FOR PRESIDENT!":** Letter from Newburgh, N.Y., to Art Buchwald, February 1, 1980, AB Papers, LOC.

141 **"As usual Mr. Buchwald":** Letter from New York, N.Y., to Art Buchwald, January 29, AB Papers, LOC.

141 **"As a mother of a normal":** Letter from Midland, Mich., to Art Buchwald, February 11, 1980, AB Papers, LOC.

142 **"Please don't get discouraged":** Art Buchwald to Irwin Shaw, March 25, 1980, AB Papers, LOC.

142 "I worship the very quicksand": *The Daily Tar Heel* (Chapel Hill, N.C.), October 3, 1977.

142 "At least 50%": *South Bend* (Ind.) *Tribune*, October 30, 1980.

142 "There will be some marvelous": *News-Press* (Fort Myers, Fla.), January 22, 1981.

142 "You can say what you will": Art Buchwald, "Hair by Julius, Clothes by Blass, Pretzels by Mary," *WP*, February 3, 1981.

143 "Well, Old Paint": Buchwald, *You Can Fool All of the People All the Time*, 237; *WP*, October 19, 1983.

143 "The Three-Martini Lunch Crowd: Let Them Eat Ketchup": *WP*, October 22, 1981.

144 "I've been meaning to write": Senator Gary Hart to Art Buchwald, October 28, 1981, AB Papers, LOC. Senator Gary Hart's bill to cut the business lunch deduction was tabled by the Senate on September 28, 1981. However, three years later, Hart's longtime Senate staffer Bill Shore and Shore's sister Debbie founded Share Our Strength (SOS), a nonprofit organization to combat hunger and poverty by providing nutritional meals to school-age children. In nearly forty years SOS has provided an estimated one billion meals for indigent schoolchildren. "Access to school lunch and school breakfast is higher than it has ever been and childhood hunger is down 30% to its lowest level in 25 years. It's an astounding humanitarian mission that started from scratch," Senator Hart and Bill Shore told the author. (Note to author, November 21, 2019.) While Buchwald and Senator Hart were able to have a satirical, light-hearted exchange in 1981 about the business lunch loophole, there is little doubt Buchwald would have been delighted with the success of the SOS program.

145 By any measure: See *Current Biography Yearbook: 1982*, 57–61, and *2008*, 635–36; Hillel Italie, "Author William F. Buckley, Jr., Dies at 82," Associated Press, February 28, 2008; David Brooks, "William F. Buckley: The Grandeur of His Life," *NYT*, March 1, 2008; Geoffrey Hodgson, "William F. Buckley: The Patriarch of the Modern U.S. Right," *The Guardian*, February 28, 2008.

145 "All great Biblical": *Current Biography Yearbook: 1982*, 57.

145 Beginning in the late 1970s: In a letter to Art Buchwald, Christopher Buckley once characterized the correspondence between Buchwald and his father as a "magnificent collection of correspondence by two fine men. Someday I know the Bodleian [Library] will want them." Christopher Buckley to Art Buchwald, March 15, 1987, AB Papers, LOC.

146 "Thank you so much for the note": Art Buchwald to William F. Buckley, Jr., August 27, 1979, AB Papers, LOC. Many of the Buchwald and Buckley Hertz letters are also included in William F. Buckley, Jr., *Cancel Your Own Goddam Subscription: Notes and Asides from the "National Review"* (New York: Basic Books, 2007).

146 "I am enclosing a letter": Art Buchwald to Frank Olson, August 30, 1979, AB Papers, LOC.

147 "Thank you so much": Art Buchwald to Frank Olson, September 26, 1979, AB Papers, LOC.

148 **"usually a little more"**: Frank Olson to Art Buchwald, October 4, 1979, AB Papers, LOC.

148 **"I just received this letter"**: Art Buchwald to William F. Buckley, Jr., September 14, 1982, AB Papers, LOC.

148 **"I don't know if you received"**: Art Buchwald to William F. Buckley, Jr., November 2, 1982, AB Papers, LOC.

149 **"You ask how many"**: William F. Buckley, Jr., to Art Buchwald, November 8, 1982, AB Papers, LOC.

150 **For award-winning news anchor**: *Current Biography Yearbook: 1981*, 36–39.

150 **"Most people write to you"**: Art Buchwald to Tom Brokaw, July 12, 1981, AB Papers, LOC.

152 **"Dear Mr. Buchwald"**: Tom Brokaw to Art Buchwald, [no date], AB Papers, LOC.

Chapter 10: A Satirist Wins a Pulitzer, But Loses His Humidor

153 **Doc Dalinsky's pharmacy**: See Barbara Gamarekian, "In a Drugstore: Big Names, Small Talk," *NYT*, February 23, 1977; Barbara Gamarekian, "A Favorite Pharmacist Is the Guest of Honor," *NYT*, April 30, 1982; and *WP*, May 10, 1970, June 19, 1977, and April 27, 1992.

153 **Alger Hiss was a regular**: Gamarekian, "In a Drugstore."

154 **Dalinsky loved to tell the story**: Marguerite Del Giudice, "The Doc and His Drugstore: Two Venerable Institutions," *The Boston Globe*, March 16, 1981.

154 **"Mysterious cartons"**: Gamarekian, "A Favorite Pharmacist."

154 **He once gave Caroline Kennedy**: Del Giudice, "Doc and His Drugstore."

154 **"The whole place"**: *WP*, April 27, 1992.

154 **Harry Alexander "Doc" Dalinsky**: John Carmody, "Doc's Georgetown Pharmacy Isn't Just a Drugstore—'It's a Family,'" *WP*, May 10, 1970.

155 **"to have come with the mortgage"**: Ibid.

155 **"apparently came over"**: Ibid.

155 **"Buchwald may be funny"**: Ibid.

155 **"A lovely man"**: Del Giudice, "Doc and His Drugstore."

155 **"Doc and Art"**: Buchwald, *Too Soon to Say Goodbye*, 157.

155 **Doc's weekly Sunday brunch**: Gamarekian, "A Favorite Pharmacist."

156 **"THIS IS YOUR FINAL NOTICE"**: Copy of the notice is on deposit in the AB Papers, LOC.

157 **"When Doc first came"**: Copy of Buchwald's remarks is on deposit in the AB Papers, LOC.

157 **over the next ten years**: Carmody, "Doc's Georgetown Pharmacy."

157 **"He is one of the last"**: Ibid.

158 **"exclusive interview"**: See tagline of Art Buchwald's Commencement Address at Vassar College, reprinted in the *NYT*, June 8, 1975.

158 **"For once, I can think"**: Katharine Graham to Art Buchwald, April 20, 1982, AB Papers, LOC.

158 **"About the Pulitzer"**: Eppie Lederer to Art Buchwald, April 13, 1982, AB Papers, LOC.

158 **"I never dreamed anyone"**: Ethel Kennedy to Art Buchwald, [no date], AB Papers, LOC. The poem Mrs. Kennedy is referring to is Robert Browning's "Pippa's Song."

159 **"like an out-of-work philosophy professor"**: *NYT*, April 12, 2007.

159 **"I don't have time"**: Art Buchwald to Mr. Entrekin, May 17, 1982, AB Papers, LOC.

160 **"Have you heard from Hertz recently?"**: William F. Buckley, Jr., to Art Buchwald, January 4, 1983, AB Papers, LOC.

161 **"I can't believe you would"**: Art Buchwald to William F. Buckley, Jr., January 10, 1983, AB Papers, LOC.

161 **"What does one do"**: Art Buchwald birthday tribute to Dr. Seuss, March 2, 1984, AB Papers, LOC.

162 **"Word reached Washington"**: Art Buchwald to Irwin Shaw, April 19, 1984, AB Papers, LOC.

163 **"Thank you very much"**: Irwin Shaw to Art Buchwald, May 1, 1984, AB Papers, LOC.

164 **"colossus" of the silver screen**: Richard Corliss, "An Appreciation: Charlton Heston," *Time*, April 6, 2008; *Los Angeles Magazine*, February 1, 2001.

164 **He memorized passages**: *NYT*, April 6, 2008.

164 **He loved to play the game**: Email to author from Holly Heston Rochell, October 21, 2019.

164 **"excited as well as honored"**: Ibid.

164 **During the summer of 1985**: *Chicago Tribune*, May 17, 1985.

164 **John McEnroe**: *NYT*, January 24, 1983; *Star Tribune* (Minneapolis, Minn.), January 24, 1983.

164 **"to sit in that box"**: *The Atlanta Constitution*, June 26, 1985.

165 **"We were laughing"**: Art Buchwald, "Wimbledon's Royal Pains," *WP*, July 2, 1985.

165 **"I've done it!"**: Charlton Heston to Art Buchwald, July 5, 1985, AB Papers, LOC.

166 **"I understand"**: Art Buchwald, "The Mail Mikhail Missed," *WP*, December 8, 1987.

167 **"Fuck you"**: Citizens of Cleveland, Ohio, to Art Buchwald, December 10, 1987, AB Papers, LOC.

167 **"lived up to his reputation"**: *Chicago Tribune*, June 9, 1989.

167 **"Thank you so much"**: Art Buchwald to Donald Trump, June 23, 1989, AB Papers, LOC.

168 **"I know you weren't ready"**: Buchwald, *I Think I Don't Remember*, 112.

Chapter 11: A Matter of Honor

173 **"The humorist has a quick eye"**: W. Somerset Maugham, *The Summing Up* (New York: Penguin Books, 1938), 47.

173 **As Buchwald watched the skirmish**: *NYT*, July 28, 1980, and November 16, 1977.

173 **"I watched the scene"**: Buchwald, *Too Soon to Say Goodbye*, 68.

174 **"The only explanation"**: Pierce O'Donnell and Dennis McDougal, *Fatal*

Subtraction: The Inside Story of "Buchwald v. Paramount" (New York: Double-day, 1992), xvi.

174 **But in the midst of the negotiations:** Ibid., 13.

175 **decidedly "hard line":** Ibid.

175 **"quantum of similarity":** Ibid., 15.

175 **"with all of the facts":** Ibid.

175 **left the studio "fuming":** Ibid., xxi.

175 **With a hit now on its hands:** Ibid., 16.

175 **"like two schleppers":** Ibid.

175 **It was a "blatant ripoff":** Ibid., xxvi.

175 **To make matters worse:** Evan Thomas, *The Man to See* (New York: Touch-stone, 1991), 424-25, 439.

176 **"do what he thought":** O'Donnell and McDougal, *Fatal Subtraction*, 16.

176 **"pissed off":** "War Stories: Pierce O'Donnell on the Art Buchwald Trial," March 26, 2020, available online; author interview with Pierce O'Donnell.

176 **"brooding":** O'Donnell and McDougal, *Fatal Subtraction*, xxvi.

176 **"I just saw":** Ibid., xxvii.

176 **Pierce O'Donnell:** See Art Buchwald's introduction to O'Donnell and McDougal, *Fatal Subtraction*, xv-xvii, 4-5; and author interview with Pierce O'Donnell.

177 **"genuine American legend":** O'Donnell and McDougal, *Fatal Subtraction*, 6.

177 **a "dead-bang loser":** Ibid., 25; author interview with Pierce O'Donnell.

177 **simple "breach of contract":** O'Donnell and McDougal, *Fatal Subtraction*, 25.

177 **On late Sunday afternoon:** Ibid., 40-41.

177 **"He had the rubbery face":** Ibid., 41.

178 **"Life was uncomplicated":** Ibid., 42.

178 **"Art's smile vanished":** Ibid.

178 **"Ed died peacefully":** Ibid.

178 **"He was my best buddy":** Ibid., 44.

178 **"All right. The case":** Ibid.

178 **"bastards" in Hollywood:** Ibid., 294.

178 *not* **having to sue Eddie Murphy:** Ibid., 48-49; author interview with Pierce O'Donnell.

178 **"It might help defuse":** O'Donnell and McDougal, *Fatal Subtraction*, 48-49; "War Stories: Pierce O'Donnell on the Art Buchwald Trial."

178 **"You need to know that going in":** O'Donnell and McDougal, *Fatal Subtraction*, 49.

179 **Williams's funeral was held:** Thomas, *The Man to See*, 495, 13.

179 **"Eddie was my friend":** Art Buchwald eulogy in AB Papers, LOC.

179 **After returning to Los Angeles:** Author interview with Pierce O'Donnell.

180 **"intellectual challenge":** Ibid.

180 **Martin Davis:** See obituaries of Davis in *NYT*, October 6, 1999; and *WP*, October 7, 1999. See also O'Donnell and McDougal, *Fatal Subtraction*, 71-72.

180 **Hitler's *Mein Kampf*:** O'Donnell and McDougal, *Fatal Subtraction*, 72.

180 "Don't bother yourself, Marty": Ibid.

181 "such an expensive bottle": Ibid., 62.

181 "What the hell's": Ibid., 63.

181 On November 10: Ibid., 65–66.

181 "I read your letter": Art Buchwald to Pierce O'Donnell, November 17, 1988, AB Papers, LOC.

182 "began to sweat": O'Donnell and McDougal, *Fatal Subtraction*, 67.

182 "Art Buchwald Says": *WSJ*, November 21, 1988.

182 "I want to sue": Ibid.

182 an "outrageous breach": O'Donnell and McDougal, *Fatal Subtraction*, 69–70.

182 "I was in a post-election depression": *Newsweek*, December 5, 1988.

Chapter 12: Drama in Department 52

183 "Paramount is trying to destroy": O'Donnell and McDougal, *Fatal Subtraction*, 315.

183 "I am suing Paramount": Speech of Art Buchwald, "Dinner for Marty Davis," January 28, 1989, AB Papers, LOC.

183 "No plaintiff has ever honored": Ibid.

184 "The idea which is mine": O'Donnell and McDougal, *Fatal Subtraction*, 107.

184 "redden a bit": Ibid.

184 "bright, tough and tenacious": Ibid., 205.

184 "Is there a definition": Ibid., 219.

185 "I'll give you mine": Ibid.

185 "uneasy" feeling: Ibid., 221.

185 "snarl like a Doberman": Ibid., 123.

185 "as close as any fraternal twins": Ibid., 237.

185 "fully exposed": Ibid.

185 "You simply cannot": *WP*, December 16, 1989.

185 Referring to a *Herald Tribune*: Ibid.; O'Donnell and McDougal, *Fatal Subtraction*, 242.

185 had "stolen" his idea: O'Donnell and McDougal, *Fatal Subtraction*, 242.

185 "He was trying to turn": Ibid.

186 "black fairy tale": *WP*, December 19, 1989.

186 "positive image": Ibid.

186 "It's obviously our script": Ibid.

186 "It's very unfair": Ibid.

186 "Damn right!": Ibid.

186 Wilder told reporters: Ibid.

186 appeared "nervous": O'Donnell and McDougal, *Fatal Subtraction*, 274.

187 "First, I'd like to say": Kim Masters, "Buchwald Says He Felt 'Shafted,'" *WP*, December 20, 1989; "Buchwald Takes On Studio, Lightly," *NYT*, December 20, 1989; O'Donnell and McDougal, *Fatal Subtraction*, 277–78.

187 "And did you write": O'Donnell and McDougal, *Fatal Subtraction*, 279.

187 "trot out the Big Lie": Ibid., 280; Masters, "Buchwald Says."

187 "We are dealing here": Masters, "Buchwald Says."

188 "ideas came from experience": Ibid.; O'Donnell and McDougal, *Fatal Subtraction*, 280.

188 "bunch of baloney": Masters, "Buchwald Says."

188 "damnable lie": Ibid.

188 On December 21, Robert Wachs: Kim Masters, "Murphy's Manager Testifies," WP, December 22, 1989; O'Donnell and McDougal, *Fatal Subtraction*, 302.

188 "fairly close": O'Donnell and McDougal, *Fatal Subtraction*, 302; Robert Wachs to Jim Harrison, September 10, 1984, AB Papers, LOC.

188 "unpublished Art Buchwald story": Robert Wachs to Jim Harrison, September 10, 1984, AB Papers, LOC.

188 "Thank you for sending me": Art Buchwald to Jim Harrison, December 7, 1988, AB Papers, LOC.

188 "This is the first smoking gun": Art Buchwald to Pierce O'Donnell, December 7, 1988, AB Papers, LOC.

188 "This is dynamite": O'Donnell and McDougal, *Fatal Subtraction*, 84.

188 In response to O'Donnell's questions: Masters, "Murphy's Manager Testifies."

188 "a poor piece of work": Ibid.

189 O'Donnell also got Wachs: Ibid.

189 in "a two-sentence description": Ibid.; O'Donnell and McDougal, *Fatal Subtraction*, 304.

189 "Mission accomplished": O'Donnell and McDougal, *Fatal Subtraction*, 302.

189 After a holiday recess: Masters, "Murphy's Manager Testifies."

189 "I know I never read": Ibid.

190 "Was my subconscious": O'Donnell and McDougal, *Fatal Subtraction*, 197–98.

190 "Paramount is trying to destroy": Ibid., 315.

190 "I knew it, Pierce": Ibid.

190 "God, why did I": Ibid.

190 "most dastardly thing": Author interview with Pierce O'Donnell.

190 "Art, you have every right": O'Donnell and McDougal, *Fatal Subtraction*, 315.

190 "It's just beginning": Ibid.

190 "I'm the one": Ibid.

191 "Art, that's bullshit!": Ibid.

191 "I think he'll see": Ibid.

191 "I'm going to make you": Ibid., 316.

191 "Okay, Pierce": Ibid.

191 Thursday, December 28: Ibid.

191 "Victor Hugo once said": Kim Masters, "'America' Trial Ends," WP, December 29, 1989; O'Donnell and McDougal, *Fatal Subtraction*, 316.

192 "There comes a point": Masters, "'America' Trial Ends"; O'Donnell and McDougal, *Fatal Subtraction*, 318.

192 "I submit to your honor": O'Donnell and McDougal, *Fatal Subtraction*, 323–24.

192 "It's a lie broadcast": Ibid.

192 "Now, of course, Eddie Murphy's black": O'Donnell and McDougal, *Fatal Subtraction*, 324.

193 "But I don't really think": Ibid.

193 "victim of racial prejudice": Ibid.

193 "I don't perceive": Ibid.

193 "All right, gentlemen": Ibid., 331.

193 "the bottom of his heart": Ibid.

193 "Ed Williams had to be": Ibid.

193 In his decision: Kim Masters, "Art Buchwald Wins Suit Against Paramount," *WP*, January 9, 1990.

193 "A year ago": O'Donnell and McDougal, *Fatal Subtraction*, 333.

194 Days later, Peter Jennings: Ibid., 341.

194 "When you go through": Masters, "Art Buchwald Wins Suit."

194 "We considered ourselves": Ibid.; Dennis McDougal, "Judge Rules for Buchwald in Movie Authorship Fight," *Los Angeles Times*, January 9, 1990.

194 "There is not a scintilla": Masters, "Art Buchwald Wins Suit"; O'Donnell and McDougal, *Fatal Subtraction*, 335.

194 "This case is also": See decision of Judge Harvey Schneider in *Buchwald v. Paramount*, January 31, 1990, O'Donnell and McDougal, *Fatal Subtraction*, 533.

195 "You have done a great thing": Russell Baker to Art Buchwald, January 11, 1990, AB Papers, LOC.

195 "Now that you own Hollywood": William F. Buckley, Jr., to Art Buchwald, January 10, 1990.

196 At first Paramount's attorneys: Richard W. Stevenson, "The Magic of Hollywood Math," *NYT*, April 13, 1990; Associated Press, "'America' in the Red, Paramount Says," *WP*, March 22, 1990; O'Donnell and McDougal, *Fatal Attraction*, 363.

196 Astonished and outraged: O'Donnell and McDougal, *Fatal Attraction*, 552.

196 Judge Schneider ruled in favor: Ibid., 517; McDougal, "Judge Rules for Buchwald."

196 "This is a fantastic victory": John H. Richardson, "Contract Unfair to Buchwald, Court Says," *WP*, December 22, 1990; O'Donnell and McDougal, *Fatal Subtraction*, 469.

196 "I can't tell you": Larry Rohter, "Buchwald Gets Damages in Film Suit," *NYT*, December 22, 1990.

196 On March 16, 1992: Bernard Weinraub, "Art Buchwald Awarded $150,000 in Suit over Film," *NYT*, March 17, 1992. See also Adam Seth Bialow, "Illusory Profits: Net Profit Agreements in Light of *Buchwald v. Paramount*," *University of Miami Entertainment and Sports Law Review* 10 (1993): 51.

196 "close to four times": Weinraub, "Art Buchwald Awarded $150,000."

197 "I'm delighted": Ibid.

197 "I believe this belongs": O'Donnell and McDougal, *Fatal Subtraction*, 520.

197 "Marty was . . . the King": Buchwald, *Too Soon to Say Goodbye*, 69.

198 "I cannot live with this": Art Buchwald to Herbert Block, May 28, 1991, AB Papers, LOC.

199 "Re: the McDonald's incident": Herbert Block to Art Buchwald, June 4, 1991, AB Papers, LOC.

199 "would try to identify": *Detroit Free Press*, October 28, 1992.

200 "That's not the question": *The Palm Beach* (Fla.) *Post*, October 27, 1992.

200 This bizarre cultural-political disorientation: Art Buchwald, "The Agony of Defeat," *WP*, January 28, 1993.

201 "I've been a fan of yours": Christopher Buckley to Art Buchwald, January 29, 1993, AB Papers, LOC.

201 "Thank you so much": Art Buchwald to Christopher Buckley, February 3, 1993, AB Papers, LOC.

202 "Congratulations on getting": Art Buchwald to Russell Baker, February 24, 1993, AB Papers, LOC.

203 "You probably heard": Art Buchwald to Cokie Roberts, February 18, 1993, AB Papers, LOC.

204 Bertram Fields: Pierce O'Donnell and Dennis McDougal, *Fatal Subtraction: The Inside Story of "Buchwald v. Paramount,"* paperback ed. (West Hollywood, Calif.: Dove Books, 1996), 528–45.

204 Soon Redstone: Ibid., 538.

204 "This new Paramount crowd": Robert W. Welkos, "Buchwald, Paramount Settle Film Dispute," *Los Angeles Times*, September 13, 1995.

204 "I want to tell you": O'Donnell and McDougal, *Fatal Subtraction*, paperback edition, 533.

205 Finally, in late June 1995: Ibid., 141.

205 "Of all the lessons": Ibid., 544.

205 "I just wanted to tell you": Art Buchwald to Maureen Dowd, September 19, 1995, AB Papers, LOC.

206 "I had dinner with [Ben]": Maureen Dowd to Art Buchwald, [no date], AB Papers, LOC.

Chapter 13: Buchwald Blues

207 "Humor is the other side": James Thurber quoted in the documentary *James Thurber: The Life and Hard Times*, directed by Adam Van Doren and narrated by George Plimpton, June 17, 2014.

207 "There is a thin line": Erma Bombeck, *Four of a Kind: A Suburban Field Guide* (New York: Galahad Books, 1996), 274.

207 "the greatest defense": Buchwald interview with Wilde, August 18, 1969, 6.

207 "ability to use humor": Senator Edward M. Kennedy to Art Buchwald, June 28, 2000, AB Papers, LOC.

208 Back in the spring of 1963: Buchwald, *Too Soon to Say Goodbye*, 37–39; Buchwald, *Leaving Home*, 34; Art Buchwald to John Huston, August 22, 1963,

Academy of Motion Picture Arts and Sciences, Margaret Herrick Library, Beverly Hills, Calif.

208 "No one recognized my manic": Buchwald, *Too Soon to Say Goodbye*, 38.

208 "into a terrible black inky": Ibid.

208 "I knew I could never kill": Gary Soulsman, "Art Buchwald Finds Humor in Depression," *The News Journal* (Wilmington, Del.), April 14, 1998.

208 a "sad summer": Ann Buchwald to Edward Bennett Williams, September 10, 1985, AB Papers, LOC.

208 "Thanks for being so kind": Art Buchwald to Katharine Graham, October 28, 1985, AB Papers, LOC.

209 "I'm feeling great": Art Buchwald to Jacqueline Kennedy Onassis, November 21, 1985, AB Papers, LOC.

209 "People ask, 'Why' ": Buchwald, *Too Soon to Say Goodbye*, 35.

209 "Funny men like me": Buchwald, *Leaving Home*, 101.

209 "The price I paid": Buchwald, *Too Soon to Say Goodbye*, 38.

209 "A funny thing can happen": Buchwald, *Leaving Home*, 101.

209 "dreadful and raging disease": William Styron, *Darkness Visible: A Memoir of Madness* (New York: Vintage Books, 1990), 37–38.

210 "When Bill Styron": *Vanity Fair*, October 1990.

212 "Gray Matters: Depression and the Brain": Radio program produced in association with the Dana Alliance for Brain Initiatives, Public Radio International, 1996.

212 "He would stay with me": Ibid.

212 "I have to give Art credit": Ibid.

212 "All my buddies are split": *Sun-Sentinel* (Fort Lauderdale, Fla.), January 27, 1983.

213 "a happy marriage": Buchwald, *Too Soon to Say Goodbye*, 40.

213 "They were like two ships": Author interview with Joel Buchwald.

213 "it was best for them both": Buchwald, *Too Soon to Say Goodbye*, 40.

213 "You doin' okay?": Erma Bombeck to Art Buchwald, November 13, 1992, AB Papers, LOC.

214 "Thank you so much": Art Buchwald to Erma Bombeck, November 22, 1992, AB Papers, LOC.

214 "read passages to her": Buchwald, *I'll Always Have Paris*, dedication page.

215 "Paris had been": Ibid.

215 On July 3, 1994: *Chicago Tribune*, July 5, 1994.

215 "Art was shattered": Author interview with Joseph Califano.

215 "When a loved one dies": Buchwald, *Too Soon to Say Goodbye*, 40.

215 "perfect tribute to Ann": Buchwald, *I'll Always Have Paris*, 236.

215 "Alexandra and I": Arthur Schlesinger, Jr., to Art Buchwald, July 7, 1994, AB Papers, LOC.

216 "searing account": Robert A. Cohn, "Humor in Politics," *Jewish Life* (St. Louis, Mo.), February 16, 1994.

216 "the dark forces behind": Roy Rivenburg, "Leaving Home," *Los Angeles Times*, February 7, 1994.

216 "a compelling memoir": Dust jacket of Buchwald, *Leaving Home*.

216 "Have I got a treat": *Logansport* (Ind.) *Pharos-Tribune*, December 24, 1998.

216 "It's the story of a poor boy": Art Buchwald to William F., Buckley, Jr., December 23, 1993, AB Papers, LOC.

216 "the most honest stuff": Rivenburg, "Leaving Home."

217 "The loss of a parent": Art Buchwald to Eunice Kennedy Shriver, January 26, 1995, AB Papers, LOC.

Chapter 14: "There's Life in the Boy Yet"

218 "If laughter is such good medicine": *The Gazette* (Cedar Rapids, Iowa), December 7, 1984.

218 "If [Clinton] did it": *St. Louis Post-Dispatch*, February 2, 1998.

218 "I consider myself": *St. Louis Post-Dispatch*, February 18, 1998.

219 "Have you ever had a stress": *Orlando* (Fla.) *Sentinel*, August 28, 1999.

219 "This is sort of a plea": Art Buchwald to John F. Kennedy, Jr., May 5, 1996, AB Papers, LOC.

220 "Everyone is very excited": Art Buchwald to John F. Kennedy, Jr., May 29, 1996, AB Papers, LOC.

220 Carly Simon sang: *The Boston Globe*, August 6, 1996.

220 JFK Jr. and his bicycle: Ibid. See also JFK Jr.'s "Donor's Letter of Agreement" for "one bicycle trip around Gay Head. Time and date to be determined after auction on 5 August 1996," AB Papers, LOC.

220 "I'll be honest with you": Art Buchwald, "JFK Jr.: Charity's Dream Prize," WP, July 20, 1999; *The Morning Call* (Allentown, Pa.), August 8, 1999.

220 "He loves Martha's Vineyard": Buchwald, "JFK Jr.: Charity's Dream Prize."

220 "may attract a dollar or two": Tom Hanks to Art Buchwald, July 16, 1999, AB Papers, LOC.

221 "I'm glad you liked": Art Buchwald to Tom Hanks, [no date], AB Papers, LOC; *The Palm Beach* (Fla.) *Post*, July 25, 1999.

221 Two weeks later: *NYT*, July 18, 1999, and July 23, 1999.

221 "He was a boy": *NYT*, July 24, 1999.

221 "John Kennedy, Jr., was not an astronaut": WP, July 20, 1999.

221 "a large donation": *The Morning Call* (Allentown, Pa.), August 8, 1999.

222 "People don't take": *The Salt Lake Tribune*, September 8, 1996.

222 "I've never been a big fan": Dave Wood, "Buchwald's Latest Book Charms Doubter," *Star Tribune* (Minneapolis, Minn.), September 1, 1996.

222 "I trust": Ann Morrissett Davidon, "Buchwald Recalls Heady Postwar Days in Paris: New Fame in the Highlife," *The Philadelphia Inquirer*, September 1, 1996.

222 "Thank you for 'I'll Always'": Herbert Block to Art Buchwald, August 16, 1996, AB Papers, LOC.

222 "After reading your book": Russell Baker to Art Buchwald, July 19, 1996, AB Papers, LOC. The passage Baker refers to on page 93 of *I'll Always Have Paris* reads: "Because of my foster-home background and being deprived of a normal family existence, the idea of having a family of my own was as frighten-

ing as anything I could imagine. I saw myself as an uncle, but not as a husband and father. This was my way of avoiding pain."

223 "fascinating and extremely candid": Curt Schleier, "A Candid Memoir from the Great Detached Pillar of 'The Post,'" *Fort Worth* (Tex.) *Star Telegram*, February 23, 1997.

224 "Your wonderful book": Art Buchwald to Katharine Graham, February 11, 1997, AB Papers, LOC.

224 "Everyone on Martha's Vineyard": Ibid., April 15, 1998.

225 "a sad occasion": *Dayton* (Ohio) *Daily News*, March 31, 2000.

225 "We made each other laugh": Ibid.

225 "commitment to honesty": *The Sheboygan* (Wis.) *Press*, May 1, 2001.

225 "To be chosen": Ibid.

226 "serious, but stable": *Intelligencer Journal* (Lancaster, Pa.), June 29, 2000.

226 "I was so sorry": Senator Edward M. Kennedy to Art Buchwald, June 28, 2000, AB Papers, LOC.

226 "be better than he was": *Daily News* (New York, N.Y.), September 19, 2000.

227 "Why are you eager": Russell Baker to Art Buchwald, September 26, 2000, AB Papers, LOC.

Chapter 15: "I Just Don't Want to Die the Same Day as Castro"

228 "I laugh at Life": Robert Service, "Laughter," in *Collected Poems of Robert Service* (New York: Dodd, Mead, 1958), 697.

228 "This is what I did on my vacation": *Los Angeles Times*, November 28, 2000.

228 "I was in a world": Art Buchwald, *We'll Laugh Again* (New York: G. P. Putnam's Sons, 2002), 233.

228 "Food has always": Ibid.

228 "I'm not complaining": Ibid., 235.

229 "There's one word": Ibid., 264–65.

229 "When the going got tough": Ibid.

229 "I saw on the screen": Ibid., 3.

229 "We'll never laugh": Ibid.

229 "I watched the same": Ibid., 4.

230 On a pleasant spring day: Buchwald, *Too Soon to Say Goodbye*, 42; author interview with Joel Buchwald.

230 "the end of a long journey": Buchwald, *Too Soon to Say Goodbye*, 45.

230 "the circle had now": Ibid.

230 A few weeks later: Art Buchwald, *Beating Around the Bush* (New York: Seven Stories Press, 2005), 90.

231 As early as: Email of David Ignatius to Art Buchwald, April 11, 2003, AB Papers, LOC; email to author from David Ignatius, December 3, 2020. The author is grateful to David Ignatius for taking time to respond to several queries about Art Buchwald and the end of his *Herald Tribune* column.

231 "were getting stale": Email to author from David Ignatius, December 3, 2020.

231 **"exercise [her own] judgment"**: Ibid.; email of David Ignatius to Art Buchwald, April 10, 2003, AB Papers, LOC.

231 **The end result**: Email of Art Buchwald to David Ignatius, April 10, 2003, AB Papers, LOC.

231 **Art was finally delivered**: Email of Walter Wells to Art Buchwald, February 20, 2003, AB Papers, LOC.

231 **Walter Wells**: Ibid.

231 **"Ignatius's decision"**: Ibid.

231 **"As you can imagine"**: Email of Art Buchwald to David Ignatius, February 28, 2003, AB Papers, LOC.

232 **"I am sorry about the bad feelings"**: Email of David Ignatius to Art Buchwald, March 1, 2003, AB Papers, LOC.

232 **"As to the current"**: Ibid.

232 **"I have been at the IHT"**: Letter of Art Buchwald to Walter Wells (copy to Arthur Sulzberger, Jr., of the *NYT*), [no date], AB Papers, LOC.

233 **"bitter"**: Walter Wells to Art Buchwald, March 7, 2003, AB Papers, LOC.

233 **"say or do"**: Ibid.

233 **"exceptional run"**: Ibid.

233 **"One of the advantages"**: Letter of Art Buchwald to Walter Wells, March 16, 2003, AB Papers, LOC.

234 **"It was the only paper"**: Statement of Art Buchwald, April 2, 2003, AB Papers, LOC.

234 **"He would have paid"**: Author interview with Joel Buchwald.

234 **two grudges**: Buchwald, *Too Soon to Say Goodbye*, 11.

234 **"It was a golden age"**: Buchwald, *Beating Around the Bush*, 90.

234 **"I'm happy to be doing"**: *The Tampa* (Fla.) *Tribune*, October 21, 2003.

234 **one hundred newspapers**: *Fort Worth* (Tex.) *Star Telegram*, June 3, 2003.

234 **including a fundraiser**: Ibid.

235 **twenty-fifth consecutive year**: *The Boston Globe*, August 6, 2003.

235 **"You can't make up"**: *Fort Worth* (Tex.) *Star Telegram*, May 6, 2003.

235 **"sudden onset"**: Buchwald, *Too Soon to Say Goodbye*, 14.

235 **After conducting an examination**: Ibid., 15.

235 **To make matters even worse**: Ibid.

235 **"double whammy"**: Ibid.

235 **In December 2005**: *The Palm Beach* (Fla.) *Post*, February 17, 2006.

235 **"To hell with it"**: Buchwald, *Too Soon to Say Goodbye*, 15; Associated Press, April 7, 2006.

235 **"in the final stretch"**: *The Times* (Munster, Ind.), March 29, 2006.

235 **"We knew he was a funny guy"**: *Democrat and Chronicle* (Rochester, N.Y.), April 18, 2006.

236 **"Alexandra and I"**: Arthur Schlesinger, Jr., to Art Buchwald, March 27, 2006, AB Papers, LOC. This letter was also published in *The Letters of Arthur Schlesinger, Jr.*, edited by Andrew Schlesinger and Stephen Schlesinger (New York: Random House, 2013), 591–92.

237 **"extraordinary hour"**: Pierce O'Donnell, "Art of Humor," *Variety*, January 21, 2007.

237 "Instead of being": Buchwald, *Too Soon to Say Goodbye*, 147.

237 "So Artie": Ibid., 161.

237 "I figure, what the heck": Ibid., 20.

238 "It gave me": Ibid., 21.

238 "Against the odds": Ibid., 28.

238 more than three thousand letters: Ibid., 61.

238 Even Judge Harvey Schneider: Ibid., 72.

238 "I'm so glad": Ibid.

238 "I never realized": Ibid., 145.

239 headed to Martha's Vineyard: *The Boston Globe*, July 16, 2006.

239 "I didn't expect": Ibid.

239 "He's indomitable": Bob Hiaasen, "The Time of His Life," *The Baltimore Sun*, July 30, 2006; *The Boston Globe*, July 16, 2006.

239 "absolutely remarkable": Michael Levenson, "Hold the Eulogies, He's Not Ready to Sign Off Yet," *The Boston Globe*, July 26, 2006.

240 "Then, when it turned out": Buchwald, *Too Soon to Say Goodbye*, 180.

240 "Too soon": Song by Carly Simon. The collection of Art Buchwald materials at the Library of Congress has an audio recording of Ms. Simon's performance of the song (Digital ID# MSS 86197 178 010).

241 bringing tears to his eyes: Author interview with Tamara Buchwald.

241 "I was sort of forgotten": Hiaasen, "The Time of His Life."

241 On any given day: Ibid.; *NYT*, July 27, 2006; Levenson, "Hold the Eulogies."

241 When he wasn't working: Stevenson Swanson, "In Matter of Life and Death, the Joke Is on Buchwald," *Chicago Tribune*, August 27, 2006.

242 "He seems to be getting": Hiaasen, "The Time of His Life"; Joyce Wadler, "A Defiant Jester, Laughing Best," *NYT*, July 27, 2006.

242 On October 20, 2006: A video of Buchwald's birthday celebration was shown at the March 5, 2007, memorial service held at the Kennedy Center in Washington, D.C.

242 "Every once in a while": Art Buchwald email about William Styron, November 8, 2006, AB Papers, LOC.

242 That same month: *Palm Beach* (Fla.) *Daily News*, December 20, 2006.

242 "I had so hoped": William F. Buckley, Jr., to Art Buchwald, December 14, 2006, AB Papers, LOC.

243 "It was not easy": Email to author from Tom Brokaw, August 11, 2020.

243 Four days later: Author interview with Tamara Buchwald.

243 "I just don't want to die": Patricia Sullivan, "Satirist Made the Most of His Long Goodbye," *WP*, January 19, 2007.

243 "His life was a rich tale": Severo, "Art Buchwald."

243 "He delighted in stirring the pot": Ibid.

244 "It is with a heavy heart": Statement of Senator Edward M. Kennedy on the Floor of the U.S. Senate, January 18, 2007.

244 Several weeks later, on March 5, 2007: A video of the memorial service at the Kennedy Center is available on C-SPAN.org.

245 "May Jack and Bobby": Ibid.

245 "funny without being mean-spirited": Ibid.

245 **"Life was good"**: Ibid.

245 **"Good night, sweet man"**: Ibid.

245 **"My dear friend Artie"**: Email to author from Senator Gary Hart, November 20, 2019.

246 **"We've lost a great American Dreamer"**: David Von Drehle, "Art Buchwald's Moveable Feast," WP, January 19, 2007.

246 **"There comes a time"**: Art Buchwald's final "goodbye" column was written nearly a year earlier on February 8, 2006. After his death it appeared in newspapers around the country, including WP, January 19, 2007; The Boston Globe, January 19, 2007; The Philadelphia Inquirer, January 19, 2007; and Chicago Tribune, January 19, 2007.

BIBLIOGRAPHY

Ambrose, Stephen. *Nixon: Triumph of a Politician*. Vol. 2. New York: Simon and Schuster, 1989.

Benchley, Robert. *The Best of Robert Benchley*. New York: Wings Books, 1983.

Bialow, Adam Seth. "Illusory Profits: Net Profit Agreements in Light of *Buchwald v. Paramount*." *University of Miami Entertainment and Sports Law Review* 10 (1993): 51.

Bombeck, Erma. *Four of a Kind: A Suburban Field Guide*. New York: Galahad Books, 1996.

Bradlee, Ben. *Conversations with Kennedy*. New York: Norton, 1975.

——. *A Good Life: Newspapering and Other Adventures*. New York: Simon and Schuster, 1995.

Buchwald, Ann, and Art Buchwald. *Seems Like Yesterday*. New York: G. P. Putnam's Sons, 1980.

Buchwald, Art. *And Then I Told the President*. Greenwich, Conn.: Fawcett, 1965.

——. *Art Buchwald's Paris*. Boston: Little, Brown, 1954.

——. *Beating Around the Bush*. New York: Seven Stories Press, 2005.

——. *The Brave Coward*. New York: Harper, 1957.

——. *The Buchwald Stops Here*. New York: G. P. Putnam's Sons, 1978.

——. *Counting Sheep: The Log and Complete Play of "Sheep on the Runway."* New York: G. P. Putnam's Sons, 1970.

——. *Don't Forget to Write*. Cleveland: World Publishing, 1960.

——. *Down the Seine and Up the Potomac with Art Buchwald.* New York: G. P. Putnam's Sons, 1977.

——. *The Establishment Is Alive and Well in Washington.* New York: G. P. Putnam's Sons, 1969.

——. *Have I Ever Lied to You?* Greenwich, Conn.: Fawcett, 1969.

——. *I Chose Capitol Punishment.* Greenwich, Conn.: Fawcett, 1964.

——. *I Chose Caviar.* London: Victor Gollancz, 1957.

——. *I'll Always Have Paris.* New York: G. P. Putnam's Sons, 1996.

——. *Is It Safe to Drink the Water?* Greenwich, Conn.: Fawcett, 1963.

——. *I Think I Don't Remember.* New York: G. P. Putnam's Sons, 1987.

——. *Laid Back in Washington with Art Buchwald.* New York: G. P. Putnam's Sons, 1981.

——. *Leaving Home: A Memoir.* New York: G. P. Putnam's Sons, 1993.

——. *Lighten Up, George.* New York: G. P. Putnam's Sons, 1991.

——. *More Caviar.* New York: Harper, 1959.

——. *Oh, to Be a Swinger.* London: Secker and Warburg, 1969.

——. *Son of the Great Society.* Greenwich, Conn.: Fawcett, 1966.

——. *Too Soon to Say Goodbye.* New York: Random House, 2006.

——. *Washington Is Leaking.* Greenwich, Conn.: Fawcett, 1976.

——. *We'll Laugh Again.* New York: G. P. Putnam's Sons, 2002.

——. *While Reagan Slept.* New York: G. P. Putnam's Sons, 1983.

——. *Whose Rose Garden Is It Anyway?* New York: G. P. Putnam's Sons, 1989.

——. *You Can Fool All of the People All the Time.* New York: G. P. Putnam's Sons, 1985.

Buckley, William F., Jr. *Cancel Your Own Goddam Subscription: Notes and Asides from the "National Review."* New York: Basic Books, 2007.

Callan, Michael Feeney. *Robert Redford: The Biography.* New York: Knopf, 2011.

Daugherty, Tracey. *Just One Catch: A Biography of Joseph Heller.* New York: St. Martin's Press, 2011.

Graham, Katharine. *Personal History.* New York: Vintage Books, 1998.

Halberstam, David. *The Fifties.* New York: Fawcett Columbine, 1993.

——. *The Powers That Be.* New York: Knopf, 1979.

Hodges, Graham R. "Dark Day in November: One Hundred Americans' Memories of the Day President Kennedy Was Assassinated." Unpublished manuscript, ca. 1999.

Kennedy, Robert F., Jr. *American Values: Lessons I Learned from My Family.* New York: Harper, 2018.

Kluger, Richard. *The Paper: The Life and Death of the "New York Herald Tribune."* New York: Vintage Books, 1989.

Manchester, William. *The Death of a President: November 1963.* New York: Harper and Row, 1988.

——. *The Glory and the Dream: A Narrative History of America, 1932–1972.* New York: Bantam, 1974.

Maugham, W. Somerset. *The Summing Up.* New York: Penguin, 1938.

Merry, Robert W. *Taking On the World: Joseph and Stewart Alsop—Guardians of the American Century.* New York: Viking, 1996.

Michener, James. *The World Is My Home: A Memoir.* New York: Random House, 1992.

O'Donnell, Pierce, and Dennis McDougal. *Fatal Subtraction: The Inside Story of "Buchwald v. Paramount."* New York: Doubleday, 1992.

——. *Fatal Subtraction: The Inside Story of "Buchwald v. Paramount."* Paperback edition. West Hollywood, Calif.: Dove Books, 1996.

Oxford Dictionary of National Biography. Vol. 59. Edited by H.C.G. Matthew and Brian Harrison. Oxford: Oxford University Press, 2004.

Perelman, S. J. *The Most of S. J. Perelman.* New York: Simon and Schuster, 1980.

Reagan, Ronald. *An American Life.* New York: Simon and Schuster, 1990.

Rosen, Michael J., ed. *Collecting Himself: James Thurber on Writing and Writers, Humor and Himself.* New York: Harper and Row, 1989.

Salinger, Pierre. *With Kennedy.* Garden City, N.Y.: Doubleday, 1966.

Schlesinger, Andrew, and Stephen Schlesinger, eds. *The Letters of Arthur Schlesinger, Jr.* New York: Random House, 2013.

Schlesinger, Arthur, Jr. *Robert F. Kennedy and His Times.* Boston: Houghton Mifflin, 1978.

——. *A Thousand Days: John F. Kennedy in the White House.* Boston: Houghton Mifflin, 1965.

Service, Robert. *Collected Poems of Robert Service.* New York: Dodd, Mead, 1958.

Smith, Sally Bedell. *For Love of Politics: Bill and Hillary Clinton: The White House Years.* New York: Random House, 2007.

——. *Grace and Power: The Private World of the Kennedy White House.* New York: Random House, 2004.

Sorensen, Theodore. *Kennedy.* New York: Harper and Row, 1965.

Stein, Jean. *American Journey: The Times of Robert Kennedy.* Edited by George Plimpton. New York: Harcourt, Brace, and Jovanovich, 1970.

Styron, William. *Darkness Visible: A Memoir of Madness.* New York: Vintage Books, 1990.

Summers, Anthony. *Official and Confidential: The Secret Life of J. Edgar Hoover.* New York: G. P. Putnam's Sons, 1993.

Thomas, Evan. *The Man to See.* New York: Touchstone, 1991.

——. *Robert Kennedy: His Life.* New York: Simon and Schuster, 2000.

Thurber, James. *The Thurber Carnival.* New York: Harper Perennial, 1999.

White, E. B., and Katharine S. White, eds. *A Subtreasury of American Humor.* New York: Coward-McCann, 1941.

The Writer's Chapbook: A Compendium of Fact, Opinion, Wit, and Advice from "The Paris Review" Interviews. Preface by Nicole Rudick. New York: Paris Review Editions, 2018.

PERMISSIONS

Grateful acknowledgment is made to the following for permission to include both previously published and unpublished material in this work:

Adam West Enterprises: Letter from Adam West to Art Buchwald dated April 1, 1966. The author would like to thank Adam West Enterprises and the family and estate of Adam West for their generous contribution of material used in this book.

Mike Baker: Letter from Russell Baker to Robert Pittman dated February 24, 1970, letter of April 23, 1975, and letters from Russell Baker to Art Buchwald dated June 29, 1976, January 11, 1990, July 19, 1976, and September 26, 2000. Reprinted by permission of Mike Baker.

Matt Bombeck: Letters from Erma Bombeck to Art Buchwald dated November 13, 1992, and May 23, 1978. Reprinted by permission of Matt Bombeck.

Tom Brokaw: Letter to Art Buchwald [n.d.]. Reprinted by permission of Tom Brokaw.

Christopher Buckley: Letter from Christopher Buckley to Art Buchwald dated January 29, 1993. Reprinted by permission of Christopher Buckley.

Maureen Dowd: Letter from Maureen Dowd to Art Buchwald. Reprinted by permission of Maureen Dowd.

The Estate of William F. Buckley: Letters from William F. Buckley to Art Buchwald. Reprinted by permission of the Estate of William F. Buckley and Christopher Buckley.

INDEX

MICHAEL HILL is a historical researcher who has assisted such authors as David McCullough, Jon Meacham, Sebastian Junger, Nathaniel Philbrick, Evan Thomas, Michael Korda, Senator John McCain, Sally Bedell Smith, James Bradley, Susan Eisenhower, Michael Beschloss, and Caroline Kennedy. He won an Emmy Award for his work as a co-producer on Ken Burns's PBS series *Civil War*. He also served as a historical consultant on the HBO miniseries *John Adams*, produced by Tom Hanks and based on David McCullough's Pulitzer Prize–winning book, and the ABC miniseries *Challenger*. A graduate of the Kennedy School of Government at Harvard University, Hill also served as a press assistant to former vice president Walter F. Mondale.